W9-DGF-172

The theory is it's
never too late
to plan or plant.
Merry Christmas,
Rip & Fita

The

Betsy Lhamon

Memorial Collection

The Art of Planting

THE ART OF PLANTING

or *The Planter's Handbook*

Graham Stuart Thomas

DAVID R. GODINE, PUBLISHER, BOSTON

First U.S. edition published in 1984 by
David R. Godine, Publisher, Inc.
306 Dartmouth Street
Boston, Massachusetts 02116

First published in the U.K. 1984 by J. M. Dent & Sons Ltd
in association with The National Trust.
Copyright © 1984 by Graham Stuart Thomas

Library of Congress Catalog Card Number 84-47657

ISBN 0-87923-531-4

Printed in the U.K.

Contents

To the Director, Staff and Students, past and present,
of the Royal Horticultural Society's garden at
WISLEY
among whom I number many friends
this book is gratefully dedicated
by the author.

Acknowledgments

Various old books, including the *Encyclopaedia of gardening* by J.C. Loudon, 1827, in the Lindley Library of the Royal Horticultural Society, provided the basis for the chapter devoted to shrubs. To the Librarian and his staff the author tenders his thanks.

The majority of the illustrations are by the author, but his thanks, and those of the publishers, are due to the following in regard to certain photographs:
Colour plate II, Mike Stammers; plate XI, Paul Miles; plate XLII, Peter Kerley; plate XLIX, A.J. Hancock.
Black and white plates: 5, 6, 10, 26, 27, 28, 35, 43, 44, 45, 48, 49, 50, 52, 53, 54, 55, 59, 61, 62; The Harry Smith Horticultural Photographic Collection.

Once again the manuscript has been successfully deciphered by Margaret Neal which has earned the author's great appreciation, and Messrs Dent's cooperation has been wholehearted throughout preparation.

AUTHOR'S NOTE

Many of the illustrations depict views in large gardens which at first sight may appear to be beyond adaptation to the smaller gardens of today, but their inclusion has been deliberate. I think we can all be inspired by views of great gardens and it is my experience that it is easier to reduce the scale of planting from these than to develop large schemes from small-scale examples. This matter is elaborated in Chapter 16.

The wonder of the world, the beauty and the power, the shapes of things, their colours, lights and shades; these I saw. Look ye also while life lasts.

From *The Little Grey Men* by "BB"

LIST OF METRIC EQUIVALENTS
(approximate figures)

1 in	2.50 cm	
1½ ins	4.00 cm	
2 ins	5.00 cm	
2½ ins	6.00 cm	
3 ins	7.50 cm	
6 ins	15.00 cm	
10 ins	25.50 cm	
12 ins (1 ft)	30.00 cm	
18 ins	45.00 cm	
2 ft	60.00 cm	
3 ft	100.00 cm	(1 metre)
4 ft	1.20 m	
5 ft	1.50 m	
10 ft	3.00 m	
15 ft	4.50 m	
20 ft	6.00 m	
30 ft	9.00 m	
40 ft	12.00 m	
50 ft	15.00 m	
100 ft	30.00 m	

Introduction

Perhaps no word of six letters concentrates so much human
satisfaction as the word "garden".

RICHARD LE GALLIENNE,
contributor to *Corners of Grey Old Gardens*, 1914

This book is the outcome of a lecture I was asked to give to the Royal
Horticultural Society, being the first Fraser lecture; it appeared in print in the
Society's *Journal* for September 1970. As recorded by the chairman on that
occasion – my old friend Frank Knight – the Fraser Lecture is for horticultural students at training establishments and is to be based mainly on the
theme of how plants should be used to the best advantage in garden planning;
the series of lectures has been made possible by Mr Henry Fraser having given
to the Society a capital sum of money, the interest from which will be used to
defray the costs involved.

The thoughts put into the preparation of the lecture have surfaced again
and again during the years and are here presented much amplified, in a form
that I hope may be useful to intending planters and all kinds of students of
horticulture. The thoughts are personal, the result of my experiences during a
long life with gardens and flowers.

Gardening today is a vast subject and the only thing constant to it is the
beauty of flowers and plants. This is the fundamental which has caused the
progression of garden design in these islands through the last four centuries.
Gardening has developed into a kaleidoscope of ideas and ideals; it is like a
fan, ever opening outwards as more ideas become absorbed, or like a sponge
in which however deeply it is probed there is no finality, or like a bottomless
cornucopia, ever flowing with beauty. The changes in ideas and ideals have
been caused by historical events which in turn have been swayed by fashion
and taste. Until the beginning of this century these turns resulted in garden
design being the plaything of those with considerable means and broad acres.

For a much longer period the *craft* of gardening has continued. It started
with the growing of herbs and medicinal roots near to the dwelling; was

I

continued and enlarged by the great religious houses; became a pursuit during later mediaeval days and through Tudor reigns and has remained in cottage gardens and in the walled kitchen gardens of the great estates ever since. Here the cultivation and production of fruits, vegetables, herbs and flowers of all kinds were paramount, and so they remain. This is a great portion of gardening which I shall leave comparatively untouched in these pages.

It is the use of plants as furnishings for ornamental gardens with which I am concerned. For this reason – and because it is so large a subject – I intend to leave out the *design* of gardens except in so far as it joins hand in hand with the planting.

When I was of a tender age my tutor always impressed upon me the importance of reading a book properly, beginning with the title page and subsequent leaves and, however much I wanted to get into the book itself, always of reading whatever foreword or introduction there may have been. It is a good principle to follow, and hence these introductory paragraphs. It is important to know what is deliberately left out of a book before we start reading. A glance at the list of contents will at once show what is included.

Also in my young days I had free access to the volumes of William Robinson and Gertrude Jekyll, both of them concerned with plants and how to use them to the greatest effect; other extremes were the writings of Reginald Farrer – concerned solely with the growing and the beauty of plants – and Avray Tipping, whose great book *English Gardens* awakened my eyes and brain to the involved history of garden design. From these and the University Botanic Garden at Cambridge have germinated all the seeds of garden thought which have come to me since, fostered by observation and practice.

Whatever its short-comings – and there may well be some in so vast and almost unfathomable a subject as I have chosen – the book is at least a catalogue of my own thoughts and as such I must leave it to your mercies.

About a hundred years ago A.B. Freeman-Mitford, later Lord Redesdale, wrote in his *The Bamboo Garden* the following paragraph, which rings true today:

> I look upon gardening as one of the fine arts, and, rightly understood, not one of the least difficult. The painter or the sculptor makes his effects at once, and obliterates, or models and remodels, until he has attained that at which he is aiming. But the gardener has to consider not what his work is now, but what it will grow into in ten, twenty, fifty years hence. He has to take into account not the present aspect of his materials, but what are their capabilities in the

future and their relative powers of development. If he has a background ready made to his hand he is lucky, but if he has to make it he has to do with trees that are mostly far slower of growth than the more immediately effective plants which it is their office to set off. He has to balance questions of soil, light and moisture. All this involves not only the poetic sense, but also great and patiently acquired knowledge. . . . Colour, form, light and shade, grouping, all have to be studied in the composition of one of those living pictures which the gardener paints with living materials.

Part I

Garden scheming

1

Historical

The most exquisite delights of sense are pursued in the contrivance
and planning of gardens, which, with fruit, flowers, shades,
fountains and the music of birds that frequents such happy places,
seem to furnish all the pleasures of the several senses, and with the
greatest, or at least the most natural perfections.

SIR WILLIAM TEMPLE, *Miscellanea*, 1690

The art of planting a garden is a different thing today from what it was even
fifty years ago, and certainly widely different from its parallel ideas through
the centuries, in this country alone. The art of planting is one of the newer
arts and as it is so bound up with garden design I feel I must devote a few
paragraphs to the history of this subject. This is so that we have a firm
foundation to build upon; it is at risk of being somewhat repetitious because I
dwelt upon the subject at some length in my *Gardens of the National Trust*,
and also in *Perennial Garden Plants* and *Trees in the Landscape*. The two last
books were concerned with design from a special point of view; the first in a
general way.

It was not until Tudor days that the profession of architect began to
assume importance; there had always been builders but architects began to
influence the design of the early garden plots. During Elizabethan days
gardening was relegated to small courtyards, walled areas and other
enclosures where numerous plants were arranged in knot gardens – so-called
because of the intricate pattern of the beds and borders, resembling knots.
Edged with boards, stones, shells, bones or dwarf hedges the beds contained
all sorts of plants: culinary, medicinal and ornamental. Each plant was given a
space to itself and had no relationship to its neighbour except perhaps in the
categories mentioned. There were fruiting plants and bushes too, and the
occasional fruit tree. So far as we can learn, though the planting was generally
haphazard, the design of the beds had started on the path of "art".

When Charles II came back from his long exile, he brought with him ideas
from Holland and France where garden design had become very formal and
often excessively grand, with the accent on straight lines and clipped trees

1 Miss Jekyll's borders, photographed in 1931. From rich colours in the foreground the tone diminished to pale colours and silvery foliage, intriguingly used as the bend in the path brought them into prominence.

2 At Bulkeley Mill, North Wales, there was a good background of native trees; the planting does not detract from them.

3 The 'genius of the place' was composed of pines and water. All else has been skilfully added at Mount Usher, County Wicklow, Eire. *Aruncus*, ferns, *Lysichitum*, Pampas grass, *Cordyline* and rhododendrons.

4 Shadows add much to this view of the author's previous garden. *Eucryphia glutinosa* is seen under the leaning stems of *Betula ermanii*, with hostas, geranium and saxifrage covering the ground.

5 At Sandling Park, Kent, *Cercidiphyllum*, juniper, cedar and pines, seen across the sloping lawn, will hold the eye after the Japanese Azaleas have lost their colour.

6 Gardens started by clearing a space, today usually given to lawn. By its smoothness it acts as a tranquillizer for colourful borders and beds. Four strong components are in this picture of the garden at the Mill House, Sutton Courtenay, Oxfordshire: box edged beds, the yews and the weeping willows, and the curving border.

7 The superlative composition of tree and shrub shapes at Westonbirt School, Gloucestershire.

8 In a birch wood James Russell composed this picture solely with foliage: hostas, ferns, *Luzula maxima*, *Mahonia japonica* and *Arundinaria murieliae*.

9 This would have been a beautiful view at Bodnant even without the trees, but they give it great perspective.

10 A view at Weir House, Shropshire, enhanced by the firm textures of gate, hostas, bergenias and topiary.

11 *Hosta tokudama* 'Variegata' gives great perspective to this little view of the dovecote at Crathes Castle, Kincardineshire (National Trust for Scotland).

12 The ground-cover beds and herbaceous border at Killerton, Devon (National Trust), with *Bergenia crassifolia* in the foreground giving perspective to the whole.

13 The curving path intriguingly disappears, leading the visitor onwards; the large clump of *Genista hispanica* is impassable, but does not shut out the view.

14   A large English Yew at Exbury, Hampshire, through which climbed *Wistaria floribunda* 'Multijuga'.

15   At Wallington, Northumberland (National Trust), many silvery-leafed shrubs and plants are used along this sunny, soft-coloured old wall to blend with flowers of white, pink and cream. The shrubs are essential to prevent the eye from taking in the whole of the narrow border at a glance.

and shrubs. These ideas increased in scope and popularity through succeeding reigns. The interesting plants and beautiful flowers were left in the care of the gardeners in the areas devoted to vegetables. And then in the early eighteenth century something very important happened; this is where the art of planting really begins. The excessively inward-looking formality of the walled gardens and the subjection of the landscape to vast formal views sparked off a revulsion of taste and a new sense of values appeared. Everyone threw wide their doors as we might say and brought the countryside into the garden. Englishmen travelled abroad doing the "Grand Tour", seeing famous classical buildings in Italy and many brought back paintings and drawings depicting idyllic landscapes, usually with ruined classical buildings included in them. Thus the buildings erected in ancient Rome enthralled the painters of the seventeenth century, who in turn inspired travellers a hundred years later — aided by poets like Milton and Pope who transferred to words the pastoral scenes — to create in England a representation of the classical idyllic landscape. The transformation was carried out by gifted amateurs and also by noted professional landscape designers and architects — Bridgeman, Kent, Brown and Repton, and their followers. For roughly 100 years from 1720 or thereabouts this theme was developed in this country. Formal avenues were cut down, parterres disappeared, straight canals were "serpentined", and the natural "landskip" reigned supreme. Known as the English Landscape Garden, it became in due course imitated on the Continent, where the "Jardin Anglais" was its title. The planting of trees to govern and embellish the informal views was very much an art. The flowers were left in the walled vegetable gardens, and of course in the cottage and villa gardens which were not swayed by fashion.

THE NEW PLANTS

Meanwhile a constant stream of new plants from Europe, the Middle East, Africa, the whole of the American Continent — and from the Far East, often through Russian gardens — reached these shores in ever-increasing quantities. This resulted during Victorian times in the origin of two new gardening styles, the arboretum and the "bedding out" schemes on the lawn. We are not concerned with arboreta in these pages because the planting of the new trees was not normally dictated by art; more usually the creation of a collection was the aim. We should, however, recall here that trees and shrubs informally grouped with taste and discernment can create a satisfying picture on their own, witness the Mitchell Drive at Westonbirt — surely one of the great pieces of art in Britain — and the prospect looking north from the hill at Winkworth Arboretum, a National Trust property in Surrey.

But the Victorian bedding craze was certainly a form of art, which is not altogether dead even today; with cheap labour and perhaps smaller gardens, multitudes of tender exotic plants nurtured by cheap coal in the new, fully-glazed greenhouses (direct descendants from the classical orangeries of the eighteenth century), it was very much in vogue. The design of the lawn beds is the first instance of borrowing from past garden styles – the knots and parterres. Small evergreen shrubs replaced the tender summer plants in the beds in autumn and created the original form of "winter gardening". The gardening eye had become inward-looking again, and still the old garden favourites were left in the kitchen and cottage gardens.

MODERN STYLES OF GARDENING

We have, then, three completely distinct styles of gardening over about 300 years, with an ever-increasing number of new trees, shrubs and plants reaching our shores. It was not surprising that prophets arose who wished to use all these new-found riches in more subtle ways than bedding out or in collections: the names of William Robinson and Gertrude Jekyll immediately come to mind. Robinson edited some influential journals, *The Garden* and *The Flora and Sylva*, and wrote *The English Flower Garden* in 1883, a book that had immense influence and ran to many editions. He was the arch-enemy of the formal garden at that time, and devoted himself to evaluating afresh, for their garden worthiness, trees, shrubs and plants both old and new. In 1898 Reginald Blomfield and Inigo Triggs published *The Formal Garden in England*; they desired a return of garden design to classical and traditional formality, but paid little attention to planting.

The most influential from our point of view was Miss Jekyll, through her ability to express herself easily in prose and to put across just the sort of information that the garden owners needed at the turn of the century. She it was who wrote a book called *Colour schemes for the Flower Garden*, 1908–1910. There were no doubt other people of earlier times who looked upon flower gardening as an art, but it was her knowledge of art in general and her practical knowledge of gardening that combined to make her contributions to the art so effective in her own gardens and in the many that she designed for other people.

Until the outbreak of war in 1914 the gardens of the wealthy in this country had become very luxurious and elaborate. Miss Jekyll made us look afresh upon the whole thing. As far as one can dare to generalize on so involved a pursuit, we might say that she and others of her time were equally at home with informal as with formal designs, but that a greater awareness of the beauty and value of plants in gardens usually resulted in informal planting, though perhaps in a formal design.

What happens today? Every sort of garden can be found echoing past styles and often combining them. We in fact draw upon the past in all our plantings. Many garden owners are their own designers, and are perhaps less influenced by fashion than were the wealthy of earlier centuries. I should like to call attention to four noteworthy garden styles that have cropped up. During the 1920s and 1930s we witnessed the upsurge of the landscape rock gardens and their eventual demise owing to their being so labour-intensive in upkeep. At this same time Hidcote was brought to maturity and has had an immense influence on the design and planting of gardens in this country. Its Jekyll-style of planting coupled with firm design may, I think, be reckoned alongside the English Landscape Garden as part of our main contribution to art in general. Thirdly, there is the woodland garden, which has developed over the same period. Thanks to the influx of rhododendron species and the raising of innumerable hybrids, and the ease with which they can be grown in thin woodland on the right soils, the woodland garden has become an obsession.

Lastly, there is the restrained garden of the landscape architects; here artistry in planting reaches a different level. The planting may be subservient to the architectural features, but acts as an indispensable foil or embellishment for the great buildings of today, whether towers of flats or offices, municipal edifices or private dwellings.

But I cannot leave it there. One more style needs to be mentioned. For the last hundred years the greater gardens generally have been shrinking in size owing to the shrinkage of means. Among the ardent plantsmen of today are some who, not content with a collection of plants, seek to garden a large area by their own labour or with a minimum of help. This they do by studying the needs of each plant and ensuring that it is as nearly suited to the conditions prevailing as possible. This is what I call ecological gardening and when plants of like needs are grown together, often a restful effect is achieved. I think therefore we can call this another style of garden art. And I may add that just as Miss Jekyll influenced so greatly the choice of colour and form early in this century, so have the ardent band of flower arrangers exercised a like influence in our gardening since the Second World War.

While we owe to many other countries our gradual pursuit of gardening, it is the *design* that we owe to them; the art of planting undoubtedly stems from this country.

FASHION

The strange changes in the art of gardening are due in great part to *fashion*, often swayed by the economics of living, which are in turn influenced by international relationships. The fashion today may be to go out with your visitor and see how much growth has been achieved during the year by your *Metasequoia* – whereas a hundred years ago we should have been looking at our wellingtonia – or to inspect the newest Floribunda rose or latest hybrid plant. Two and a half centuries ago the visitor would have been standing, surprised, at the edge of the ha-ha, that innovation which enabled the landscape to approach to the house. We must remember in the potted history of gardening which I have given above, only the great garden owners set the fashion and rang the changes in styles, though today we all tend to influence them. Now that we have mini-roses and mini-dahlias we must admit also to mini-gardening. Gardening has been influenced by fashion just as much as any other art or hobby, as will be easily apparent if we turn over the pages of gardening periodicals. Furthermore gardening is interrelated with other forms of art. I need hardly point out that architecture is closely related to garden design, and sculpture figures largely in gardens; the influence of poetry and painting is no less marked though less apparent at first sight.

OTHER FORMS OF ART

The masterpiece of architecture, sculpture or painting is done once and for all and is subject to gradual deterioration. Poetry is perhaps the most lasting of all arts, because words can be so easily reprinted. The evanescent art of music can be recreated by musical artists whenever they so desire, from the thoughts of musicians hundreds of years before. But all these arts are in a way finite; garden art is infinite and far more difficult. Unlike music it can never be repeated exactly, even by skilled gardeners; it is multi-dimensional like sculpture – you have to look at it in front, from behind and from side to side. It often embodies architectural principles, as it has to have some relationship with the house: nobody in their right mind would lay a concrete terrace, for instance, in front of an old brick or stone dwelling. Planting a garden has been likened to painting a landscape, which is acceptable so long as we look at one view from one given point, but this is seldom possible or desirable. The planting must run smoothly in, shall we say, a musical or poetic progression. Many of the rules which in their various ways govern different forms of art are gathered into the art of gardening.

In addition to all these aspects of study, gardening has one great and fundamental difference from all. The art of planting is never static. It varies through each year and from year to year. The effect desired can never be guaranteed and a successful garden-planting scheme can never be repeated exactly on any other plot, because of the varying soil and microclimate which affect the already variable health of each plant. I think therefore we must write down that gardening is the most difficult of all the arts and is a very complex subject for study.

CATEGORIES OF GARDENERS

Those who plant gardens can be primarily divided into three fairly clear-cut categories. There are the collector, the artist-plantsman and the landscape architect. With the collector, the plants are his objective, the be-all and end-all, and he is not concerned with their arrangement. Landscape architects often go to the other extreme, treating their plants in a subjective way. The collectors and artist-plantsmen are probably more in evidence in Britain than elsewhere, because, or partly because, our climate enables us to grow an almost unparalleled range of plants from all over the world, or at least from the north and south Temperate Zones. We can equally claim that our prowess in the Landscape Garden, the Hidcote-style garden and the woodland garden have given great opportunities to the landscape designer and artist-plantsman. The collector can be left out of this book but these other two categories concern us very much; they are closely related because we have to exercise *taste* in arranging and using the plants.

TASTE

Taste is difficult to write about. Perhaps it is best summed up by saying that we must educate ourselves so that we can make a pleasing picture, either for ourselves or to please others, without transgressing any of the special ideas that underline art in general. That is at least how I regard it. It is normally considered quite useless to criticize a point of taste, because two people will seldom agree, but one must try to be honest and satisfy oneself. I once heard it said that good taste is most easily acquired by knowing as much about bad taste as good.

The fundamentals, then, in our research into the art of planting are fashion, taste and economics – which go hand in hand with the dictation of the climate, exposure, soil and all those difficulties with which gardeners have to contend.

2

Consulting the genius of the place

And so I am content with what I have, and make it richer by my fancy which is as cheap as sunlight and gilds objects quite as prettily.

ALEXANDER SMITH,
contributor to *Corners of Grey Old Gardens*, 1914

The title of this chapter is taken from an often quoted, even hackneyed phrase written by Alexander Pope in 1731. It is the fundamental upon which all other ideas and maxims hang. To ignore it is to court disaster which no amount of fashion, taste or economics will alter.

It is consulting the genius of the place which dictates the siting of the dwelling, the placing of paths and other features and the choice of plants. To be consulted therefore is the soil and micro-climate, the terrain, the view (if any), the prevailing wind, the light and many smaller points. To word it differently I might write that we must be led by Nature and never try to drive her or go against her. That usually brings disaster or untold expense, work and worry. In addition to the soil and climate we must also consider any established features – such as trees, stream, rock, etc.

As we journey about the country the "genius" varies enormously. The first thing we are likely to note is whether the soil is limy or acid, or perhaps it may be neutral. As a very general rule most of our limy areas are in the south-east of the country, though there are outcrops of limy rock in the west and north as well. Any student of the British Flora will be able, by examining the wild plants in the district, to say whether the soil is limy or not. Any experienced gardener could arrive at the same conclusion by studying the contents of local gardens.

SOILS

Let us first of all imagine a limy garden; there is a great choice of plants available for all but the most chalky areas, so long as one excludes rhododendrons, camellias, kalmias, *Hydrangea macrophylla* and *H. serrata* forms and cultivars, most heathers and a few other plants and shrubs. *Aubrieta* and *Lilium candidum* will thrive, also various kinds of *Buddleia, Cotoneaster, Berberis* and all the plants associated with our chalky and limy hills. They include *Viburnum*, wild roses, *Prunus spinosa, Crataegus, Euonymus europaeus* and all those lovely "weeds" like the Harebell, Knapweed, Scabious and Agrimony. Having lived for most of my life in a lime-free district I sometimes yearn for the smell of the air sweetened by these delights. As you go from the Woking area, redolent of pines and cypresses, and approach the Downs by Guildford the different air is noticeable. But then on second thoughts I remember that practically all lime-loving plants will flourish or can be made to flourish on acid soil, so that I am comforted. But it would go very much against Nature to attempt a grouping of lime-hating shrubs and plants on a chalky hill.

There is no doubt that a plant growing well in the conditions given to it is a far more satisfying sight than one which barely exists. Thus on a garden of acid sand one's thoughts would turn to heathers and gorse, pines and brooms and end up with all the acid-loving shrubs and plants as well.

In strong loams and good light soil we can grow more or less what we like; roses and popular flowers and all kinds of shrubs and plants. Clay is difficult to cope with and will dictate those few days when it is in a suitable condition for working in, so that it does not turn into bricks or a swamp. And swamps, whatever the conservationists may say about altering the environment, are, from a gardener's point of view, only there to be drained, unless the idea is a garden for bog plants. Clay must only be caressed and improved by vegetable waste, cinders, broken brick and the like. By vegetable waste I mean any sort of compost, leaf mould or peat, and funnily enough this is just the kind of thing which will also improve poor sandy soils, and when dealing with chalky soils it disappears fast and is always needed.

Sometimes in gravelly soil the water-table deposits iron which makes a "hard pan" through the subsoil. It is vital to break this before planting.

TREES

Likewise we may claim that the presence of trees has some equally surprising effects. On poor sandy soil – so long as they are not surface rooters like the pine and beech – the casting of shade across the garden during the day is highly beneficial. The same may be said of wet sites; trees drink up a lot of water and give it off through their leaves and so help to drain the ground. This of course points to the fact that though their branches may help to cool the ground, they also dry it. This was borne in upon me very forcibly on light sandy soil where stood a great oak. Having always been taught that the roots of oak trees delve deeply, I thought that rhododendrons would be well suited in its shade, but they drooped badly every summer. For other reasons it became necessary to fell the oak, and, in spite of sudden exposure to sunlight, the rhododendrons never drooped again except in periods of severe drought. Their own foliage shaded and kept cool the ground, and the thin, greedy surface roots of the oak had rotted.

THE CHOICE OF PLANTS

If we had to choose plants solely from our natives our gardens could still be interesting and full of beauty through the year. But fortunately we have a superabundance of imported and highly bred plants to choose from. This rich source enables us to do more than just repeat the heather- or chalk-complex and extend our choice of plants to give point to the association of ideas. The style of architecture and the materials used for building, the style of summerhouse, the paths, pergola or other features add up to an almost indefinable something, which with thought can be turned to advantage. So are gardens of different character born, and the plants used in each will prove to be in different categories. This is particularly noticeable where the garden has some formal pretensions. With the key plants chosen to accentuate the association of ideas, the remaining choice can be more catholic.

3

Styles of planting

This garden full of leaves and flowers;
And craft of man's hand so curiously
Arrayed had this garden, truly
That never was there garden of such prys
But if it were the very paradise.

GEOFFREY CHAUCER,
The Franklin's Tale, 14th century

Lancelot – or "Capability" – Brown, having designed many great landscape
parks for thirty years, died in 1783. He, with the earlier Charles Bridgeman
and William Kent, had changed the fashion of gardening in this country,
with his lakes, serpentined waters, expanses of grass for grazing and clumps
and belts of trees. It was Humphry Repton who returned us to sanity and
sought to have at least some garden, preferably formal, around the house. In
general Repton was the originator of today's garden design.

In Chapter 1 I declared that this book would not be concerned with
garden design, but I must ask to be excused in this chapter. I cannot avoid
writing about the planting in general without calling attention to how the
design affects it.

Immediately outside a house on the garden side the need is felt for some
sort of dry area – gravelled or paved – where a seat and perhaps a table can
be placed. This acts as the first outside room of the house, assuming that the
garden is to be an extension of the home and give delight and refreshment.

The design of the paths and paved area, and any walls, fences or hedges
outlining them, are best designed parallel with or at right angles to the lines of
the house. Exceptions may be found, of course, to this general rule. It is a
good place, perhaps the only place, to indulge in formal planting. Close to
the house we can accept bright colours from flowers in plenty. Immediately
we step on to the lawn, which is generally the next feature, or walk down a
side path, the planting can be less formal or balanced, and so it continues in
gentle transition to the further garden. This is a usually successful scheme for

most gardens under one acre; a larger one would provide endless possibilities with cross-vistas and surprise areas.

The idea of formal planting in formal beds and borders on or near a terrace has a long history. It started in Elizabethan days and was revived in part by Repton and elaborated in Victorian times. It has never quite left us, in traditional gardening. But it leaves of course endless possibilities for variation, just as Francis Bacon's ideal garden left much to interpretation, of which he wrote in his essay *Of Gardens*, in the late sixteenth century.

Formal planting can be just a balanced composition of firm, perhaps clipped, bushes or conifers, augmented by a balanced composition of attendant beds and borders. The plants used, upon which so much depends throughout the year from the windows, can be mainly evergreen, interspersed with balanced or echoing planting in between. I like some sense of orderliness as I step from the house to the first "outdoor room". It can be achieved by a pair of garden ornaments, as well as by planting.

Formal planting is of very varied kinds. Avenues, hedges, hedged alleys and the like take us back to Caroline days and are not infrequently used today where there is space enough for them. A drive could be planted formally by using separate rows of shrubs, backed perhaps by a flowering and fruiting tree, the whole so chosen that flowers would greet one for at least six months of the year, to say nothing of the varied tints of the foliage. A lawn can also be shaped and treated formally and perhaps this should be so immediately beyond the house while the more distant part of the garden can have curves and informal planting.

LAWN BEDDING

The most formal of all planting is bedding. It, too, has a long history. I think we can trace it back to the development of the true greenhouse, as mentioned earlier, which grew out of the eighteenth-century orangeries. It was discovered that the opaque roofs of orangeries, with consequently light only from the side, were insufficient for the plants. As soon as glass roofs were invented, the nurturing of the new tender, floriferous plants became easy and they were produced in quantity, thanks to ample labour and cheap coal. The advent of the lawn mower – as opposed to the hand-scythe – resulted in beautiful lawns and the obvious temptation came to provide a pattern of beds on them to take the "bedding plants". The patterns were very often borrowed from the parterres of the seventeenth century. This is an eclectic style of gardening which is, even so, a form of garden art. Originally when the summer-flowering plants were taken up in the autumn, the beds were saved from looking too empty through the winter by dotting in small evergreens – laurels, hollies, aucubas, cypresses, box and mahonias. But the idea of having a spring bedding season as well as a summer display started about 1850 through the energy and enterprise of the head gardener at Cliveden, now a property of the National Trust, but then owned by the Duke of Sutherland. This has been the pattern in this form of art ever since. It is still practised in many a public park, also in the National Trust's Lyme Park, Cheshire, and at Kew. Here of late years much ingenuity by the Assistant Curator, Mr Brian Halliwell, has been exercised. He has brought the whole thing into the realm of fine art. Having at his disposal an unrivalled collection of plants from which to choose, he has rung the changes on tender and also hardy plants and every year tantalizes us with carefully worked-out colour schemes. They are worthy of watching and noting year by year.

Although abhorred by Robinson and Jekyll, bedding had – apart from anything else – at least the "elaboration within the idea" which was at the bottom of so much Jekyll thought. In *The Wild Garden* (1870) William Robinson mentions that twenty years earlier, hardy plants had been given their due in gardens but that since then it had become the fashion to do most of the floral work with tender plants. He cites the awful, crude colour-schemes and monotony of the idea. He had just written two books on French gardens (*Gleanings from French Gardens*, 1868, and *The Parks, Promenades and Gardens of Paris*, 1869) and no doubt saw much of it done over there. However, in his *The English Flower Garden*, 1883, he brought all his guns to bear – as was his wont – to shoot down bedding in all its then popular styles, and in his own formal garden near the house, practised what he preached, using mainly hardy plants. In this he was following greatly in the footsteps of J.C. Loudon earlier in the century.

In private gardens today bedding is seldom practised, being labour intensive and therefore expensive, but its overtones remain, witness the vast quantities of bedding plants that are sold every year.

It is worth noting here the impact that modern bush roses – Hybrid Teas and Floribundas – have made on the decoration of lawns. Grown in beds solely devoted to them, they have in many places usurped the position held by bedding plants with the fond thought they cause less work. But their flowering season is much shorter than two relays of bedding plants. In their search for vigour and size the breeders have rendered them totally unsuitable for lawn bedding: it is unfortunate to say the least to make use of bushes reaching often to 4 ft in height to give a pattern of colour on the average lawn. Their height destroys the design. Only in the largest schemes are plants of 3–4 feet suitable, but fortunately I think the breeders have sensed this and some are now turning their attention to dwarfs, such as the admirable 'Marlena'.

I shall not be alluding to the art of bedding again in these pages but hope that these few paragraphs will bring home to gardeners in general that "bedding out" does not necessarily have to be the expensive product of greenhouses – nor need it be ugly.

FROM THE FORMAL TO THE INFORMAL

As we progress away from the house the need for formality of design and planting decreases. In large gardens the formality may eventuate into rough-mown grass with trees in it, the whole softened by shrub planting around the perimeter. This is our next step – informal planting, such as Miss Jekyll loved. I believe her examples and writings and the development of Hidcote were inevitable. They were part of the upsurge of horticulture. Horticulture is, as I have said, like a fan or a sponge; its popularity made it the plaything of fashion and taste. With so many styles of planting and design already part of history, something new had to crop up for fashion to feed upon. With riches in plants galore and less left to the traditions and whims of the garden staff, what more likely than that the new pursuit, so adequately explained by Robinson and Jekyll, should be taken up by the owner and his wife? I am not claiming that either worthy necessarily influenced Lawrence Johnston at Hidcote but that the time was ripe for that sort of garden to crop up. Judging by the numerous gardens that have been laid out since, it is obvious that the mood was in the country; moreover it started a new fashion.

The fashion was that within a firm, small or informal design the planter should use all the plants he wanted which were available, cheaply, from numerous good nurserymen, and should arrange them with taste to embellish to the full a preconceived idea in colour and form. I have long ago given up that misconceived idea that cottage garden planting was the form at Hidcote and elsewhere; cottage gardens gloried in their mixture, stemming from the knot gardens of four hundred years ago, and were seldom arranged artistically. But their plants, the old garden favourites, were brought out of obscurity by Robinson and Jekyll and used side by side with all the new plants from the four corners of the world.

GROUPING

It is one thing to create a definite colour scheme but quite another to know how to group the plants. Miss Jekyll gave us lasting instruction in the border plans in her books. She favoured not the succession of clumps, but an interweaving of drifts. These have two advantages: when looked at from one end of the border these drifts – narrow and gently laid obliquely to the line of the border – each present small areas of colour; looked at from the other end they overlap in a medley of graded tints. The result is that when a certain plant has spent its flowers it presents the minimum of a gap in the scheme from either direction. To carry on her schemes of colour Miss Jekyll had of course the advantage of a head gardener, and his staff, and also a *garden boy*, and so cutting down a spent plant and training another over the gap, or whistling down to the nursery yard for a potful of this or that to fill the gap was a simple matter! It is different today. . . .

Things were done rather differently at Hidcote. Here the long drift pattern was not used but interplanting was helpful in filling gaps during the season. And every part of Hidcote not only had its own plants, colour scheme or feeling, but also produced floral colour throughout the season. This it still does, and it is something which was not to the fore at Munstead Wood, Miss Jekyll's own garden, where different parts of the garden were often devoted to displays for separate times of the year – spring borders, summer borders, Michaelmas borders and the like.

When I first started helping the National Trust at Hidcote in the 1950s there were some old gardeners who had worked at Hidcote for many years and knew Lawrence Johnston's methods. One, Walter Bennett, stayed with us until he retired, over age, and he had a happy knack of planting in a different kind of way. There would be a fair-sized planting of A with a similar group of B adjoining it, each being composed of several plants for major effect. But here and there he would put an odd plant or two of A overlapping with B and vice versa. It is a real art to do this and is very effective. It gives the impression of each plant having been long established and having seeded itself around. And like as not an isolated A or B would be popped in some distance away to reinforce the supposition.

Some areas at Hidcote are given to isolated shrubs, with a through-plant-ing, or ground-cover, of some plant which would make a great display either in contrast or sympathy with the shrubs, to subside into respectable greenery for the rest of the year. This is because one of the great arts in planting for effect during the whole year, or at least for the growing months, is to choose plenty of plants whose foliage presents a good appearance the whole time, and specially after the flowers have faded.

If we accept that much of the Hidcote style of planting – and Jekyll's as well – is rightly called informal, this leads us on to the ultimate stage of so-called "natural" planting, though of course no deliberate planting really deserves this term. And all the time we must visualize ourselves walking farther from the house, to a bend in the path or lawn, or, to those who are really fortunate, to a view of the countryside.

COVERING THE GROUND

We may note here another Robinsonian admonishment. I think he may be looked upon as the original instigator of natural planting, in *The Wild Garden*. Here he advises: "The chief rule should be – never show the naked earth: carpet or clothe it with dwarf subjects, and then allow the taller ones to rise in their own wild way through the turf or spray." He advises too that with such treatment of covering the foreground with flat junipers, *Iberis* etc., no digging is necessary. This was of course the main theme of my *Plants for Ground-Cover*.

The lawn is one method of covering the "naked earth". Though mowing is a chore, it too can be done with artistry. In a rectangular plot the stripes of the mowing should obviously be done to follow the main lines, but an informal garden can easily be marred by the stripe following a wrong line in relation to the design. In almost every garden where the house leads on to a lawn, the stripes should leave the formal terrace or building at right angles. Thereafter the lawn can be adjusted to the lines of the planted areas. In an informal garden too much close-mown lawn can be boring; but if the main ways are indicated by close-mown wide paths through a rough-mown surrounding area much boredom can be relieved.

I THE COLOUR CHART

The main part of the colour chart overleaf is arranged in three concentric circles.

The inner circle of colours shows two reds at the top; to the right, two blues and to the left two yellows. Somewhere between these pairs are true red, blue and yellow of the spectrum – the three primary colours. Still in the central circle of colours in between the three primary colours are the results of mixing these three primaries with their neighbours, thus red with blue gives violet, red with yellow gives orange and blue with yellow gives green. Note that it is the tint of the primary colour nearest to the tint of the text primary colour which is used for mixing.

It may be taken that any five consecutive tints around the circle will make a blend if skilfully used, but more may cause undesirable clashes. Particularly is this found with the tints on either side of the central red and blue.

The next circle shows the same colours thinned by white. These are all soft and are known generally as pastel shades (such as would be found by using crayons composed of tinted white chalk). Few colour clashes occur with these tints. They are never dominant in a colour scheme.

The outside circle shows the same original colours toned down with black. Again, these are not dominant colours but act as a foil to brighter colours and often represent shadows over a clear colour.

Nearly all colours are found in the rainbow. Some that are outside of its sequence are found in the four *outlying panels* of colours. Left, top: brown, obtained by mixing red with green; mid-brown is shown, also clouded with black. Right, top: magenta, also its pastel relative, thinned by white. Left, bottom: two tints of jade or emerald green. Right, bottom: purple, and thinned with white to a pastel tint.

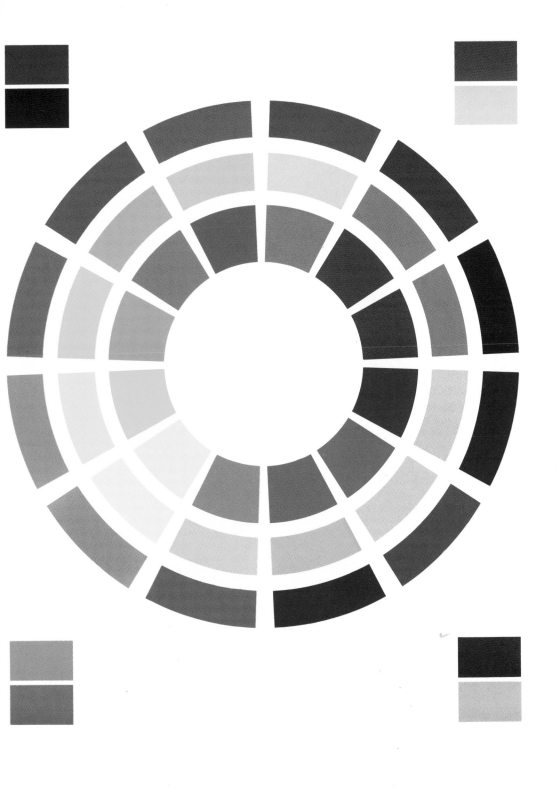

II Roses in a bowl, by Frank Galsworthy, see Chapter 4. The roses depicted are 'Ulrich Brunner Fils', 'Madame Abel Chatenay', 'La France', 'Mrs Herbert Stevens', 'Madame Alfred Carrière', with 'William Allen Richardson' lying on the table.

III The 'tapestry' hedges at Hidcote, Gloucestershire (National Trust). They are composed of green beech, copper beech, green holly and variegated holly, yew and box.

IV Formal excellence in the rose garden at Bagatelle, near Paris.

V Formal excellence at the Roseraie de l'Haÿ, near Paris. Both of these rose gardens were planted towards the end of the 19th century and are extremely well maintained.

VI At the Hotel Pompadour, Fontainebleau, France, the Vicomte de Noailles planted this array of *Robinia* (Acacia) *pseudacacia* 'Inermis' to create a chequering of shadow on the lawn beyond the Oriental Plane trees *(Platanus orientalis)*.

VII At the Hotel Pompadour the vegetables were arranged in an ornamental pattern in the square, hedged garden.

VIII The perfection of clipped Box (*Buxus sempervirens* 'Suffruticosa') in the parterre at Edzell Castle, Angus, Scotland. The castle was built in the late 16th century; the parterre is a modern effort at providing a garden within keeping. It is maintained by the Department of the Environment.

IX The soft, pale murrey-coloured paving, and the grey lead tank at Knightshayes Court, Devon (National Trust), dictated the planting scheme. The colours are all soft, with much grey foliage; most plants are under 10 inches in height in order to reveal the pattern of the beds.

X Scarlet roses (mostly 'Frensham'), coppery leafed *Prunus* and *Berberis* vie with the yellow of *Cornus alba* 'Spaethii', throughout the summer months. Bulbs and Honesty give colour in spring. At Tintinhull House, Somerset (National Trust).

XI and **XII** The pool garden at Tintinhull has a pair of flanking borders each with a background of yew hedge. Small plants and bulbs brighten the verges in spring. One border facing east has brilliance with flowers of scarlet, yellow and white; the opposite border has flowers of apricot, soft yellow, pink and mauve. Both borders have clumps of grassy foliage.

4

Colour, its values and uses in the garden

"Just as an unassorted assemblage of mere words, though they may be the best words in our language, will express no thought, or as the purest colours on an artist's palette – so long as they remain on the palette – do not form a picture, so our garden plants, placed without due consideration or definite intention, cannot show what they can best do for us."

GERTRUDE JEKYLL,
'A definite Purpose in Gardening'
from *The World*, August 15, 1905

Earlier in this century when people spoke about a colourful garden they would have meant a garden full of flowers. Today a garden can be colourful with variegated plants as well as with flowers, so increasingly popular have they become. In fact colour in a garden is taken to mean any colour other than green, though it should be remembered that green is a colour too. Indeed it is the most important colour in the garden, from any point of view, for without greenery, plants could not live. To a certain extent the colours in the room, giving access on to the paved area or terrace, affect, or are affected by, the most prominent flowers in the immediate garden. A brown carpet will enhance the greenery outside; but the most striking example of carpet colours I have seen used – and the same would apply of course to curtains – was a rich wine-purple. It was amazing how all greens came to life outside. It gave them so much clarity and brilliance that I could imagine I was in the Irish countryside, where all outdoor colours are clarified by the clear air.

Colour is a very personal matter; it is one which we bend to our way of delight. Who is to say that one colour is better than another? Our preferences are bound up with prejudice, personality, association and fashion as well as with taste. I remember differing from a fellow horticulturist when judging a competition for cut rhododendrons at one of the Royal Horticultural

Society's Shows; he wished to suggest first prize to one because, he said, "it is a better colour" than another which ran it close in quality. This seemed to me to be wrong; our own preference for a colour may not be agreed by another person. What we were clearly asked was to recommend the first prize to the vase best presented and in faultless condition. I cannot remember whether I won the day, but I could see that my remark had shaken my friend.

I think we enjoy different colours at different times of life. I knew a keen gardener who wanted everything to be of the brightest; particularly red, flame, orange and startling yellow. Later in life an ardent flower arranger came to live with her whose choice in colours was just the opposite – the soft pinks and mauves, lavenders, blues, palest yellow and white. Gradually my gardening friend changed her ideas and the fierce colours were thrown out. Her former colours were *exciting* colours; her choice in later life was of the retiring tints. Perhaps many of us change like that; young boys love red, particularly red engines which they yearn to drive.

THE CLASHING OF COLOURS

There is a difference of opinion about whether the colours of flowers clash in gardens. Here again it is a personal matter, but in my opinion it is a case of defeatism to claim that colours do not clash. It is an example of being careless and leaving to chance that which should concern us deeply. As intimated in the first chapter, we have all been educated by the flower-arranging sisterhood in these matters of late years and much of it stems from Miss Jekyll's own books (including one on *Flower Decoration*) and, of course, her follower in so many ways, Constance Spry. A lot of the success in using opposing colours is governed by proportion. I call to mind seeing two flowers which I should never have thought of placing in juxtaposition – common wild red poppy and French Willow Herb – looking superb together in one of Constance's groups. Because of the proportion of each, the colour of the container and the background, the arrangement "came off" in no uncertain way. Likewise on our long borders at Sunningdale I planted the fierce magenta *Geranium psilostemon* under and around Rose 'Scarlet Fire'. This "came off" too, mainly, I think, thanks to the black centres of the geranium flowers. But these are exceptional instances,

Frank Galsworthy's water colour painting of roses (Plate II) illustrates the importance of proportion. He told me that having painted all the soft mauve and similarly tinted roses he decided the vivid emerald green book was the right contrast, but that the picture still needed its third colour and so he added a bloom of the bright orange Rose 'William Allen Richardson', without which he felt the picture was too dull. Here was a strong clash carefully used.

When can flower colours be said to clash disagreeably? Here again I just offer my opinion: I believe it is a very simple matter. If we represent the spectrum – that is, all the colours of the rainbow – as a circle with red at the top (Plate I), it is my belief that so long as none of the red shades with blue in their composition are used with those which contain yellow, no clashes will occur. This seems to me to be a basic fact, but it eludes many people, especially those who have not thought about it and do not understand their preferences. Still more is this true if they have never spent a half-hour with a box of water-colours, observing by mixing how colour-tones are formed. I find quite a few people cannot name the sequence of colours in a rainbow: red, orange, yellow, green, blue, indigo, violet. This is easily memorized by the initial letters ROYGBIV or, in reverse, VIBGYOR.

These three primary colours (red, yellow, blue) and their immediate derivatives (orange, green, violet) are not the end of the matter. There are infinite variations to be taken into consideration, whatever our walk of life. There is intensity of colour or its opposite, paleness. Strictly, the terms red, yellow and blue refer to pure colours and should only be used to describe the tints at the three equidistant points in the diagram, and do not have any suspicion of the other primary colours in them. But really pure colours are seldom seen in gardens. We could achieve them with solid flat paint on a board, but colours in flower are so muted and adjusted by shape, shadows and textures that each colour is usually composed of several tints. An example which comes to mind here is Sargent's portrait of the famous cellist, Madame Suggia. In order to present her flowing red velvet dress he used all colours from orange to purple. And that "comes off" too! The first realization of this is an excitement of great value, and may be compared to the strange fact that a bed of mixed colours of zinnias, though they may contain every hue from yellow through red to almost purple, presents to most eyes a reasonably happy blend. This is because their petals are matt-surfaced and because many of the tints are muted and thickened; if the same range of colours were developed in the buttercup's petals with their polished surfaces, trouble would ensue.

In addition to the three primary colours and three main headings for the intermediates, there are many gradations. If we were representing them on paper with water colours we should need an admixture of white in some, and something approaching black in others. These two extra "colours" are not in the spectrum. White and black are not really colours; both are complete negatives to the eye, but are marvellous for showing up real colours.

The palest greys or white mixed with water-colours will achieve a range of what we often term pastel tints while the darker admixture will produce sad receding hues, of flowers in shadow. Brown (red and green), grey (yellow and violet) and black (best represented by equal quantities of red, blue and yellow used in full tone) are only occasionally found in flowers in their relatively pure state and need not concern us here.

DESCRIBING COLOURS

As with scents and flavours, it is well nigh impossible to convey a colour exactly by the written word when we attempt to describe the involved and mixed shades. It *is* possible to describe the pure colours because we can invoke the spectrum. Beyond those we resort to imagery and similes, like pillar-box red, azure blue, buttercup yellow; or the intermediates, orange, grass-green, violet; or, still more involved, brown and grey.

RED TINTS

There are some fairly clearly understood colours such as the following allied to red:

flame (yellowish)
poppy-red
garnet (*granat*, a dark red)
blood-red
red-lead (oxide of red)
rust
terracotta (burnt earth, brick)
wine-red (claret, Bordeaux or dark port)
crimson (carmine, *cramoisi* as derived from the cochineal insect)
beetroot
cerise (a bluish bright pink)
old rose (a bluish dull pink)
rose pink (pure light spectrum red)
scarlet (hunting "pink"), a bright red verging on orange

BLUE TINTS

A similar series is found among blues:

ultramarine (sky or azure blue, pale or dark)
cobalt (opaque, cold)
cornflower (true blue)
sapphire (dark blue)
Delft (China) blue
Royal blue (a dark true blue)
midnight blue and indigo

Prussian blue (just on the yellow side of spectrum blue)
turquoise (greenish)

Blue is the most misunderstood colour. Many people refer to lavender-blue and heliotrope and even mauve (all of which have some red in their make-up) as "blue". Bronze-blue is a printer's ink which dries with a metallic sheen.

YELLOW TINTS

Yellows are equally involved and sometimes vague in the terms used:

buttercup or sunflower yellow (cold and warm respectively)
Chinese yellow (contains a little blue)
sulphur (much more vivid and cold than lemon or citron)
Nankeen (a buff tint)
lemon or citron
cadmium or chrome (strong true yellow)
maize (warm, orange-tinted)
saffron (rich orange-yellow (stigmata of Saffron Crocus))
primrose (of the wild Primrose, a constant tint)
raw sienna (the tint of young oak foliage)

The term "golden" is used in general for plants, shrubs, conifers and other trees with yellow variegation, as well as for flowers. It is in an effort to call attention to the brightness of the colour, though of course in reality no gold is as bright as a strong yellow. It is best therefore to drop the term.

GREEN TINTS

Greens may vary from blue-green to true green such as:

verdigris (corroded copper)
emerald (pea-pod)
jade (usually applies to the pale blue-green variant of this stone)
pea-green
parsley (true green)
grass-green
lime-green (creamy yellowish green)

BROWN TINTS

With so much variation in the colours that can be combined it is not surprising that the next step, i.e. the combination of various reds and greens which create browns, is equally variable – Vandyke, chocolate, ginger, snuff, mahogany.

VIOLET TINTS

The violet shades have their own titles too: lavender, heliotrope (both ambiguous like many other terms above because there are pale and dark varieties of both), Royal purple, and all the mauve (from *Malva*, mallow) shades, to startling magenta.

Those who wish to delve deeper into this complexity of complexities should read the *Handbook of Colour* by Kornerup and Wansher and *Colour* by Enid Verity. There is also the British Standard of colours followed by decorators, and *The Colour Chart* of the Royal Horticultural Society. But there is no unanimity of terminology to be found and therefore in my writings I usually use water-colour names or close imagery. It is about the best that a mere gardener can do without referring continually to the Colour Chart, but this is the best guide for us when undertaking careful identifiable descriptions.

FASHIONS IN COLOURS

In addition to all the ambiguities and inaccuracies in the terminology, colours are also subject to fashion. Today's fashion in colours runs to the sharper colours – the flames, salmons, corals, bright yellows and clear blues. I think this fashion first began to be felt in the 1920s. I remember well the gossip that was engendered in Cambridge when a house was redecorated in the "new" clear and pastel shades. Still more I remember the gasp of astonishment when the curtain rose on the daring combinations of colour in some university stage productions by Madame Gwen Raverat: lime-green, salmon, pale yellow and *magenta*. The use of these clear light colours – apart from magenta – was always the choice of Mr F. Tustin, head gardener, for the scintillating effect he used to achieve in the great parterre at Abbotswood. The colours were seen *against* the light and thus gained added brilliance. He used no "hard" or "heavy" colours.

Magenta has for long been a controversial colour. My first introduction to the "anathema" of it was in books by Reginald Farrer. It was a colour he could not abide. I recall his fulminations about plants of magenta or vivid crimson-purple colouring, and he was by no means the only writer of his time – and earlier – who disliked this tint. Since one colour is as beautiful as the next except in the eye of the beholder, whence came this dislike? Judging by what is left to us of some Victorian tastes, there were plenty of heavy thick colours for twentieth-century people to dislike. Magenta of course needs grey foliage to set it off and perhaps those plants not having this complementary advantage offended Farrer. He was, too, writing before the silver-grey plants had been taken to heart by gardeners.

In describing colours we have to remember that they can vary under different lights. I always felt a little guilty of booking orders for the very free-flowering old Ghent Azalea called 'Fanny' or 'Pucelle' in the marquee at the Chelsea Flower Show. Bluish pinks were always cleared to an extraordinary degree of brightness in the dimmed light. The same happened more recently in an exhibit in which was the staring light carmine 'American Pillar' rose – which in the shelter of the canvas appeared bright salmon-pink.

Dimmed light can play strange tricks. Sir Francis Bacon noticed much the same thing in the late sixteenth or early seventeeth century. In his essay *Of Masques and Triumphs* he wrote: "The colours that shew best by candle-light are white, carnation, and a kind of sea-water green. . . . As for rich embroidery, it is lost and not discerned."

We must admit that the classification and description of colours, like botany, is not an exact science. Even chemical or crystal substances, such as a few cited in the foregoing lists, are variable. Rarely today is a book published in which colour photographs can be said throughout to be true representations of the originals. It is to me amazing that with perhaps only one red, one yellow, and one blue – all fairly near to the spectrum tints – plus black, the average publication of only three colours succeeds as well as it does. Very involved colour printing needs far more colours and therefore is more costly work. Some of the trouble accrues from using artificial light for the photographic process; it has not the "white" clarity of daylight. This is extremely important; most artists in colour prefer a constant north light for their work. My old friend Frank Galsworthy, so that he could carry on painting after dark, made himself a large white paper shade for his standard lamp; on it were painted little squares of different blues, greens and reds which, he claimed, counteracted the yellowness of the electric light. It was a very successful piece of experimental work; his colour representations after dark were remarkable. Some of us can look back to the disappointment when seeing in the morning what we had painted by the aid of a gas lamp the previous evening!

COLOURS IN THE GARDEN

I started this chapter by speaking of garden colour and stressed the value of greenery of all kinds as opposed to floral colour. It may however come as a surprise to some that there are no colours in leaves which are not found in flowers, and very few floral colours other than true blue which are not found in leaves. There is no doubt though that the majority of leaves are green and the majority of flowers are other than green.

Colours can be used with different effects in garden placing; a colour in bright sun will appear quite different in shade, and will be equally affected by the type of background, foreground and its neighbours. If we accept that all of us would like to make our gardens *look* as big as possible, while not altering their size beyond our capabilities, much can be done towards this with colours.

Bright colours on leaving the house and softer colours beyond will enhance the distance. We all know how far-away hills look bluish; soft cool tones of blue and lavender, mauve, subdued pink, and soft apricot-yellows will appear to recede in the distance, especially if contrasted with vivid colours in the foreground. A favourite scheme of Miss Jekyll's was to start a long border with clear blues, soft grey-blues, white, palest yellow (always a valuable colour in the garden) and clear light pink, then work towards richer yellows and orange and red; this would be the climax of the border after which the colours would grade from strong yellow to pale yellow, white and palest pink, ending with blues, purples and lilacs softened by grey foliage. In her own main border the planting was backed by plants on the wall, and shrubs such as Golden Privet and purple-leaf *Prunus*. This sort of thing can only be achieved in a really long border – perhaps of 150 ft. I like sometimes to vary the scheme after the red climax by then using rich purples, followed by cool lavender tints to white and grey foliage. Either scheme would appear to lengthen the border when seen from the first end. To manage such a planting effectively, it is almost impossible to make it last for more than about six weeks of July and August unless we are going to rely on "popping in" plants in pots to fill up gaps from time to time. In short borders such colour schemes tend to look forced and disturbing; but instead a portion of the scheme can be taken and elaborated in greater detail so that the colours still present a sequence.

It is in such instances that borders of a few, selected colours are effectively made. At Tintinhull one of an opposite pair is of clear bright colours: red, white and yellow, while its fellow is of muted tones of yellow, apricot, mauve and wine-red; both are augmented with grey foliage and a dark background of yew hedge. At Cliveden one border has cream, yellows, oranges and hot reds and the other blue, lavender, pink and white. Both of these gardens are owned by the National Trust, likewise Powis Castle, where the pair of long parallel borders are of cool tints at one end and finish with strong reds and oranges against dark yew hedges. The Red Borders at Hidcote are often cited: here the colours include orange and all shades of red supplemented by dark purple delphiniums and purplish foliage. These borders at Hidcote are Suggia's dress brought to life. In Lady Kleinwort's garden at Eyford House, Cheltenham, we devised a blend of crimson (avoiding orange-biassed reds), dark pink, purple, with some grey foliage in the foreground, all merged with coppery purple foliage; the grey stone wall at the back has the Claret Vine and *Clematis × jackmanii*, while 'Hidcote' Lavender edges the foreground parapet. The choice is almost endless. In the same garden are soft peach-coloured roses and yellow Day Lilies sharpened by lots of good greenery such as *Alchemilla* and orange roses.

At Mount Stewart, in Northern Ireland, a property of the National Trust, Lady Londonderry had inaugurated certain colour schemes in the series of splendid terraced gardens around the house, which she designed in the 1930s. Some time after the garden came to the Trust I was asked to refurbish the borders which had lost their impact. There are two opposite parterres in the Italian garden on the south front. The design to the east is devoted to strong reds, yellows and orange tints, that to the west has cool pinks, lavenders and mauves. Both are supplemented by coppery foliage, and, separately, pairs of beds are edged on the one section by dwarf shrubs such as *Berberis thunbergii* 'Atropurpurea Nana', yellow-leafed heathers and *Thuja orientalis* 'Rhein-gold', and on the other section with greyish *Santolina* and rue. It was noticeable that with this original re-planting the weight of colour was mostly on the strong coloured side – not surprisingly. To augment the strength of the cooler toned assortment we had to increase white and clear pink. Below this great array is the Spanish garden, so called because of the blue-green Spanish tiles with which the summer-house is roofed. Here we have developed a colour scheme of glaucous-leafed *Kniphofia caulescens* and hostas while the floral colours are lemon-yellow, salmon-pink and wine-purple. The foliage covering is echoed through the tall cypress arches by glaucous-leafed rhododendron species, chosen also for their blending flower colours.

On the west front is the Sunk Garden, designed by Gertrude Jekyll, with lawn beds, wall beds and pergola; every plant used contributes purple, blue, orange and yellow colourings. It is a scene of particular splendour when the orange azaleas are in flower.

These formal areas of Mount Stewart rank with Hidcote and Sissinghurst, Tintinhull and Newby, and many more gardens created earlier in this century where colour, as well as design and form, has been a guiding principle.

People of all tastes make gardens, including those who are oblivious to clashes of colour, and I must admit that all such attitudes are very much at the whim or preference of the beholder. Some people desire to exercise their artistic capabilities by arranging borders or beds of one colour only. The easiest to arrange is one devoted to white flowers; these can be coupled with silvery and grey foliage but I think very dark green is needed as well. You can hardly go wrong with a white border; having done it you will be surprised how few truly white flowers there are. Most of them verge towards blush or cream or green. There are many white gardens about the country, Sissinghurst containing one of the most noted. It is at its best in full summer, likewise the highly successful purple border. This is aided by a gorgeous backcloth of clematises and by the clash of red from the flowers and fruits of *Rosa moyesii*. Blue borders have been attempted in several gardens partly because true blue is scarce and always much desired; the schemes usually become adulterated with purple and lavender, however, because of the scarcity of true blue. In any case true blue amongst green foliage needs clear pale yellow or perhaps white to enhance the blue.

I have never felt that areas peopled solely with yellow flowers are successful; yellow is too near to green. Such a scheme needs toning down with cream and white or toning up with orange flowers or coppery foliage, or both. Pink and white allied with coppery foliage are a delight; grey foliage could be added to taste.

A scheme which I have long had in mind but have never found the opportunity of using is coppery purple foliage with a foreground of orange flowers and lime-green leaves. One can think out endless schemes, but the right setting has to be found for them.

Strong yellow, pure white and bright red are the most obtrusive colours, standing out from their fellows. For this reason they should not be used in the distance, at the end of a vista. The eye at once leaps to them, shortens the perspective and is not left wondering what happens at the turn of the path. The view is finished with one glance. The imagination is not stimulated. At the beginning of this paragraph I referred to "strong" yellow. This was deliberate because in discussing this sort of thing one day with an artist I mentioned "hard" yellow. She informed me that to her all yellows were soft. Which to me was surprising, and may be the reason for some gardeners who deliberately choose some definite bright colour to make a focal point, as they would a garden ornament or seat. This is not the lesson learned at Hidcote.

THE COLOURS OF STONE AND BRICK

Often the environment aids selections. Colours can blend with and lead up to an already established Copper Beech for instance, a Copper Nut or *Prunus*, or a bright variegated holly or Silver Willow. Turning back to the house, the colour of the stone or brick must be taken into consideration. Stone itself can vary much from a cold grey to fawn and brown and the rich warm yellowish tint of Ham stone in Somerset. Montacute is built of this stone and even after hundreds of years' exposure the house still dominates the garden by its colour as much as by its bulk. The borders were planted with all the soft colours and grey foliage plants by Vita Sackville-West (Lady Nicolson) for the National Trust many years ago. Phyllis Reiss lived nearby at Tintinhull, a house of the same colour around which she had gardened for some years. Her taste indoors was for the strong colours. When she undertook to look after Montacute garden some years later than Lady Nicolson, she gradually replaced the soft tones with rich reds and purples, lemon-yellow and some coppery foliage. White, another strong colour, was not forgotten. The borders came alive and did successful battle with the house. I recall much the same at Bramham Park, Yorkshire, where there was a paved court by the house which is of dark honey-coloured stone. Lavish plantings of every warm rich colour for spring display were used – purple aubrieta, many-coloured polyanthus and tulips vied with each other and created a scene of splendour. It quite subdued the house. The soft brown Hornton sandstone of which Upton House (the National Trust), near Banbury, is built was given a lovely complementary planting of Catmint (lavender-blue) and yellow roses by Miss K. Lloyd-Jones in the 1950s.

Brick needs just such careful attention. The "stone" coloured bricks can be treated like stone itself; the "red" bricks need a lot of care. One hears the phrase "old pink brick", but I have never seen a pink brick; they are every tone of soft to dark terracotta, the most difficult being those nearest to red. There are many stock bricks of blended tones. My own contain every tint of fawn, terracotta, to dark cinder, with rather yellowish mortar courses, and I find I can only enjoy white, yellow, blue or purple flowers against the walls; anything of a mauve or pinkish tone is out of place. Other examples of violet and white against red-brick walls are found at Dunham Massey, Hatchlands and Clandon Park, all properties of the National Trust. As a general rule I think it best to keep to this scheme against red bricks, though on occasion a clear pink rose will be successful. I have never had to garden with the dark liver-coloured bricks which are being used so much today; probably the light pinks would suit them well. Apparently their colour is brought about not by normal baking, but by gas heating.

Terracotta is an old, old term for baked earth, such as we find sometimes in the ash-heap of a bonfire. It is surprisingly sympathetic to a variety of colours, like human flesh. When the orangery at Blickling Hall, a National Trust property in Norfolk, was redecorated in soft terracotta, we found that glaucous greenery was most sympathetic. It made a beautiful contrast to the dark shining green of camellias. We also used the creamy-white variegated privet *Ligustrum ovalifolium* 'Argenteum', which in the subdued light became luxuriant and very beautiful. Though the building was unheated, *Cupressus cashmiriana* managed to thrive, its lacy drooping grey-blue foliage making a remarkable contrast to the broad leaves of *Hosta sieboldiana elegans*. I thought *Rhododendron cinnabarinum* and *R. concatenans* might have thriven also, to display their blue-green young foliage, but they would not grow in the restricted light.

MIXED COLOURS OF ANNUALS

In these days of specialization – as opposed to proliferation – the availability of seed-raised strains of plants is much at risk. Hand in hand with the scientific aids to production seems to go a determination to get everyone to grow annuals in mixture. Many of the self-colours of the past are vanishing from the lists and as a consequence a medley of colours is the result from mixed strains. I suppose it is all a matter of cost of production. It is however a sad development. Annuals are essentially colour givers, rather than (as I have stressed elsewhere) plants of personality to be looked upon as individuals. Only in certain parts of the garden will a medley of colours look well and we should continue to ask for special colours for our schemes, in an effort to keep them still in cultivation. It is a strange fact that whereas these foreigners were introduced from their native countries in somewhat variable colours, through many decades our expert seedsmen have first developed and then discarded self-colours of reliable strains, just when gardening as an art is coming so much to the fore.

FOLIAGE COLOURS

In my book *Trees in the Landscape* I devoted a paragraph or two to the danger of planting copper beeches and other trees with coppery-purple leaves right away from the house. Foliage of this colour is, in any case, no use except when brought to its full tint by bright light. I have the same reservations about this colour in the garden: I like to keep it fairly near at hand and do not find it sympathetic in a woodland glade. This is of course purely a personal point of view, and there are many variations of this tint, some rich and blatant like the copper beech or well-known *Prunus* and *Acer palmatum* varieties, others only with a hint of the purple tone like *Weigela florida* 'Foliis Purpureis'. I call to mind particularly the careful blending of all sorts of purplish and grey tones in Brenda Colvin's garden at Filkins in Wiltshire. Here was an assembly dominated by the grey-green of *Pyrus elaeagrifolia* and the subdued purplish tone of *Prunus spinosa* 'Purpurea', with a foreground of Jackman's Blue Rue in the sun and *Hosta sieboldiana* in the shade.

This reminds us again of glaucous foliage which, though often used with it, is of quite a different value from the woolly or silky silvery-greys. Miss

Jekyll's favourite Seakale is the most splendid of glaucous leaves, and the Cardoon and Scots Thistle the most magnificent of silvers. I find the silvers are the best possible foil for all the mauves, pinks, soft purples, etc., while the softer more receding hue of the glaucous plants assorts specially well with clear blues, purples, whites, and even yellows. Glaucous and silvery foliage, be it noted, is best in full sun; this includes conifers.

It will be seen from the above that we need never be defeated in our colour schemes by lack of variety in foliage colour, for sun or shade. While flowers to many of us are paramount, we cannot make a successful garden without carefully considering the foliage; fortunately some flowers carry with them the ideal foliage colour when it is other than green. Those who look askance at too much green in a garden may take heart from the fact that a considerable area could be filled with plants with foliage of every tint other than green, and many would produce flowers as well. This might be worth a trial in a public park where visitors are always looking for a diversion, but I should not want to live with such a scheme myself.

Leaves may be plain green; dark, medium or light; shiny or matt. Every variation has a special merit or significance in the garden. But there are many other colours to be found among leaves. The most strident are those with yellow variegation. Not only can the area of yellow in the leaf vary but so can the hue. 'Golden Queen' holly or *Elaeagnus pungens* 'Maculata' are two of the most commonly seen of really bright variegation. Being evergreen they are with us for the whole twelve months. The most startling in early summer are the deciduous yellow-flushed *Ribes sanguineum* 'Brocklebankii' and *Philadelphus coronarius* 'Aureus'. Theirs is a brilliant lime-yellow, but since their leaves are apt to burn in hot sunshine they are best grown where they are shaded for the hottest part of the day, where their colour will be somewhat muted towards lime-green. This sort of shelter should be provided for any such coloured deciduous plants. On the other hand yellow-flushed counterparts among evergreens – such as *Ligustrum vulgare* 'Vicaryi', *Lonicera nitida* 'Baggesen's Gold', *Ilex crenata* 'Golden Gem', and the yellowish conifers – are at their most brilliant in full exposure. The same is true of all yellow-variegated shrubs.

Practically all white-variegated shrubs give their most telling colour in part or full shade. This gives them a special value to planters because they lighten dark shady backgrounds. In sunny places the best lightness comes from the so-called silver plants whose green leaves – and perhaps stems – are clothed in a white woolly or silky covering.

Sometimes I am asked to prepare planting plans for a pair of borders running east and west. It frequently happens that one is shaded from the south. Thus the lightness of grey foliage in the south-facing border can be echoed by white-variegated plants on the north-facing one. And here in the shade which is not enjoyed by grey or silver plants is the place for that invaluable *Rosa rubrifolia* – or *R. glauca* as we are now told to call it. In the shade its leaves become luxuriant and of a cool, pale, leaden green tint, whereas in sunshine the prevailing tint is purplish.

Purplish-brown foliage, often termed copper or coppery purple, is a valuable addition to our colour planting. It can be used to give depth and richness to reds and oranges; it is equally delightful with pink and lavender-pink. In the first combination it will be retiring and in the second dominant. Although variegated plants and shrubs and those with tinted leaves have come to the fore so much in recent years, it may be interesting to recall that Miss Jekyll designed both a "silver" border and a "gold" border for the garden at Pyrford Court, Surrey. They were highly successful.

I have heard it said by people with small gardens that there just is not the space available to arrange borders or areas of specific colours. This is of course often true, though much can be done with a bulky shrub, evergreen probably, to make the division, but too much segregation of colours can create a worrying effect in a garden of limited extent; it is just the opposite of what is desired. On the other hand I have found it invaluable to deny certain borders one or more colours but to allow them elsewhere. In my book *Three Gardens* I enlarged upon this: in one border, dominated by a large variegated *Elaeagnus*, all pinks and mauves were left out. This therefore became a mixture of white and yellow, blue and purple with some glaucous (bluish) foliage. In the rest of the garden these colours were omitted and pink and lavender were linked to silvery-grey foliage. I find it helpful to be governed by such gentle rules; it makes it much easier when finding places for kind gifts – for I am, I must confess, an ardent plantsman as well as having ideas about colours!

On one occasion I was asked to design flower borders to run along each side of crossing central paths in a large walled garden which was otherwise devoted to produce of all kinds. The owner wanted them all filled with old French roses, with lots of bulbs for spring, and fondly thought the old roses would continue to give their whites, soft pinks, mauves, purples and maroons until autumn. Having explained this could not be I set to work, arranging that one walk would have the roses that did repeat in later summer and that they would be augmented with herbaceous plants and shrubs of like tones for the whole season. The cross walk would follow these same colours while the once-flowering Gallica and allied roses were in flower until about July 10th, after which the herbaceous plants and shrubs would provide only yellow, orange and true blue. Both vistas were bolstered with grey and coppery foliage.

I was asked to go and see the borders two years later in August, "because they are looking so splendid". I found that the head gardener had filled every available space in both walks with a mixture of colours from bedding plants of all kinds – antirrhinums, salpiglossis, gaillardias, zinnias and all the rest. . . . But, seriously, I think this art of making an area of the garden change colour in mid season is a great ploy and it should appeal to owners of small gardens. The crux of the matter is to choose the tints of your foliage plants first, so that they will act as complements to varied colour schemes.

Finally let us return to plain green. One cannot very well have a garden without green. Today's predilection for bright colours is the very antithesis of a "green thought in a green shade". If our garden is large enough to be divided into "rooms" or compartments, we might make a tour of it, through all the colours mentioned, and eventually arrive in an area devoted to greenery, eschewing all its extremes and concentrating on the mid tone of true green. There would be an ample range of tones from grass green to the black-green of certain ivies and *Helleborus foetidus*. There would be leaves of every shape and size, rounded, narrow or filigree, and the plants would give different habits: the firm round bergenias, the drooping Day Lilies and grasses, the grace of bamboos, and soldier-like cypresses. There is no limit when we start looking for variety, but this sort of thing is best achieved in full or partial shade. This is merely an attempt to take advantage from nature's own expertise in semi-woodland. For open, sunny areas brighter colours can be enjoyed. The use of greenery as a complete furnishing leads us on to the next chapter.

5

Perspective, texture and continuity of interest

The size of a garden has very little to do with its merit. It is merely an accident relating to the circumstances of the owner. It is the size of his heart and brain and goodwill that will make his garden either delightful or dull, as the case may be, and either leave it at the monotonous dead level, or raise it, in whatever degree he may, towards that of a work of fine art.

GERTRUDE JEKYLL, *Wood and Garden*, 1899

We hear a lot about plant association these days; it is closely linked with the effect of leaf-mass. It is something that has grown up during the last half century or so and is nearly always associated with contrasts, which make a mixed planting "interesting". I am not disputing this in the least, but we must also remember that contrasts, if repeated too often, begin to pall and that the Jekyll idea of variation within the theme is equally valuable. I do not think she actually wrote these words but it is a maxim picked up from her writings and photographs. "Interesting" mixtures of leaf shapes is certainly a comparatively new concept in garden planting; in fact not so many years ago, Miles Hadfield, the noted garden historian, remarked to me that "this is the only thing all you fellows are interested in today". He did not mean this unkindly, I am sure, but it made me realize how deeply steeped he was in the broad history of garden planting and, also, how much we owe to the landscape architects and flower arrangers. It is they who have awakened us all to the value and contrast of foliage and it is not difficult to see why.

Evergreen leaves are with us for the whole year and deciduous ones for half the year. This statement alone brings us to the inescapable fact that they are far more important in garden furnishing than flowers. Only a few plants of any kind flower for more than one month; many for even less.

Getting down still more to fundamentals we must recall that we all have to garden with the same basic things. There is the house and the soil, the paths, the lawn and perhaps some masonry. All these are static; giving them life and

FORM IN BORDER PLANTING

16 The famous border at Kiftsgate Court, Gloucestershire. The Copper Beech hedge acts as a rich back-drop for flowers of blue and yellow with coppery foliage intermingled. *Rodgersia podophylla*, delphiniums of clear bright blue, *Miscanthus sinensis* 'Gracillimus', *Hypericum* 'Hidcote', hosta, *Thalictrum speciosissimum* and coppery *Berberis*.

17 Herbaceous plants were allowed to sprawl over the gravel path in Lady Moore's garden near Dublin. *Veronica teucrium* 'Trehane', *Geranium psilostemon*, pinks, peonies.

18 At St John's College, Cambridge; daffodils planted by the "spadeful" method, but sufficiently closely to merge into generous drifts.

19 *Narcissus cyclamineus* at Wisley, Surrey (The Royal Horticultural Society). They have spread by seeding into random groups.

20 A scattered grouping of daffodils at Chobham Place, Surrey, with plenty of lawn space to accentuate their embroidery.

21 This kind of intimate, small-scale planting is best done by hand and trowel, immediately after flowering. *Erythronium dens canis, Narcissus obvallaris, N. pseudonarcissus.*

22 Daffodils. Lavish planting of this kind leaves little to the imagination.

23 This is the fatal result of the "spadeful" method of planting daffodils, fortunately softened by blue *Anemone apennina.*

24 Old garden ramblers never look so well as when allowed to hang from natural supports. 'The Garland', *Rosa multiflora*, etc.

25 At the Roseraie de l'Haÿ, near Paris, roses are trained up the rope swags (instead of down them) for which their growth is best suited. 'Madame Alfred Carrière'.

26 Conifer shapes. *Cupres-socyparis* × *leylandii* makes a shapely, tapering column very quickly; its companions are dark green *Cupressus sempervirens* and *C.s.* 'Swane's Golden'.

27 A pleasing assortment of conifer shapes at Dane's Cottage, Surrey. *Picea pungens* glaucous form in foreground, backed by *Chamaecyparis* and *Thuja*, with an interplanting of heathers.

28 Irish Yews respond well to clipping and here at Williamston House Aberdeenshire, they are given a conical outline, as opposed to the usual truncated shape.

29 Panelled and buttressed Yew hedges surround the Iris garden at Bagatelle, near Paris. The June-flowering Bearded Irises in the dry outer beds act as a prelude to the marsh beds in the middle, filled with forms of *Iris laevigata* and *I. ensata* (*I. kaempferi*), with clumps of *Caltha* for contrast and early flowers.

30 Where water lilies are planted they should be kept in check to ensure that at least two-thirds of the surface of the water is free, since the whole idea of having water in the garden is to see it. At Bedgebury Pinetum, Kent.

31 Pleaching is much used in France to create formal avenues. These are Lime (Linden) trees at Mottisfont Abbey, Hampshire (National Trust); *Chionodoxa luciliae* is spreading beneath.

32 *Magnolia sinensis* is one of the great beauties of the year and is deliciously fragrant. Nodding flowers or drooping growth of shrubs is most appreciated when the beholder can look up to them.

Sensitive grouping of shrub shapes at Bulkeley Mill.

Remarkable contrast of shrub shapes at Lanarth, Cornwall. Compare this
analytical sketch with colour plate XVI.

Contrast of tree, shrub and plant shapes at the head of the Second Lake, Sheffield Park garden, East Sussex (National Trust).

The bare ingredients of an association at Bodnant, North Wales. Compare with colour plate XIII (National Trust).

movement are all the plants, from tall trees down to tiny creeping plants, bulbs, and perhaps water. I think the desire is within us all to use these constituents to make some sort of paradise or haven away from our daily chores, which by skill can be made to look larger, perhaps infinite, without providing unnecessary work. In the last chapter we saw how colours can help; here we are concerned mainly with growth and shapes, known by the hard-core of gardeners as the "habit" of a plant.

Various ways of using leaves to lessen work were explored in my *Plants for Ground-Cover* book. This was concerned with small- and large-scale plantings, but in *Trees in the Landscape* I made suggestions for the creation of apparently limitless space. In gardens (as in landscapes) the boundary is often only too apparent, but we will leave this until a later chapter.

TYPES OF FOLIAGE

Just think what we command in terms of foliage. Carpets of moss, close mown or rough mown greensward; vigorous carpeters such as *Cotula, Sagina* and *Acaena*; the whole range of herbaceous plants from the tiniest to the biggest like *Rodgersia, Peltiphyllum, Rheum, Heracleum, Cynara* and the giant *Gunnera*. Among shrubs tiny-leafed *Erica* and *Buxus* to broad-leafed *Viburnum davidii*, laurels, rhododendrons, *Rhamnus imeretina, Fatsia* and many more. The same range is available in trees: almost fern-like *Nothofagus menziesii* and *Carpinus turczaninowii* to the large blades of *Aesculus, Paulownia* and *Catalpa*, not forgetting a huge range likewise of pinnate leaves. There are the conifers, too, with their tiny or slender leaves and needles, and dramatic outline.

It is a notable trait of engravings of earlier centuries, depicting landscapes, that nearly always there is a group of Burdock or other large-leafed plant in the foreground. Nothing so clearly gives a sense of scale and perspective apart from figures or buildings. The same sense can be achieved even in small gardens by keeping large-leafed bergenias, hostas and *Viburnum davidii* in the foreground and decreasing the leaf-size in all sorts of plants the farther we go from the house.

It is equally true to say that while size is very important the texture of the leaf is vital too. The illusion of distance can be fostered by using glossy leaves in the foreground and matt in the background. Because silvery-grey plants thrive best in full sun, they are usually well-lit, and appear to come forward as a consequence in spite of their leaves being of matt surface. Glaucous leaves likewise need the sun but there is a range of size from large (Seakale and *Hosta*) to filigree (Rue) to be conjured with.

As with colour, size and texture, so with the growth-shapes, particularly of shrubs. Those of dramatic shape – horizontal, columnar or merely characterful such as pinnate *Rhus typhina* – when placed near at hand can cause the eye to travel away to gentle, arching or dense, small-leafed shrubs in the distance. The same is true of trees.

But all these paragraphs have been concerned with deception. Sometimes we are not dependent on deception to please the eye. All the examples I have chosen are calculated to show variations within a theme. Sometimes a strong contrast will hold the eye with great delight. Take for example that most noted contrast of wide arching parrotias and columnar Incense Cedars (*Calocedrus* or *Libocedrus*) at Westonbirt. As well as their differing shapes there are their differing textures: the parrotias are broad-leafed, deciduous, the Incense Cedars evergreen with tiny dark leaves. The grouping has been repeated for the future at Wisley on the far side of the Trial Ground. The same sort of contrast can be arranged in very small scale with *Alyssum spinosum* and a miniature vertical juniper. *Deutzia* × *rosea* and *Juniperus* 'Skyrocket' would have the same effect in a larger size which extends ever upwards to oak trees grouped with Lombardy Poplars. Those are examples of the rounded with the vertical; a similar scale can be found using prostrate plants with rounded, or indeed with vertical. The example of the Irish Junipers in the heather garden at Wisley comes to mind.

TINY GARDENS

Many people today garden in tiny courts and my examples may seem out of their reach and comprehension, but so great is the variety of plants available that suitable groupings can be chosen for the smaller plots. While it may not always be successful in a tiny courtyard to achieve any sense of perspective in varying the size of leaf, much can be done by planting one big shrub which will prevent the eye from taking in the whole extent in one glance. This is a lesson learnt in big old gardens, where something has obviously reached out-of-scale size, but which at the same time adds majesty and mystery. In much overshadowed town gardens it will be found that glossy leaves, of any size, are most advantageous; they reflect whatever light is available.

I must not presume however that the yearning of all garden owners is to deceive – to plant so that their gardens appear larger than they really are, or limitless. Some are content with the rich contrast or blending that can be achieved with careful plant association. Where there is masonry of any sort – walls, paving, steps – something with bold leaves is very effective. There are hostas for shade, bergenias for sun or shade; the crisp contrast of evergreen *Waldsteinia* or London Pride. The filigree of ferns adds a delicacy that few other plants provide; they are all best in shade but similar delicacy is found in

Sweet Cicely, *Ferula* and *Selinum* for sunny places. A plant of particularly noble proportion of leaf-blade is *Silphium terebinthinaceum;* unfortunately its flowers in August are disappointing, just small yellow daisies on tall stems. Many of our best herbaceous plants have good characterful leaves – for instance peonies, lupins, delphiniums, the larger geraniums, species of *Acanthus, Helleborus, Cimicifuga* and *Rodgersia.* There are also the sword-shaped leaves: *Iris, Yucca, Crocosmia, Curtonus* and the evergreen, nearly hardy *Phormium.*

All these and others are mentioned later in this book and are fully described and categorized in my *Perennial Garden Plants* to which I will ask you to refer to save repetition.

THE FOLIAGE OF SHRUBS

Shrubs – and I should really include yuccas with them – offer just as much variety. Compare for instance the great shining blades of laurels with the rough surfaces of the leaves of *Viburnum rhytidophyllum*; and splendid mahonias, *Fatsia* and *Magnolia grandiflora*; *Eriobotrya* and large-leafed species of *Rhododendron.* There is enough there to satisfy all cravings for big leaves among the evergreens alone. I have a soft spot for the big, jagged, vine-like leaves of *Rubus odoratus* and *R. nutkanus* which bring us to deciduous shrubs, also the great pinnate leaves of *Rhus glabra* and *R.g.* 'Laciniata' (which are superior to the far more common *R. typhina* and *R.t.* 'Laciniata'), the sorbarias and *Aralia elata.* A sprinkling of shrubs such as the above will give character to any mixed planting.

Of late years two cultivars of laurel, *Prunus laurocerasus*, have come to be appreciated, 'Zabeliana' and 'Otto Luyken'. The former is an old plant, raised in 1898, the latter is of recent origin. Had it not been for today's interest in foliage 'Zabeliana' might well have remained in obscurity. It is of mid-green, of graceful arching or horizontal habit, a study in submissiveness, while the latter is of very dark green, a dense upward-thrusting, dominant shrub in any position. While 'Zabeliana' is wider than high in maturity, 'Otto Luyken' is about equal in either dimension and both have small, glittering leaves and thrive in sun or shade. I mention these as an indicator of how we must search through the lists for extremes of growth for different uses and positions, even in the forms of one species. The same is true of the tree that has excelled all others in its variation from seed in habit and colour – the Lawson's Cypress of North America, *Chamaecyparis lawsoniana.* It is available from a dense bun-shape ('Tamariscifolia') to the tallest of columns, in a variety of tints.

If we wish to avoid striking contrasts there is ample scope for interest in small-leafed shrubs. The grouping that immediately comes to mind is of course the numerous heathers and allied plants, prostrate junipers, dwarf hebes, small-leafed ivies and the little carpet-making evergreen fern *Blechnum penna-marina*, all of which are so effectively used at Knightshayes Court in Devon (the National Trust). I have never seen the North American prostrate bluish junipers used to better effect than in Mr Hillier's garden, Jermyns, in Hampshire; here they make wide mats of steely grey and blue against a totally different texture and colour, that of shingle.

In these days of shortage of labour, ground-cover of different kinds is much to the fore. It can be plants, peat, leafmould, pine needles, pulverized bark, or shingle; all are effectively used to avoid cultivation, preventing weeds from seeding, especially at the Savill Garden, Windsor; also they are materials on which one can walk and yet avoid making foot-marks. There is no doubt that for sun-loving shrubs and plants shingle has much in its favour. I recall a special use for it at Merrist Wood, Surrey, where a wide variety of grassy and sword-leafed plants is used in dramatic combination, creating a desert or savannah effect. The shingle can be graded quite small for small areas, or rough and ungraded – containing some quite large stones – for bigger areas. This is how it is used in the Savill Garden where John Bond has made a most successful gravel and stone area; not only does the background sharpen the outlines of the plants, but it also gives them excellent drainage and dry "necks" in the winter. Wherever possible the local material should be used; for this purpose one gravel is as good as another, except for the fact that some may be limy.

LONG INTEREST IN LESSER GARDENS

Earlier I mentioned how some famous gardens such as Hidcote are divided into separate "rooms" or compartments and that each of these is devoted to separate assemblies of plants – dictated by colour and other considerations – and that they produce flowers throughout the season. Few of us have gardens today that can be divided into so many sections as Hidcote, in fact quite likely there is only one section. It is into this that one looks, walks and works and its interest should be sustained throughout the year. As described in my *Three Gardens* I have got over some of the difficulty by planting my front garden for display mainly from November until April, while the back garden is for enjoyment during the warmer months. This primary division simplifies matters considerably. Thus the front is given autumn, winter and early spring bulbs along the paths, and is in the main carpeted with winter-flowering heaths, with shrubs like *Mahonia* × *media* varieties for late autumn to be followed soon after Christmas by early rhododendrons, sarcococcas, viburnums and skimmias. Here and there are hellebores and of course the yellow Winter Jasmine, variegated ivies, *Euonymus* and other evergreen shrubs. It is remarkably work-free and full of contentment. Further details may be found in my *Colour in the Winter Garden.*

This assembly of winter joys leaves me free to plant for late spring until early autumn in the back garden, where I like to sit and see and eat as well as to work and study. After all, we do not often sit out of doors during the winter months unless the garden is particularly cosy, so this arrangement seemed sensible to me. It does however take some forethought to make the whole of the back garden floriferous for six or seven months. I do not propose to go into the detail of the planting here – it is fully covered in *Three Gardens* – but merely to indicate some of the more important ideas.

We shall be considering boundaries in a later chapter so it is only necessary here to say that one has the walls of the house, garden shed, fences and hedges to clothe as well as the ground. These backcloths can help considerably when we remember how long roses and honeysuckles, for instance, flower and are followed by clematises.

There are always some deciduous shrubs in flower or berry or providing early autumn colour; under them is a good place for Lenten Hellebores, pulmonarias, primroses, Lily of the Valley and other early flowering carpeters interspersed with spring bulbs.

But we do not want all the spring things at the back of the borders. Small bulbs – crocuses, scillas, miniature daffodils – interplant quite happily among the later spring plants along the fronts of the borders. These plants are what I should call large rock plants such as violas, London Pride, *Cerastium biebersteinii*, and pinks. There is another opportunity of planting larger daffodils and tulips around standard roses; also around peonies with whose brownish-purplish young foliage they contrast well, and around hostas (whose later foliage will cover up the decaying daffodil leaves), and agapanthuses which appear late. This all means that the front verges and the shrubby background are in beauty at least until May, after which the main masses of herbaceous plants start, to be overtaken by roses, and later by Tree Mallows, fuchsias, indigoferas and *Ligustrum quihoui* towards the autumn.

The shady portions can be treated likewise with an equally rich assortment of shrubs, plants and bulbs which actually thrive in shade. We should never look askance at shady areas unless they are overshadowed by the most dense and rooty of large trees. A big beech tree, with its dense canopy and greedy surface roots, inhibits everything.

With so intensive a coverage of plants the soil must be kept in good heart by applying fertilizer in spring before spreading the weed-excluding mulch.

We nearly all plant too thickly and as a rule shrubs always exceed the sizes we imagine they will attain. A shrub can be constantly thinned and thus kept under control, but if due to neglect it has to be cut back severely it will be some years before it is really presentable again. If a shrub gets too large *it should be enjoyed* is the message of old gardens, so long as it pays its rent in beauty. As shrubs grow the borders will become increasingly shady and the choice of herbaceous plants may have to be altered.

In small gardens therefore one needs to interplant to economize in space, and plants of good foliage should be to the fore. Nobody wants to see a solid mass of graded shrubs and plants. There should be an in-and-out and an up-and-down outline creating an irregularity which can be enjoyed walking around, or sitting in one spot. It is a living picture which we are attempting and every year it must be re-interpreted allowing opportunism to be the watchword.

Part II

Garden plants in their classes, historically and today

6

Trees

I like flowering plants, but I like trees more – for the reason, I suppose, that they are slower coming to maturity, are longer lived, that you can become better acquainted with them, and that in the course of years memories and associations hang as thickly on their boughs as do leaves in summer or fruit in autumn.

ALEXANDER SMITH,
contributor to *Corners of Grey Old Gardens*, 1914

In the days of the first Elizabeth, and subsequently through the Caroline period, the only trees that were tolerated in gardens were those that bore fruit. In Elizabethan gardens these were loved and cherished along with all other garden treasures. In fact at that time the Seasons were deeply observed and created a firm pattern in the lives of mankind; jobs were done "at Candlemas" or "at Michaelmas". By Michaelmas – in fact even by July – practically all the cultivated garden flowers would have been over and fruits of all kinds were not only desirable but gave the garden interest. The fruit trees were left in the mixed, produce-gardens for the next 200 years or so and with them might be grown the May or Hawthorn perhaps tinted with pink, and the Laburnum with of course the Crab apple, the Sloe, the Bullace and the wild pear. These early fruits with the Apricot and Peach and all other fruits have been grown ever since; their qualities have been raised by selection from seed to our modern fine varieties. Currants, gooseberries and raspberries have followed along similar lines. Their history is wrapped up right through the centuries until 1914, in the great walled gardens which have always contained the garden craft of the nation.

But in the eighteenth century a new type of tree was accepted as a thing of beauty. The big native trees, with which the country had been more or less covered long ago, had been thinned by commercial demand since they provided the most popular material for building and making of practically every aid to mankind's livelihood. With the awakening to beauty – as opposed to use – trees took a new place in British affections and the great

Landscapists planted them in hundreds of thousands, creating what today are still some of our most superb landscapes.

J.C. Loudon in his *Encyclopaedia of Gardening* of 1827 is somewhat reticent about garden trees, contenting himself with a paragraph on the matter followed by a tabulated list in which the value and colours of the quite insignificant flowers of some trees are greatly exaggerated. On the other hand he writes exhaustingly about trees in the landscape.

But I think we must go farther back than Loudon to find the beginnings of our modern tree gardening, and like so many things in our Western civilization, the inspiration comes from the Chinese. It was 1772 when Sir William Chambers wrote his *A Dissertation on Oriental Gardening*. Here are a few of his observations on the ideas and ideals to which the Chinese adhered: "The perfection of trees for ornamental gardening consists in their size, in the beauty and variety of their forms, the colour and smoothness of their bark, the quantity, shape and rich verdure of their foliage, with its early appearance in the spring, and long duration in the autumn; . . . their hardiness . . . in making no litter, during the spring and summer, by the fall of blossom; and the strength of their branches to resist, unhurt, the violence of tempests." I think today many of us enjoy the moment when the ground is strewn with fallen petals; in fact I have heard it said that this is the greatest moment in the life of a 'Kanzan' cherry! But here was a new concept for the *garden* value of trees which, during that century, had been relegated merely to the role of shaping the English landscape mostly in belts and clumps.

By Victorian times great trees were collected from all over the world and perhaps interplanted among our native trees, or spaced out on lawns or in fields to make an entirely new contribution to the landscape. Those planted on lawns around the great houses – the cedars, wellingtonias, Douglas Firs, cryptomerias and other splendid foreigners – are now accepted as the embellishment of many country seats, and town parks. Although many of them strayed into smaller gardens, there they usually look incongruous, the sense of scale not having been appreciated in the excitement of growing these new foreign conifers. Likewise natives such as oaks and beeches came to be planted within the larger gardens.

Later and during this century something very different has happened. A stream of what are generally known as "flowering" trees were introduced. The Weeping Willow, the Tree of Heaven, the Copper Beech and American oaks noted for their autumn colour had been known and grown since the eighteenth century, but now was the tide altered, bringing the smaller trees from America and the Far East: thorns, crabs, rowans, whitebeams and the like, all eminently suitable for the smaller gardens and apart from their flowers they mostly excel in autumn colour. In fact until this century little was done to make a feature of autumn colour from trees and shrubs in gardens.

The last great influx of flowering trees was that of the Japanese cherries – hybrids and garden forms of ancient lineage in that country. In terms of blossom only the hybrid Crab Apples could compete with them and the last sixty years or so have witnessed their rise and fall in popularity. They were, many of them, introduced by Collingwood Ingram, who was their chief advocate and soon they were being listed by Waterers of Bagshot with all the enthusiasm of the inter-war years for flowering trees. They have two big disadvantages: one is that by degrees bullfinches discovered their toothsome buds with the result that in some districts both cherries and crabs present a poor appearance at flowering time; the other disadvantage is their roots. Practically all Japanese cherries are grafted on rootstocks of our wild cherry or Gean, a much more vigorous tree, which is coarse in growth above and below ground. On this rootstock they are most unsuitable for planting on a lawn: the wide-spreading roots travel near to the surface and in due course heave themselves up, making mowing a difficult, sometimes impossible, job. In addition the roots form suckers.

Whereas at one time they were the most popular of flowering trees of garden size – with two 'Kanzan' being planted to one of any other kind – and indeed are still planted, we have watched their decline. At the same time it must be granted that they make a superb display; collectively their season is long, starting with *Prunus subhirtella* 'Autumnalis' in autumn, followed by *P. incisa* forms and *P. conradinae* soon after Christmas; *P. yedoensis* with the almonds and plums, and then the main mass at the end of April and into early May. The whole series, together with the Crabs, blend in a haze of white, blush, pink and carmine and provide one of the tints needed to add variety to the general spread of yellow daffodils, causing the garden to be as colourful as at any other time of the year. Like the coloured thorns and the laburnums they provide such a mass of colour that the garden appears emptied after they are over.

The single-flowered thorns, mostly white apart from the pink and red forms of *Crataegus oxyacantha*, the rowans and whitebeams are mainly for autumn display and have added a new dimension to our gardens, together with many maples. I have seldom indulged in planting for autumn colour, being avid for actual *flowers* throughout the year, but enjoy what comes from trees and shrubs planted probably for their other attractions. Autumn colour is seen perhaps best when the sunlight shines *through* it. Berries and coloured barks need the sunlight *on* them, otherwise they are seen merely as silhouettes; this is an important point in siting. Everyone seems to glory in the brilliant scarlet of autumn leaves but bright yellow is equally important. In fact I feel that red can be overdone and we need the clear yellows to give the best contrast against evergreens.

The laburnums flower mostly with the thorns and to me one of the most offensive colour combinations is the brilliant brassy yellow of laburnum with the pink and scarlet of the thorns such as 'Paul's Scarlet' and 'Rosea Plena'. The laburnum is well worth a place in a garden when surrounded solely with greenery, for its yellow bears a hint of this tint. All types are rather stiff and upright in growth, but lose this later, particularly when shaded by higher trees. 'Vossii' can then become a gracious and lovely thing in thin woodland, spread beneath, perhaps, with white bluebells; together the green and yellow and white make a delicious blend for a short while. Thinning out the branches of a laburnum as it grows saves it from becoming a dense vase-shape; it is not until the branches bend outwards that the flowers can hang free of them and reveal their greatest beauty. Likewise the crabs and thorns repay well some thinning of branches.

SCREENING

We have to be circumspect in planting even small trees in a small garden. There is perhaps the neighbouring unsightly building, lamp standard or pole to screen. Either to me would be a compelling factor in tree planting, but it is a mistake to put in a screen of quick-growing fastigiate conifers without first considering how they will fit with the rest of the garden scheme. There is no surer way of indicating that there is something that needs hiding than the planting of even a short row of conifers. Sometimes I think we have recourse too freely in choosing evergreens for screening. Though they do it effectively for the whole year, the summer, when one mainly enjoys the views for long hours of the day, is really the testing time for unsightly objects. In winter densely twigged trees create something of a screen without being so solid and dominating as a conifer or other evergreen.

THE VALUE OF SHADE

The shade cast by a tree has enormous value. Many people prefer to sit in the shade so that the planting of a tree indicates that under its branches will be a place for a seat after a few years. Others prefer to sit in the sun. As the years pass there is the gradual reorganizing of the underplanting to be done; for some years sun-lovers will thrive, but in due course the shade will provide homes for those plants which prefer shade, and there are many. But wherever possible a tree should be so placed that it casts its shade across the flat lawn in the morning or evening. That dark shadow moving across the grass, changing in shape as the day passes, is a magical addition to a garden view.

The choice of trees for a garden must be governed, if aesthetics are to be considered, by the type of tree in neighbouring properties, whether gardens or the countryside. Trees, in common with all plants, have personalities whose potentials are brought forth or neglected by the environment. To take but an obvious example: if you garden in an oak-dominated neighbourhood it is unwise to decorate your garden with pines and birches; likewise if the garden is given character by its old fruit trees, Japanese Maples will not fit well as an addition. No exercise so brings out such things as experimental sketching, even in pencil, and getting to know the main characteristics of trees. It may be added that, such is the wealth of plants at our disposal, the least promising sites all have their own possibilities. In the choice of trees must come the proportion to the building apart from all the practical considerations of the site. What size, what weight of foliage is required for the best results?

Every tree has a character of its own, which it will give freely with the passing years. Some of us may be said to own trees, if we have planted them; if we inherit them as like as not they will exceed the length of our lives and it may then be said that nobody owns them. They dominate and outlive us giving forth their amplitude and beauty to succeeding generations.

STRAIGHT STEMS OR CROOKED

There is no doubt that in a large garden or park a great tree with a straight lofty bole is an inspiring object. In fact a series of straight-stemmed trees in the form of an avenue or grove takes the same place in the world of gardening as stone pillars do in the realm of architecture. Nevertheless a tree with a leaning, crooked or forked trunk evokes such adjectives as "quaint" or "picturesque" and is often looked upon with affection. In any formal planting such an object cannot be tolerated. But in planting our lesser garden trees I feel it a mistake to select nothing but perfect nursery-grown standards with straight 6–7 ft stems. Better by far to exercise our judgement regarding where such trees are needed – on the lawn perhaps – and to choose something which will add another character to the garden in different positions. What is a slight crook or bend or irregularity today will, when it matures, develop into a characterful, sinuous trunk.

Sometimes the need is felt for a tree with several trunks springing from ground level. As often as not the desired tree is a birch because of its conspicuous white bark. If such a tree can be obtained, all well and good, but it is useless to plant, say, three very closely together to simulate a tree with three trunks, because the one whose roots are mainly below the others will thrive at their expense and in any case three seed-raised trees will grow differently and exhibit different bark characteristics. If a three- or four-stemmed tree cannot be obtained (it can be produced by cutting down to ground level and training up the required number of stems) it is best to plant three or four trees a few feet apart to give the effect of a little grove, or of the trees having seeded themselves.

7

Shrubs

He told of the magnolia, spread
High as a cloud, high over head!
 The cypress and her spire;
 – Of flowers that with one scarlet gleam
Cover a hundred leagues, and seem
 To set the hills on fire.

William Wordsworth, 1770–1850

The history of the use of shrubs in our gardens follows much the same pattern as that of trees. They, like the trees, were slower in reaching our country from abroad than bulbous and fibrous rooted perennials. Nor was there much enthusiasm for the few that were known; they would be awkward extras to include in the kitchen garden borders with all the popular flowers; moreover, very few of them provided fruits.

The great influx of North American shrubs was mainly during the last quarter of the seventeenth century and the first three-quarters of the eighteenth century; they were promptly followed by other plants and shrubs from the Southern Hemisphere – sparked off by the discovery of Australia by Captain Cook in 1770. With the opening up of Japan to commerce after the middle of the nineteenth century plants began their major flow from those islands to Europe and their astonishing variety and beauty were only eclipsed by the riches from Western China in the early part of this century. It is amazing that so many plants from all over the world flourish in these islands, aided, of course, by our equable climate. By reference to old books and records we can trace the effect on our gardening of the enthusiasm for growing all these new shrubs, to say nothing of the numerous herbaceous and bulbous plants. It was not until the great landscape gardens of the eighteenth century had begun to wane that this sort of interest, for so long confined to the walled gardens, began to have free reign and to become a gardening enthusiasm of the nineteenth century. Though there are old books which call attention to shrubs a hundred years earlier, we have to refer to Thomas Whateley's *Observations on Modern Gardening* of 1770 to get our first real

XIII A beautiful grouping of shapes and tints at Bodnant, North Wales (National Trust). Two magnolias provide lightness against the dark background of conifers and the spire of *Cupressus sempervirens* leads the eye from the grassy walk to the distant hills.

XIV At Heaselands, West Sussex, azaleas light the woodland scene. The strong, vivid pink and white in the foreground give way to light salmon and soft orange in the distance.

XV The planting at Ynyshir, Powys, gives way and blends perfectly with the distant hills. The photograph shows how strong the spot of white is in the distance; it upsets the otherwise gentle colours.

XVI To analyse this successful essay in shrub planting at Lanarth, Cornwall, please refer to the sketch on page 39. It is a satisfying arrangement of shapes and soft colours but the perspective is destroyed by the scarlet azalea.

XVII The naturalizing of bulbs in a small area requires much thought and is best done immediately after flowering, when one can visualize the colours, heights and periods of flowering. In the picture are *Narcissus* 'Beryl', 'Piper's Barn' and 'Larkelly', with *Scilla lilio-hyacinthina,* in the author's previous garden.

XVIII This whole vista owes its low maintenance and serenity to a concentration of conifers and heathers; the Weeping Willow provides light relief. At Great Comp, Kent.

XIX A rocky bluff at Stagshaw, Cumbria (National Trust), planted by Cuthbert Acland and the author. In the foreground are dwarf *Rhododendron impeditum* (in bud) and allies; the bulk of the planting is of Japanese Azaleas and White Broom *(Cytisus multiflorus, C. albus)*. It is the white of the azaleas that is the strongest colour and gives the picture its sparkle.

XX Planting for vertical effect. Out of a tall holly pour the long trails of a Synstylae rose, reaching down to *Philadelphus* 'Belle Étoile' below. At Nymans, West Sussex (National Trust).

XXI In the cool dell at Hinton Ampner House, Hampshire, the lowest plant *(Aruncus dioicus)* is about 5 feet high. Above it stands the giant Cow-Parsley *(Heracleum mantegazzianum)*, while a Synstylae rose hangs out of a holly yet higher.

XXII Winter colour from sere fronds of *Osmunda regalis* (Royal Fern) and *Cornus alba* (Red Dogwood) at the Savill Garden, Windsor Great Park.

XXIII A February picture at Wisley, Surrey; the assembly of tree shapes is accentuated by the tranquil lake.

glimpse of shrub gardening. Before then — if we take this as a convenient date to start with — shrubs were used incidentally not only in the walled gardens, but also in some of the greater landscape gardens, such as Stourhead and the Rievaulx terrace.

In his *Observations* Thomas Whateley suggests that it is right "To range the shrubs and small trees so that they may mutually set off the beauties, and conceal the blemishes, of each other; to aim at no effects which depend on a nicety for their success, and which the soil, the exposure, or the season of the day may destroy; to attend more to groups than individuals; and to consider the whole as a plantation, not as a collection of plants, are the best general rules." He also suggested the grouping of shrubs for foliage colours. Here were some quite advanced ideas, but they were seldom followed. In fact as late as 1812 Walter Nicol, in his *The Gardener's Kalendar*, complains that "indiscriminate mixing prevails" and recommended that judicious grouping should be employed, and that in the "shrubbry" all shrubs should stand distinct.

Loudon in 1827 refers to the design of the shrubbery, quoting Nicol from one of his books. "The conducting of walks through the shrubbery is a matter of convenience and taste. . . . In the former case the walk should be simple and direct: in the latter case it may be circuitous; and if there be any variety in the ground, it ought to lead to particular points of view. The walks, however, should seldom cross one another; they should rather take off at oblique angles; nor should one run parallel to another within view. It is proper to *show off the shrubs* [my italics], but too many walks perplex."

We get a general idea of the sort of garden Loudon was envisaging by his remark, "The walks in the pleasure ground should generally exceed a mile or two for the sake of recreation; but what proportion of these should be in open lawn, and what in flower garden, or along the margin of a shrubbery, is too vague a question to receive any useful answer". These are the guidelines towards our modern gardening being expressed very clearly. He continues: "It may be mentioned as a characteristic distinction between the ancient and modern shrubbery, that the former was of limited extent, compact form, situated near the house, and that the length of walk was made up by repetition of parallel and cross walks. The whole of these had little distant prospect . . . whereas, in the modern shrubbery, the length is made up by stretching out the walk to a distance; and air and ventilation, as well as views and prospects, are obtained by its being chiefly planted on one side. Such shelter and shade as is deemed requisite for the walk is obtained by the introduction of scattered trees along its margin."

Our present-day ideals for shrubs had their precursors in his remarks that

"The perfection of shrubs consists not only in most of the above-mentioned particulars, but also in the beauty, durability, or long succession of their blossom; and in their fair appearance before the bloom, and after it is gone. We are sensible, the Chinese say, that no plant is possessed of all good qualities; but choose such as have the fewest faults." Is not this exactly what we do today? Some of us are collectors, others selectors in what we plant; this divergence between two types of gardeners seems to have been evident to John Abercrombie in 1816 who in his *The Practical Gardener's Companion* claimed that there were two rival systems: "One proposes the indiscriminate mixture of many different species; the other deliberately groups those only which have some marks of affinity"; further that "the principle of unity may be consulted, without losing sight of the advantage of variety".

Thus we have not only advice on the use of shrubs within the garden, but on their grouping and their use in their own right, as well as for screens. Considering that both shrubs and trees during the seventeenth and eighteenth centuries had been relegated to purely subsidiary positions, first in the control of walks by clipped hedges and alleys, and later in the embellishment of the landscape, these few extracts that I have given trace the beginning of our modern garden planting. From henceforth the shrubs in particular came into their own not only as things of great beauty themselves, but as the necessary ingredients for actually shaping the garden in their own natural way.

It was left therefore to the Victorians to appraise first the value of shrubs in the garden. This was for more than one reason. It is difficult to know which was the major influence that pointed the way: whether it was boredom with the fashion of landscape gardens, where the grass – kept short by deer or livestock – came right up to the house, or whether it was a recognition of the possible use of shrubs, perhaps outgrowing their welcome in the walled gardens, as major embellishment for the proper lawns around the house. At all events the new style of gardening tended to bring the hardy and tender exotics nearer to the house and thrust the untamed meadows and native trees away from it.

Shrubs are very much linked with the term "Gardenesque", invented by Loudon as a change from the Picturesque, to indicate a garden designed, through its often curving walks arranged through the new shrubberies, to display the new delights. At first the welcome was very much towards evergreens, our own resources being so limited in this class of plant. Hollies and yews had for long been grown in green or variegated forms, but imagine for instance beholding the magnificent broad green glossy foliage of laurels and the spotted aucubas for the first time! With them were deciduous and evergreen shrubs grown for the beauty of their flowers. This gradual new appraisal of plant-form to create an entirely new style of gardening is breathtaking. We are apt to take shrubs for granted, and think we know quite well how to use them. But this was a great experiment which succeeded and which has lasted far longer in success than that other great fashion (which now has mostly gone) of carpet bedding.

In Victorian times much stress was on the new pursuit of botany and many shrubberies were designed to illustrate the botanical affinities of all the new shrubs. In other gardens the shrubs were grouped more aesthetically. But in either way the stress was on the new-found value of shrubs, for screening and providing solid backgrounds to walks and groves, with some smaller plants, perhaps grouped in the foreground, and surmounted here and there with evergreens. Some of these would have been tree-like shrubs. *Phillyrea latifolia* had a great vogue in planting about the turn of the century. Most specimens of this noteworthy glittering evergreen small tree which we see today are of approximately the same age. They, the Laurustinus and the Bay Laurel joined the hollies and yews, overtopped by laburnums, thorns and the like, together with cypresses and Arborvitae of various kinds. Altogether it was an impressive assembly. But the specimens were admired as much for their individual beauty and interest as for the general effect they created.

INDIVIDUAL BEAUTY

It fell to William Robinson to awaken gardeners to the horrors of carpet bedding and also to the amazingly varied shrubs grown for their separate values. He was a very great exponent in his garden and through his books and journals of the almost unbelievable richness that had fallen on our gardens. He sought to extol the grace and line of every plant, shrub and tree and was the first important teacher of what has become the twentieth-century style of gardening. His precepts were followed and further exemplifed by Gertrude Jekyll and the two of them led Edwardian gardeners along new paths. They both were exponents of the herbaceous border.

The drifts and clumps of designed herbaceous borders were, later in this century, unfortunately adapted to large borders of shrubs. Many of the most dull and repetitious of public park shrub borders owe their character to this. By enlarging the scale of a herbaceous border, and using shrubs instead of perennial plants, groups of separate kinds of shrubs were placed with no regard to the individual grace of each species. Groups of say six or ten Flowering Currants, box bushes, forsythias or deutzias make, each of them, the same kind of effect; the dense mass of twigs obscures one group from another. Since most of the usually planted shrubs achieve 6 ft or more those at the back are completely obscured and a general lumpishness obtains. But this is the easy way to fill a large border, or to make a long screen, of shrubs. It requires little thought. Such schemes are far from the ideas brought forth by Robinson and Jekyll. I think a genuine evergreen shrubbery, looked upon entirely as a screen for curving walks, was better than this prostitution of the beauties of individual shrubs.

Salvation was at hand from more directions than just the admirable teachings of Robinson and Jekyll. With the gradual shrinkage of the average garden more shrubs were used singly and so their own individual beauty became more appreciated. And there were increasingly more shrubs to choose from. As I intimated above, this century was to see the great influx of Chinese shrubs and these in particular swamped, so to speak, the shrubs already in cultivation. Many were not less lumpy and perhaps even dull – except in autumn – than the older shrubs; take for example the great enthusiasm for species of *Berberis* and *Cotoneaster* which created so much interest and were so freely planted during the 1930s. And in addition to having all these foreign species to take under his wing, what does man do but start hybridizing and selecting colour forms! Famous French nurserymen like Lemoine of Nancy led the way with numerous new kinds of lilac and *Weigela*, Mock Orange and *Deutzia*, and talented amateurs and nurserymen in this country bent their energies in the same direction. Never before had so many new shrubs burst upon intending planters.

RHODODENDRONS

Together with all this was the arrival of the Chinese species of *Rhododendron*. Splendid Himalayans and some North Americans had led the way and among deciduous species (azaleas) as well as true evergreens a new enthusiasm had arrived. In common with the other shrubs these too were brought into being by crossing some of the hardiest species by the Waterer nurserymen and others; the progeny were used to decorate every garden and shrubbery where they could be grown. Since the soil in many parts of Surrey and Berkshire is lime-free, and because they flower into the usual date for Ascot, their fashionable popularity spread quickly.

Besides these hardy open-air rhododendrons came masses of species from the hinterland of China, ranging in size from tiny dwarfs to giants of 18 ft or more. The dwarfs were quickly absorbed by lovers of the then fashionable rock gardens; they were also used in quantity for the fringe planting of shrub borders and heather gardens. But the bigger species mostly came from damp cool climates and in these islands, especially in the drier south-east, needed woodland conditions. In this way was another great British contribution to the history of garden planting born. Many large estates with a mansion and a big garden, formal or otherwise, at their heart also had belts of trees, spinneys and woods which with a little thinning provided ideal homes for the new species that flowered from earliest spring until late summer. This sort of planting by the wealthy was helped on its way by a declining interest in woodmanship. I think there is no doubt that the woodland gardens, primarily made to accommodate rhododendrons, but which gradually absorbed so many lovely shrubs and trees, were the natural outcome of too intense gardening in such styles as bedding, herbaceous borders and kitchen gardening, which were brought to such a pitch of excellence during Edwardian days.

The rhododendron woodlands had of course been foreshadowed by the American Gardens of the nineteenth century; in these areas were congregated the various calcifuge shrubs and trees from North America such as *Kalmia*, Blueberries, *Gaultheria shallon*, *Gaylussacia* and the like. Until as late as 1939 it was not unusual to find such plants in nursery catalogues under the heading of American Plants, though the lists often contained plants from the Far East as well.

Botanists continue to argue about the actual specific standing of many of the Himalayan, Burmese and Western Chinese rhododendrons. Some new rhododendrons collected from one great valley have since proved identical to, or mere variations on, earlier ones collected from another valley. But each consignment of seeds from great travellers and collectors such as Forrest, Wilson, Kingdon Ward and Farrer was given the greatest care and the resulting progeny were planted by enthusiasts in their woodlands regardless of the effect that might be given in, say, fifty years time. The result is that rhododendron plantings tend to be overcrowded. We have to go to High Beeches in West Sussex or to the landscaped expanses of Lochinch in south-west Scotland to see rhododendrons so well spaced that we can enjoy their vast beauty. Despite its great potential as a landscape plant in its infinite variety, the rhododendron has been planted as much as a collector's piece as it has in thoughtful planting design. In the fullness of time it may even be considered that, with its ease of cultivation and its magnetic attraction, the rhododendron has had an adverse effect on garden design in these islands.

And so today, apart from these specialized shrub gardens, the trend is to fill our gardens with shrubs to accentuate the design, provide small trees to give greater height, and to interplant the shrubs with hardy plants and bulbs. Climbers may cover fences and buildings and ascend into trees. We are in a way back to the general mixture of plants of the Renaissance days, with the great exception that, in gardens where arrangement of all these riches takes

precedence over mere collection, the design of the planting is the first
consideration. It is a long story, but the shrub and garden tree, to say nothing
of the lesser plants, are in a very dominant position.

In our smaller gardens of today shrubs play a very important part. The
boundaries and bare walls need covering. Shrubs give a totally different effect
from morning to evening, as the sun passes round them. Yet they are always
there, shaping the views, leading us round the corner and screening unsightly
things.

In considering the planting of a garden the boundaries, the trees and the
shrubs are paramount. We are dealing in the skyline, the relationship of house
to garden, and scale in depth, breadth and height. It is obvious a garden
would be dull without shrubs. Never should we be able to see round an angle
or the curve of a border, nor look over one bed or border to another. Our
shrubs are there to accentuate the necessary and to obscure the unnecessary.

DOMINANT SHRUBS

If we look upon our hardy plants and bulbs as the personal trivia of our
garden rooms, the shrubs are our major furnishings. Very seldom should the
height of a herbaceous plant overtop its shrubby background. This statement
has more to it than is obvious at first. Most herbaceous plants are flimsy, even
ephemeral things, compared with shrubs; few of the taller kinds will stand on
their own without support. I cannot think of a more inappropriate planting
than to find some good shrub obscured by such a tall perennial even for a
couple of months. In some places we can grade our single great shrubs down
to clusters or drifts of dwarf shrubs, or alternatively to dense ground-cover-
ing plants. In this way our predilection for an assembly of many varied shrubs
is pulled together as it were by the foreground planting, which saves a spotty
effect engendered by choosing too many individuals.

It has often been said that we should select a shrub − or any plant for that
matter − very carefully for every given position. The last thing to do is to go
to a garden centre and choose a number of things and then wonder where to
put them. Just as the garden depends on its shrubs for its overall shape, so does
our choice of shrubs make or mar the garden design. I was taken to see a small
garden not long ago; the owner had recently been to a garden centre and had
been tempted by a tiny bright plant of *Elaeagnus pungens* 'Maculata'. She
had proudly planted it 2 ft from the path in a small corner, oblivious of the
fact that it would achieve in time some 10 ft × 10 ft, though we must not
forget that for 4 or 5 years that little plant would give pleasure. It does
nevertheless bring me to the warning that shrubs require *much* thought if we
are settling down to real gardening for a lasting period. Even the most

far-seeing and circumspect of us almost always err in not giving shrubs enough room. Few things, other than trees, are more unsightly than a shrub reduced in size. But how many of us have enough faith and patience to give our elaeagnuses 10 ft diameter of space? The answer is of course that ultimate thinning of the planting is preferable to lopping; meanwhile our ground-cover has likewise become overshadowed and benefits from replanting. We should try to regard a shrub as static, yet expendable, and here again an answer is to interplant our valuable, best shrubs with quicker growing temporary things like cistuses and brooms, and herbaceous plants. It remains true however (and I repeat this) that almost any shrub, if well suited, will exceed the expectation of growth in our mind's eye.

If we look at a successful and satisfying piece of planting – perhaps a small garden or a portion of a large border – as likely as not we shall find that it is dominated by one thing. It may be a tree or a large shrub, or perhaps a piece of masonry, a vase, steps or a seat. The lesser items are arranged round it and grade down to the foreground which is finished off with prostrate junipers or other ground-cover plants. There in that one area is a whole range of growth in all sizes. Size is not the only thing to be taken into consideration however. A general sense of harmony must pervade throughout the planting. Within this general harmony comes a selection of contrasting shapes, of colour and of texture. This sort of successful composition could never be approached by the lumpy Victorian shrubbery, composed so often of shrubs of approximately the same size. It was a subject to which I devoted several pages in my book *Colour in the Winter Garden*. It is not a thing which can be achieved by unthinking visits to a garden centre. It is a deliberate piece of art, carefully studied. On canvas we might be confident of achieving our aims, but in the hazardous venture of garden art it is dependent on choosing plants that are likely to succeed.

For all such schemes, and indeed in almost all garden planting, the shrub is the most important ingredient after one has chosen the trees and screened the formal boundaries. We might compose such a picture solely by using shrubs, from giants of 10 ft reaching up to the trees and the dwelling, down to dwarf creeping shrubs to fill the foreground and to flow around the larger shrubs. It is this flowing, even repetitive, foreground that is the saving grace of many an indigestible assembly of larger shrubs, selected purely on account of acquisitiveness. But whatever success may be attained by groupings of woody plants, I think the most satisfying result is to be had from a judicious mixture of shrubs and low herbaceous plants. Then do we achieve a full covering of nature and a richness unattainable otherwise. There are, it is true, large gardens, and indeed certain small gardens, where something more austere is the aim. This particularly happens where bald modern architecture is apt to set at variance all but the most severe and bold planting. Then the shrubs, coupled perhaps with a gravelled foreground and relieved by grassy plants, come into their own.

MAKING MOST USE OF THE SPACE AVAILABLE

I have heard it said by owners of small gardens that they cannot afford the space required by shrubs and that once they have flowered they are just dull greenery. They no doubt have in mind large lilacs, weigelas and philadelphuses, and have no conception of the great range of species and sizes available. They ignore too several other important points. Shrubs, like garden trees, can often be chosen to give two or three seasons of beauty: tinted spring foliage, flower, berry, autumn colour or winter twig. This is not all. Under deciduous shrubs can be grown a great variety of lowly plants which flower in the early year – snowdrops, hellebores and many spring bulbs. It is a very satisfactory way of growing spring-flowering bulbs, because we can see the flowers under the bare twigs and the shrubs' later foliage obscures the untidy leaves of the bulbs. Moreover, by putting the bulbs into such places they are safe from errant forks and spades. They add further to the claim that the same area can be made to yield floral and other beauty more than once during the year. And a further embellishment can be added to spring-flowering shrubs which are not also contributing autumn colour: over them can be trained clematises and some other climbers for August and September display. These climbers, if chosen from a select list of kinds that benefit from being cut down to about 1 ft above ground level every January, will not get into a heavy untidy tangle and spoil the shrubs.

PRICKLY SHRUBS

I referred earlier to the extraordinary wave of popularity accorded to species of *Berberis* during the 1930s. The bulk of them owe their charm to their undoubted prowess in autumn, when colourful fruits are hung among brightly coloured foliage. It was all very well in the days when we all had gardeners, but today the owner-gardener is not likely to fall for their charms. Anything more calculated to drive an embryonic gardener away from gardening could not be chosen, unless it is some of the roses with hooked prickles. Probably because I am so fond of roses I can forgive their grasping ways, but anyone who has had to work under prickly shrubs will do all he can to avoid such unpleasantness. It is surely inimical to happy, pleasurable gardening. The anwer is of course – if we cannot resist planting a prickly shrub – to choose a good, weed-smothering ground-cover for underplanting, which will get rid of all work apart from a little pruning or extracting the odd bramble or tree seedling.

It must be admitted that prickly shrubs do have special uses. There are lazy commercial visitors who will not keep to the path from gate to front door, where a strategically placed prickly shrub will prove to be worth all the discomfort it provides for the gardener. And on a larger scale, in public parks, where hooligans and dogs may abound their uses are only too obvious.

SELECTION

So many shrubs are at our disposal that on assessing a new site, or augmenting an old one – of any size – we should I think begin by making mental or written notes of the possible choice, eventually to thin these down to the select few. A garden picture is built best by selecting the dominant characters and adding slowly the extras which appear to us to be in keeping and which will give us beauty through the year. Even if we are greedy and add shrub to shrub with little thought to their character and habit, we have the solution of uniting them by the underplanting which, if chosen well, will bring cohesion to a chaotic mixture. This is the danger of today.

8

Perennials

Anyone can cultivate an herbaceous border but to grow a natural
garden is an art and a science.

F.S. SMYTHE,
The Valley of Flowers, 1938

Though no gardens remain, in this country, of the Renaissance period, we
have contemporary pictures to help us realize the inventiveness that had
given rise to the geometrical beds and borders, of "curious design",
surrounded by arched alleys. These knot-gardens as they were called – from
the intricacy of the pattern of the beds – formed a repository for all kinds of
plants. The new desire for beauty in all things led people to study and copy
foreign art; most of the learning and the plants came from countries that lay
around the Mediterranean. Herbs and simples having already arrived for the
sake of their value to health, the purely ornamental plants followed, though
often all sorts of magic properties were conjured up for them. Versed in the
study of all sorts of living creatures and of plants, men travelled far and wide
seeking for the rare and new. Plants, bulbs and seeds reached the gardens of
north-western Europe, particularly Holland and England.

The outline of the story of the introduction of foreign perennials is told in
my *Perennial Garden Plants*; it followed the sequence of the discovery of
different parts of the world and the development of international trade.

It will be obvious from earlier chapters of this book that herbaceous
perennials, bulbous and fibrous rooted, were nurtured in the real gardens
– the walled kitchen gardens – through the long intervals of fashionable
formal and informal gardening, to be released, reappraised and used for the
embellishment of the garden around the dwelling by the energetic examples
and writings of William Robinson and Gertrude Jekyll. Thereafter they have
remained the principal colour-givers in most gardens, and particularly those
of lesser extent. They are as popular today as they have ever been but today's
accepted term "herbaceous border" is not old as gardens go.

There is no doubt that the Jekyll-style border of graded colours is one of the highlights in the art of planting. Though always referred to as herbaceous borders it should be borne in mind that at the back of her own great border – and some of the lesser ones – were grouped certain shrubs and climbers which would augment the succession of colours along the whole length. Choice new rarities were not so often chosen by her as her own well-tried favourites. The general sameness of herbaceous plants was broken by such characterful plants as yuccas and *Acanthus*, bergenias or lavenders in the foreground. Thus many of the areas were what we should today call mixed borders. My own preference is for mixed borders, where there are some trees giving retreats for shade-loving shrubs and plants, and casting their dappling of shade across the lawn; groups of larger shrubs on corners and elsewhere to give shape to the view and to create surprises, and a general mixture throughout of dwarf shrubs, perennials and ground-covers, with bulbs interplanted to provide added interest at different seasons. This has been called gardening in four layers and I believe it to be the most satisfying form of gardening. It provides the greatest enjoyment over the longest season with the least work. I devoted some pages to it in *Plants for Ground-Cover* and also in *Colour in the Winter Garden*.

If we read J.C. Loudon's books and others of the early nineteenth century we shall find that, though in many ways these writers indicated the trend of gardening towards today's ideals, they were only just feeling their way. Thus was it recommended to grade plants in borders strictly according to their heights. And while heights were given this attention, colours were destined to follow one another in regular sequences along the front, middle and back rows of the borders. Today we have the courage to take things much more liberally, and one of the things that is borne in upon us is that it is the height of the *foliage*, not necessarily the *flowers*, that dictates the position of a plant in a border. A classic example of this is *Campanula latiloba* whose erect stems achieve about 3 ft; they appear in June and for the rest of the year we enjoy the rosettes of good greenery only a few inches above ground. A forward position is therefore desired; the flower stems only last a few weeks in any case.

Purely herbaceous gardening has been brought to a fine art by Alan Bloom in his own-invented scheme of island beds at Bressingham, Norfolk. As a whole – it has some shrubs and trees as well – it is possibly the most beautiful piece of planting in the country, helped considerably by the skilful artificial moulding of the contours. There are island beds of perennials also at Wisley, graded according to colour. But one must have considerable space for island beds; they can soon obtrude upon the principal *space* which is the basic reason for all gardens. Beth Chatto has provided another superlative piece of planting in her own garden at Elmstead Market, Essex, though it is enriched by shrubs in general.

Perennials are very much concerned with background which is normally provided by shrubs in borders. But, borrowing the idea of island beds, some of the most vigorous – filipendulas, Globe Thistles and the greater species of *Acanthus, Ferula* and *Cynara* and grasses – will establish themselves in rough greensward and when grown in large clumps give a majesty to the scene during the summer which cannot be achieved by anything else.

Because herbaceous plants come early to maturity from seed they have been chosen more than any other plants except annuals for hybridizing and selection. While I should not be so rash as to claim that this has spoilt all plants by increasing the size of flower and range of colour, it must be admitted that the species themselves, in most instances, are the best self-reliant things to grow, stalwart and free of disease. It so happens that the bulk of perennials that have been "improved" by our hybridizing belong to the Daisy Family (Compositae) and the bulk of these have rather uninteresting foliage. Take for example *Helenium, Aster, Gaillardia, Erigeron, Solidago, Chrysanthemum* and *Heliopsis*; add to them popular genera of other Families such as *Phlox, Fuchsia, Monarda, Campanula* and *Veronica*. Compare them with yet other genera which have been freely hybridized like *Paeonia, Lupinus, Astilbe, Iris* and *Hemerocallis* and the difference will at once be apparent. These few last genera, together with *Dianthus, Hosta, Bergenia, Sedum* and less favoured plants like *Trollius*, Japanese Anemones, *Kirengeshoma, Crambe, Echinops, Helleborus, Geranium, Peltiphyllum* and *Rodgersia*, with the beautifully contrasting ferns and grasses, present a range of leaves that is at once surprising, inspiring and gratifying.

There is another point of vital importance to be considered: if they have good foliage both *before and after* the flowering period their presence in the garden is a great asset. With such plants can satisfying and long-lasting pictures be made.

There is a sequence of colour-giving plants which is perhaps too readily accepted in gardens. We start the year with bulbs followed closely by flowering trees and shrubs, then by herbaceous plants and roses, hydrangeas and fuchsias, after which it is the turn once again of shrubs, this time for their autumn colour and berries. But if we look hard enough there are perennials to flower and augment the garden display in every month of the year.

A bulbous plant is simply a herbaceous perennial with a food-storing kind of root, though books and catalogues usually treat them separately. I shall be writing about the naturalizing of bulbous plants in Chapter 9 and this is, to me, the ideal way of growing them. It does inhibit us from growing the summer-flowering bulbs, as I shall explain, on account of the difficulty of mowing, and such plants are best included in the mixed borders, grouped particularly through and round other plants with a short flowering season.

In a formal design bulbs come into their own in spring bedding in particular; the more formal of them – hyacinths and tulips – do not naturalize well and are best in formal planting. But wherever bulbs are grown they are best displayed and appreciated where they spear through other foliage – grass or ground-cover plants. In such methods the impact of their fading, untidy foliage is minimized.

Colour was the subject of Chapter 4. In *Perennial Garden Plants* I covered it fairly exhaustively in connection with those plants and feel it unnecessary to repeat here all the lists of different borders in gardens throughout the country where good examples may be seen.

In spite of their comparative ease of growth perennials offer us quite as much in the way of habit, distinctiveness and rarity as do shrubs. They are however looked upon more as givers of colour than as rarities. Specialists in them would not, I think, agree with this and their devotees have got off the ground first in the present age of Conservation. The Hardy Plant Society has done a remarkable job in conjunction with the National Council for the Conservation of Plants and Gardens in locating and listing rare and fast-disappearing plants.

9

Bulbs and bulb planting

Beneath the crisp and wintry carpet hid
A million buds but stay their blossoming;
And trustful birds have built their nests amid
The shuddering boughs, and only wait to sing
Till one soft shower from the south shall bid,
And hither tempt the pilgrim steps of spring.

ROBERT BRIDGES

Although bulbs grow throughout the world, there is a great concentration of them in the wilds of the Middle East, where long dry summers occur, but where the autumn, winter or spring transforms the landscape with new growth after the rains. The cradle of our civilization is in the same region and from very early times bulbous and other plants were transported to the gardens of the herbalists and apothecaries in Europe, particularly in Italy and Holland, but also in England. In those days of lengthy travel both seeds and bulbs were easy to transport during their dormant periods and as a consequence foreign bulbs became well known in our gardens.

Treated as rare gems – which indeed they are – they were planted and tended in beds and borders where rare plants were grown, to be admired, studied and assessed for their supposed qualities to benefit the human race. Special forms were grown simply for their beauty in Renaissance times and later, and tulips, as is well known, created a passionate enthusiasm in Holland during the seventeenth century – never before accorded to any growing plants, new and rare sports commanding vast sums of money.

For many years bulbs were grown in the walled kitchen gardens until the awakening of the nineteenth century, when colour from flowers was demanded near to the house. After 1850 bulbs were used for spring display, together with double daisies, forget-me-nots, wallflowers, etc. This spring display originated, I believe, through the energies of a noted head gardener at Cliveden, Buckinghamshire, a property of the National Trust, as recorded in my book *Gardens of the National Trust*. Before that time small plants of evergreens decorated beds for the winter and spring, which were given to a range of plants for summer bedding. For this work tulips were the ideal plant, their single stems growing easily through the shorter plants and making a level, colourful display at flowering time. They are still just as popular.

With the advent of the many shrubs and trees to our gardens from foreign countries during the last two centuries, less formal planting became more general. Trees and shrubs planted in rough grass made the ideal companions for daffodils and of course native bluebells which have always been with us, though the Spanish Bluebell, *Endymion hispanicus*, was not introduced until 1683, and has proved a wonderful colonizer, particularly for drier places where the native does not thrive. Snowdrops and *Crocus vernus*, the species from which the modern crocuses have been bred, are still found more or less unadulterated in gardens, as at Lacock Abbey (the National Trust), from very early introduction. All these together with fritillaries, dwarf scillas, chionodoxas and aconites appear in drifts of great beauty in less formal gardens; this fostered the old idea of *millefleurs* tapestries and thus was the very earliest form of gardening re-born.

In this century, with many countries closed for long periods to foreign travel, collecting has again concentrated on the Middle East and the bulbs less tractable in cultivation have become the darlings of the alpine house and unheated frame. Meanwhile hybridizing and selection have led to great specialization, particularly among daffodils — whose newer creations, some with a combination of pink and white, the yellow colouring excluded, command great prices when new. Today bulbs of all kinds, like roses, find their way into garden decoration and the bulb fields of Lincolnshire and Holland — to say nothing of the great displays at the Keukenhof, Holland — bring bulb culture to the approbation of the millions.

THE PLACING OF BULBS

I know of nobody — of a gardening or non-gardening persuasion — who is not delighted with the sight afforded by spring-flowering bulbs. After the drear winter days to find the greensward dotted with snowdrops, aconites or *Crocus tomasinianus* is perhaps a somewhat esoteric delight, but when the daffodils appear, then winter's curtains are drawn and the spring is disclosed, be it ever so fraught still with icy winds and storms. There is no doubt that the daffodil as a flower is taken deeply to heart by everyone because of its season, intriguing shape, wonderful clarity of colour, glistening texture, and resistance to bad weather. As the years go by our commercial florists bring the daffodil ever earlier before our eyes, even at Christmas. Personally I like my flowers in season and although there are miniature species and hybrids of

Narcissus which will flower in the garden in December, it is the multitude of genuine spring kinds that are in our minds when we think of daffodils.

Some bulbs, like hyacinths, tulips and Spanish Irises, are, I think, best displayed in beds and borders; moreover they do not generally thrive in grass. But, to me, daffodils and many other bulbous and tuberous plants – crocuses, scillas, anemones – are best enjoyed in informal plantings in grass. Where the soil is sticky and cool, snowdrops and aconites are also likely to thrive in sparse grass under deciduous trees, but they do not take so kindly to acid sandy soils. The other generally used bulbs seem happy in a variety of soils, heavy and light, in the open or under deciduous trees, anywhere where the grass is not composed of coarse tussocks such as those of Cocksfoot.

It is not desirable to plant bulbs in the actual mown lawns of a garden, because of the difficulty of spring mowing. Further, if rough-grown grass is intended it must bear some relationship in area to the total area of the garden, and, as envisaged in Chapter 1, the transition from the formal or fully gardened part to the rougher area must be thoughtfully conceived. Even in gardens of a quarter of an acre the transition can be suitably contrived with a tree or two and a few shrubs disposed apparently at random. It is this transition, which leads the senses on from formality to informality, which can create the illusion of countryside beyond. Even so, with the greatest imagination brought to bear, the amount of bulbs to be "naturalized" in grass must be carefully considered also. I think that we can adopt the same scale as is the rule for floating plants in relation to the open surface of water in any pond or lake: that two-thirds should be free of planting.

In the naturalizing of bulbs there are two difficulties to be overcome; one is the upkeep and the other the planting.

UPKEEP OF NATURALIZED PLANTING

Let us deal with the upkeep first. The grass through which bulbs and flowers grow in spring cannot be mown before the first week of June, preferably later. It is a lovely thought to follow the spring bulbs with say clumps and groups of *Lilium martagon* (which, when suited in good soil, will seed itself) or other later flowers which will grow in grass such as *Buphthalmum speciosum*, or native orchid; these will not harm the early bulbs, but will make mowing if not impossible at least difficult before the end of September. Meanwhile the whole area will look like a hayfield. In a *very* large garden this sort of thing can be tolerated.

I think the answer is to concentrate the bulbs into those which flower in the first four months of the year, and, if the area is sunny, to provide

33 The Mitchell Drive at Westonbirt, Gloucestershire; a remarkable planting achieving the maximum of contrasts by using trees and shrubs alone on flat terrain.

34 Stiff columns of dark green from *Calocedrus (Libocedrus) decurrens* at Westonbirt, contrasted by the arching branches of *Parrotia persica*.

35 Small and young conifers create a delightful, lively effect.

36 *Trachystemon orientale* will grow satisfactorily in almost any situation. Its big, hairy leaves are specially useful in places too sunny for hostas. Deciduous.

37 The dappled greenery of *Vancouveria hexandra*, for shade.

38 Contrast of foliage in miniature: *Bergenia cordifolia* 'Purpurea', *Sedum populifolium* and *Antennaria tomentosa*.

39 A carpeting, dark green fern for moist shady positions: *Blechnum penna-marina*.

40 *Asarum europaeum* has firm, crisp, dark green leaves, the ideal foil for lawn or paving.

41 The bold leaves of *Cardiocrinum (Lilium) giganteum yunnanense* add dignity to this view at Rowallane, County Down (National Trust). The artistry of this picture owes much to the smaller group across the path from the major group.

THE VALUE OF BOLD FOLIAGE

42 Bergenias seem to be the ideal complement to paving or gravel. Here is *B. × schmidtii* 'Ernst Schmidt', in full flower in early spring. Clear pink.

43 At Cobblers, Sussex, there is this pleasing assortment of foliage plants – *Euphorbia wulfenii*, *Centranthus*, *Euphorbia mellifera*, and others, dominated by *Hosta fortunei* 'Obscura Marginata'.

44 *Yucca gloriosa* and *Santolina chamaecyparis* make a firm, contrasting foreground to a shrub garden.

45 It is not generally realized that *Hydrangea sargentiana* and *H. villosa* and its relatives thrive on chalky or limy soil. Large velvety leaves and lavender-blue flowers in August. For cool positions.

46 Moisture-loving *Rodgersia podophylla* takes control of a view in Alan Bloom's garden at Bressingham, Norfolk.

47 The foliage of *Anemone tomentosa* – and its relatives the Japanese Anemones – is handsome from early summer until autumn and thus they can occupy a frontal position.

colchicums and crocuses for September. By avoiding the usual "grandiflora" type of hybridized daffodils the growth of the earlies will be sufficiently decayed to make mowing possible by June 15th; this is what I practise in Surrey. Another mow will be necessary at the end of August (or before if the season be wet) so that the grass is short for colchicums and autumn crocuses. It is essential for it to be cut again after the autumn flowers, to make leaf raking easy; if autumn bulbs are included and the cutting is done by a rotary mower this will cut up the fallen leaves to so that the whole lot can be raked up in one operation.

BULB PLANTING

With regard to planting, the cheapest way of covering a large area with drifts and patches of bulbs is (i) to purchase cheap kinds (they are cheap because they increase freely), (ii) to plant them on receipt in nursery rows, (iii) to lift them directly after flowering two years or so later and plant them where and how they are required. They will have at least doubled, perhaps quadrupled, their quantities and their seasons, heights and colours will be fresh in the mind. Moreover the fact that they still retain their leaves means that their positions in the ground are marked during planting, whereas directly a dormant bulb is planted its position is set out of sight and lost. I may add that I have never noted any kinds of spring-flowering bulb to suffer from lifting and replanting after flowering. It is in fact a recommended practice to give this treatment specially to snowdrops. There is also human comfort to be considered; it is more enoyable planting bulbs in spring than on a dank, dark autumn day!

My suggestions above come of my own experience and are suitable for following in gardens of small to medium size. Where planting is on a really big scale, with perhaps hundreds or thousands of a kind, autumn planting is best and quickest.

Many gardens are flat; sometimes one is blessed with a slope or undulations. While such things would be reduced to a convenient level where formal beds and plots were intended, when it comes to informal planting advantage should be taken of even the most meagre of slopes, hillocks and valleys. I was at some pains to point out the value of bringing the planting *down* a slope in my book *Trees in the Landscape*. It makes a tiny slope appear more definite and helps to shape the grouping. A shrub of arching (not stiff or upright) growth, or a tree placed on a slight knoll will gain in importance. The lie of the land can be used too, to choose special positions for plants. For instance *Narcissus cyclamineus* and *N. bulbocodium* both prefer damp positions, whereas colchicums and autumn crocuses such as *C. speciosus* and *C. kotchyanus* grow best, seemingly, where it is dry. Primroses will naturalize in thin grass in the moister places, while Cowslips prefer it drier, both of them so long as the soil is of a retentive nature, preferably limy for Cowslips.

Many of the smaller daffodils and narcissi have been bred from *N. cyclamineus* and *N. triandrus*. 'Jana' is one of the earliest in light yellow followed by *N. pseudonarcissus* – our native Lent Lily – and the corresponding Welsh species *N. obvallaris*; after these come many hybrids such as 'March Sunshine', 'Rockery White', 'Beryl', 'Golden Cycle', with *N. triandrus* derivatives – 'Thalia', 'Rippling Waters' – leading on to hybrids of *N. × gracilis* such as 'Skylon'. The whole series may extend from the end of February to mid-May if the late white Pheasant Eye, *N. poeticus recurvus*, be included. Many are very fragrant. There is no doubt that these miniatures suit the smaller garden admirably and add great charm to larger gardens. Their lengthy flowering period is a great contrast to those bulbs which are usually listed in catalogues specially for naturalizing, mixed "grandiflora" types with large flowers often of bizarre colouring, which all come into flower during a fortnight or so of April. They are fine to have in borders for cutting, but are not suitable, in my estimation, for creating a semi-wild planting in grass. Moreover few of them will reproduce themselves from seed as many of the smaller species do; they wax into ever denser, heavier clumps where they are planted.

THE ART OF BULB PLANTING

I went fairly fully into this whole matter of bulb planting in my *Three Gardens* and will not belabour the points now except for two. One is colour and another is distribution. Early in the year we are much beset by yellow from daffodils of all kinds, also yellow crocuses, polyanthuses, wallflowers and *Forsythia* and I like to add to my bulb planting as many small bulbs as possible of blue and purple colourings. Purple and white crocuses (not the common yellow), *Scilla biflora* and *S. sibirica* 'Spring Beauty', chionodoxas, *Scilla lilio-hyacinthina*, pinky-mauve *Erythronium dens-canis* come first to mind. They make all the difference in the world to a sprinkling of daffodils. Anemones, too, offer good colour – white and blue of our native *A. nemorosa*, blue *A. apennina* and *A. blanda*; few spring flowers have more charm or are more long lasting. In the early year the rough grass is still pale and wan, and I like the big rich green leaves of colchicums at this time; it is a most welcome tint and they are not to be eschewed on account of size.

It is not easy to get a carefree natural effect. I referred in Chapter 3 to Walter Bennett's skill in planting so that it appeared as if the plants, once put in a single clump, had perhaps spread by seed. This is exactly the effect desired. The groups should overlap and intermingle, but yet at the same time have each a focus where they are thickest to give maximum effect. This applies as much to a few dozen as it does to hundreds or even thousands. When it comes to really large quantities I am afraid such counsel will be neglected; the time taken to plant carefully by hand is not likely to be permitted. Often big quantities of bulbs are planted by lifting a spadeful of turf and throwing in a handful of bulbs and repeating the same at every yard or so. The pattern will never disappear unless free-seeding sorts such as *Narcissus pseudonarcissus* are used. Likewise trying to meet each requirement half-way by lifting strips and areas of turf and planting irregularly in the soil beneath is obvious at flowering time. It is, however, preferable to the spadeful method. But I am really writing from the small or average garden point of view and I repeat that too much thought and care can hardly be given to achieve the right assortment rightly disposed by the aid of a trowel after flowering; in fact I consider that the planting of bulbs to simulate a natural effect is a high form of art and it draws out all our latent abilities.

All the bulbs mentioned thrive under deciduous trees and the larger shrubs; they therefore make double use of an area devoted perhaps to trees which flower with them or later, or which provide an added bonus of autumn colour. A few clumps of Common Male Fern are all that is needed for the summer months, to relieve flatness. If, on the other hand, it is intended to have a summer meadow of Marguerites, orchids, Day Lilies and various turf-lovers, it is essential for it to be in full sun. This kind of thing is practised very successfully by Christopher Lloyd at Great Dixter in East Sussex.

CYCLAMENS

To return to the shorter grass, many of us will be tempted to include hardy cyclamens. Though we sometimes find them successfully naturalized in grass, it is wise to keep them away from the bulbs I have mentioned. This is for two reasons: damage may be done to the growing points of the corms only just underground by walking on them when dormant, and their foliage appears out of season. That of *Cyclamen hederifolium* (*C. neapolitanum*) appears at the end of September and lasts through the winter; some of the others produce leaves later and even in spring. The planting of dried corms from bulb merchants is seldom successful; as like as not they are imported from the wild. It is far better, in spite of much greater cost, to purchase from a nurseryman (specializing in rock and alpine plants) who will have raised them from seed and will have them established in pots. Much as I like to see cyclamens established in grass, I think they are more healthy when grown with an annual topdressing of leaf mould under trees, even in rooty places; then will their beautiful foliage be best enjoyed.

The sort of planting I have described above need not be done all in one season; we can seldom get it right at the first try. It is enjoyable purchasing fresh lots each year and distributing them as desired. It is rather like touching up a picture, every touch adding to the whole.

10

Roses

The true gardener, fickle lover that he is, should grow as many
roses as he can find space for, that he may wander as the mood will
take him, here and there from Rose to Rose, and in happy
moments of imagination feast on a very Nectar and Ambrosia of
scent and vision, and take his fill of happiness.

FRANK GALSWORTHY,
from *Flower Grouping* by Margaret Waterfield, 1907

Frank Galsworthy gardened and painted flowers for over fifty years in his
one garden at Chertsey, Surrey; the paragraph above, taken from *Flower
Grouping* by Margaret Waterfield, serves well to remind me of evenings with
him, wandering from flower to flower. He could conjure up from his
paint-box a true representation of any flower he picked or was brought but I
wonder sometimes how he would have fared if I had taken him a bloom of
'Super Star' or 'Trumpeter', or one of today's dazzling yellows. He might
have done his best as a challenge, or have thrown it away in despair or
disgust. To him, though, every colour was beautiful and I have stressed this
point in Chapter 4. I am not afraid of colour and guarantee to find right
companions and backgrounds for the most strident of today's roses if
required; I can see them used to great advantage in certain parts of a garden,
where, not warring with adjacent soft colours, they could be found with
companions of lime and bright green together with the strongest of purple
foliage. It is a case of making a selection and building up to it with the right
colours. It could be shocking and I should not want to feast my eyes upon
such a group all day. It might be compared to a double whisky.

I doubted whether I should get through this book without a chapter on
roses. As I have written three books on the roses of the last century and the
species from which they sprang, many people seem to think I have no use for
modern roses. They would be entirely wrong. I was brought up on Hybrid
Teas and have grown them all my life; many have given me the greatest
satisfaction. In their rich dark crimsons, clear yellows and subtle pinks of a
coral or salmon tone they provide tints which are not found in the old roses;

many are exceedingly fragrant, too, with as different a combination of odours as they have in colours.

Roses come into use in so many parts of the garden. We like them around the house, to enjoy their scents. In particular they are specially suited, through association with the kind of gardening envisaged in Chapter 3. Here, with all the garden favourites, they will charm us with their colour and shape when growing and when gathered into such a nosegay as can only be made in a garden of mixed flowers. Here can be grown the moderns in twos and threes to delight us specially with their autumn flowers; here too will walls and arches reveal that special beauty of climbing and rambling roses, which, having been trained up the supports, will hang down. No upward-trained branches can ever capture that lovely beauty; "correct" pruning must be bridled and the full grace of the plants must be allowed.

ROSES ON TREES

The other special way of appreciating the strong lax growers was pointed out by Gertrude Jekyll in her *Roses for English Gardens* of 1902. "For spaces between the garden and the wilds . . . the rambling and free growing Roses seem to be offered us by a specially benevolent horticultural providence. . . . When they begin to grow freely among bushes and trees, if it is desired to lead the far-searching growths one way or another, it is easily done with a long forked stick. . . . It is like painting a picture with an immensely long-handled brush, for with a fourteen-foot pole with a forked end one can guide the branches into Yew or Holly or tall Thorn into such forms of upright spring or downward swag as one pleases."

There are many great rose species of the Synstylae section which are best used in this way and the fragrance from their multitudes of small flowers will flood the garden. So far the only one of several that has seized the popular imagination is *Rosa filipes* 'Kiftsgate'; it is frequently recommended for growing over old apple trees. Anyone who has seen the gigantic specimen climbing 50 ft into a Copper Beech tree at Kiftsgate Court will realize that this recommendation is highly suspect. Fortunately there are plenty of strong rambling roses with fancy names such as 'Albéric Barbier' and 'Princesse Louise', together with 'Treasure Trove' and 'Brenda Colvin', which will be less vigorous. But there is no doubt that the growing of such roses into trees is one of the most satisfying if the space is available. In smaller gardens we must consider the less vigorous – but sturdy – newer roses in various colours which will comfortably cover an arch or house wall.

A rose of almost any kind creates its effect by spottiness, by which I mean the flowers are small for the size to which some kinds grow, especially the superb species such as *R. hugonis* and its relatives and hybrids. For this reason roses need a dark background. Miss Jekyll had this in mind, you will note, from her mention of yew and holly. There is no doubt that the effect of roses is much enhanced by large evergreens in the vicinity or dark green hedges, and also to a lesser degree the smooth quietness of a mown lawn.

The three paragraphs above are concerned with the greater roses in the wilder parts of a large garden. Apart from this sort of scheme roses seem to me to be more suitable for what we may perhaps call the "home" end of the garden. Here they blend happily with other old favourites. To go to Mottisfont, Hampshire, a property of the National Trust, at the end of June is to see one of the ways in which the roses of a hundred and more years ago can create an overpowering effect of scent and colour. Colours of white, pink, mauve, carmine-purple and maroon, which were innate in roses, were bred until the late nineteenth century when the pale yellows of the Tea Rose invaded the old races, followed quickly by the dazzling yellow and orange of the Austrian Briars after 1900. But I have written all about this before and there is no need to repeat it here. What we are concerned with is how to use roses in the garden.

This century has seen the most astonishing strides in rose breeding. The growth – sturdy and resilient; the foliage – large, often glossy and richly coloured; the flowers – shapely after the new bud-formation had been bred from the Tea Rose; the colours – embracing a gamut like the notes in a scale, including white, cream, yellow, orange, flame, coral, pink and dark crimson; in addition to which many newer varieties have been selected which hark back to the mauves and purplish tints inherent in the majority of roses. It amuses me to be wearing in my buttonhole at a rose show a flower of 'Reine des Violettes' dating from 1860, when some new variety with the prefix of 'Blue' is much vaunted, knowing full well that no modern rose has yet been raised which is as near to blue as that old stalwart!

Roses are great favourites with gardeners and I count it as very fortunate to be living at this time when, through selection and breeding, a rose can be found to augment any colour-scheme in any garden. It will not do, however, to look upon the rose just as a colour. Each rose must be looked at as a plant; a plant for a particular purpose or position; a plant with its own personality to be displayed to greatest advantage. Many of the moderns regretfully fail in this respect.

The history of gardening is full of anomalies. I have ventured to suggest that the present fashion for growing roses massed together in beds on a lawn stems directly from the parterres of the seventeenth century through the carpet bedding of the nineteenth century. Since we cannot afford enough greenhouses and gardeners to carry on with carpet bedding we use roses instead. And it must be admitted that for six months of the year the beds look forlorn and uninteresting unless they are given some permanent underplanting of small bulbs and dwarf plants. From all this stems the dazzling display of bedding roses in the splendid garden of the Royal National Rose Society at St Albans and in many public gardens, Kew and elsewhere, where the rose is subjugated to the position of merely a colour-giver without its own individual personality being allowed to obtrude. But, as I intimated above, this is only one way of enjoying roses; and enjoy them thus many of us do in spite of the fact that the robustness and vigour of today's varieties give them so much height that any actual pattern of beds in the grass is obscured. This applies just as much to some of the softer colours of today as to the more brilliant.

11

Conifers

But that which is more remarkable, is the virtue of this famous
timber of this noble tree [Cedar], being proof against all human
putrefactions of human and other bodies, above all other
ingredients and composition of embalmers; and that by a pretty
contradiction, giving life, as it were to the dead, and destroying
the worms which are living. . . .

JOHN EVELYN,
Silva, or a discourse of forest trees, 1801 edition

Though this country has only three native conifers, it is nice to feel that two
of them are in the very front rank among the great range of species that are
found around the Northern and Southern Temperate zones. They are the
Scots Pine, *Pinus sylvestris*, which I consider to be not only the most beautiful
of all pines but among the most beautiful of all conifers, and the English Yew,
Taxus baccata, which is by common consent, I think, regarded as the most
excellent of all hardy evergreen hedges. The third native is *Juniperus
communis*, but except in its selected prostrate and columnar forms this is
seldom grown in gardens. We have to go to the wilds of the north-west
Highlands to see it at its wayward, untidy best.

Many books have been written on conifers alone, so large and so varied is
the subject. The term broadly covers trees and shrubs, some with fleshy fruits
(not cones), and contains some species which are deciduous. "Gymno-
sperms" would be the correct title for this chapter, but I adhere to the readily
understood "conifers".

Early in our island history the Norwegian Spruce, *Picea abies*, was highly
desired for ship masts, and as a consequence it was introduced to this country
around 1500. Other European species of spruce and fir (*Picea orientalis, Abies
alba, A. cephalonica*) and pines (*Pinus pinaster, P. nigra* and its relatives, *P.
cembra*) followed it into cultivation, until in the nineteenth century a flood of
species arrived from far away and in great part not only gave rise to an
upsurge in forestry but also were the mainspring of the fashion for arboreta.
From the mid seventeenth century onwards the lawns of great houses became

characterized by the Lebanon Cedar, which was undoubtedly the favourite great conifer for gardens until the arrival of the Wellingtonia and relatives in the middle of the nineteenth century. Since that date the most common conifer in this country has been the Lawson's Cypress (*Chamaecyparis lawsoniana*) which, coupled with the Western Arborvitae (*Thuja plicata*), has given rise to almost countless forms varying in colour and habit; the Woking area in particular, thanks to its local nurseries which have been so abundant during this century, can, on suitable humid days, have a distinct resinous smell in the air.

Since the Second World War, all these genera and more besides have yielded an astonishing lot of colour- and habit-forms, and far from being the Edwardian and Victorian gloomy conifers of churchyards and cemeteries, must be ranked today as some of the most brilliant of evergreen shrubs and small trees. All the cypresses, the yews, junipers and spruces contribute particularly to this new conception of the conifer. And therein lies their danger from our present point of view. On sandy lime-free soil the dwarf and slow-growing conifers, coupled with an equally astonishing array of coloured foliage from the native Ling or Heather (*Calluna vulgaris*), can be given a most varied planting and during summer or winter are able to compete in brilliance with any assembly of shrubs or plants that we grow. Being evergreen and easily grown in containers, both groups are best sellers in garden centres and are tempting to a degree. The foliage of the conifers varies from the normal dark green, through light to yellowish green, khaki and vivid yellow to coppery orange and brilliant blue-grey. The heathers include all these tints except the last, but add bright red. Here then are two groups of plants which, coupled with many heaths (*Erica*), bid fair to assume great popularity. In addition to all this we might add the almost sinister fact that it is the dwarfs and semi-dwarfs that have produced the greatest colour range, making them suitable for gardens of all sizes. We find, indeed, brilliant yellow semi-dwarf conifers described in catalogues, glowingly, with the additional words "should be in every garden". Now, I admit that I have been guilty elsewhere (*Three Gardens*) of saying that the Winter Jasmine is one of the six best plants and should be in every garden, but can you imagine what our gardens would be like if every one contained brilliant yellow conifers?

Great as their attractions and uses are, I feel conifers are unsuited to the sort of schemes envisaged in Chapter 3, except as a dark green hedge. On the other hand they assort well with the type of planting in Part IV, Group 10. Adrian Bloom has been to the fore in popularizing conifers and heathers and some of the colour photographs in his little booklet *Adrian Bloom's guide to garden plants, book 2, Conifers*, would be an eye-opener to many of us. A journey to Wisley, Wakehurst Place or the Savill Garden would serve us in the same way, or to Great Comp in Kent. The results there achieved are a concentrated form of comparatively trouble-free gardening with the variations played on foliage-colour and shape of bush, with the bounty of tiny bloom from *Calluna* and *Erica*. It is an extraordinary outcome of the vigilance of growers in propagating errant sports and seedlings in one kind of ideal – as if we were having a meal entirely of savouries, and had omitted the contrasts of what are known as "starters" and also sweets and cheese, to say nothing of fruit, nuts and wine. It is up to you to decide whether this would appeal to your taste. Within a certain amount of variation of tint the garden composed of these few ingredients – with the flat, small details of mown grass or gravel – would remain the same year in, year out. It would certainly be classed as garden art, of a high order, but I should find it monotonous. Its upkeep would be minimal.

I think conifers can do better for us when grouped or used singly in the garden to add a vertical or flat line, a rounded or conical shape, in a variety of tints to highlight a piece of garden planting. As intimated earlier in this book, the tiny leaves of conifers fit them very well for accentuating distance; this effect would of course be completely minimized if the foliage were of a brilliant tint. In our planting schemes I feel we have to ground ourselves on great dark green trees, and select the variants when we need a solid feature – for the bulk are indeed solid – of any shape or form. We know the sort of effect we can achieve in an assembly of these plants; the greater skill lies in selecting a variant to give just that touch needed to contrast with a loose, broad-leafed shrub or plant, in one of the colours available. Equally the slender upright growers can act architecturally in a formal vista, or those of more open growth will assort well in informal plantings.

In the sections of this book devoted to fastigiate and weeping trees, and to coloured foliage, I have called attention to many of the conifers of specialized appeal, but have hardly touched upon the numerous forms of more normal growth and colouring.

Seeing them in the dry air and clear light of Bloom's nurseries in East Anglia can bring home to us better than anything else the extraordinary brilliance of many of the "coloured" forms. Anyone would fall in love with the almost unbelievable steely blue-grey of some of the piceas and junipers, the yellow of some pines and cypresses and the orange tint of Arborvitae. They have every compelling attraction; call it sales-appeal if you like.

There is also the enormous satisfaction of acquiring a shapely specimen, ready made. The difficulty comes when it gradually gets larger and larger, until you realize that you must start all over again. This is indeed what we have to do because few of them will respond to hard cutting. It is a fashion in the United States to plant a border under the house with these hardy, attractive evergreens and to enjoy them so long as they are in proportion to the dwelling, and then to get rid of them and start with a fresh grouping. It is called foundation planting. Let nobody think that by choosing what are called "dwarf" conifers he will defeat this growth potential. The great gardens of these islands contain many assemblies of dwarf conifers which in time get the bit between their teeth, so to speak, and rear and gallop upwards or sideways at an ever-increasing speed. Examples are to be found at the National Botanic Gardens, Glasnevin, Dublin, where Murray Hornibrook's collection can no longer be called a collection of dwarfs; the same is on the way in Mr Nisbet's collection at Wisley and Mr Welch's at Devizes, Wiltshire; no doubt the same will happen in due course at the Savill Gardens where John Bond is building up a most comprehensive collection.

We must admit that it is when these "dwarfs" are half-grown that their greatest beauty is shown. In a nursery, in rows, they have great appeal; when half grown they have a splendid dominating effect; in old age they may become bare beneath, or may even achieve grandeur. I have in my garden a small grafted specimen of *Pinus sylvestris* 'Moseri', propagated from the great old plant at the University Botanic Garden at Cambridge; mine is nearly 2 ft high, a dense mass of growth; its needles in summer are green, but during the winter turn to bronzy-yellow. I shall never see it displaying grandeur on its gnarled old trunks as at Cambridge, but hope to enjoy its yearly increase of growth. This illustrates what I want to point out: that these plants, many of them, must be looked upon as plants of almost ever-increasing size and beauty. As such they are a very different proposition from a herbaceous plant, or a shrub which by repeated pruning can be made to give the same effect year after year, or even a tree which by degrees makes a tall stem and delights by the shade it casts. The dwarf and slower conifers are plants of great personality and there is enough variation among them to be able to select a specimen to accentuate most plantings, apart from the old walled gardens where the craft of gardening reigns supreme. There they would be out of place.

Part III

Garden features

12

Boundaries, hedges, screens and formal matters

Is it not a pleasant sight to behold a multitude of trees round about, in decent form and order, bespangled and gorgeously apparelled with green leaves, blooms and goodly fruits as with a rich robe of embroidered work, or as a hanging with some precious and costly jewels or pearls, the boughs ladened and burdened, bowing down to you, and freely offering their ripe fruits as a large satisfaction of all your labours?

RALPH AUSTEN,
A Treatise of Fruit Trees, 1653

No matter how large the property, there will be a boundary around it somewhere. As far as possible the principal view should not be curtailed by a line of wall, fence or hedge. Somewhere in between these two sentences lie all the gardens and garden boundaries of plots both large and small.

Very large landscapes are treated in my *Trees in the Landscape*, in which I called attention to the value of the haha and fence screened by spinneys and trees. Some of us are lucky enough to own a plot which looks over natural scenery; here a deep haha or *clairvoyée* will keep intruders out.

But this book is about the average garden of today, which may be bounded by wall, fence or hedge. I think the essential is to soften them so that the hard line is less obtrusive. A wall is a precious adjunct to a garden, no matter which way it faces. Some walls are so old and beautiful that it would be a sad thing to cover them completely with climbing plants: some brickwork should show through here and there. Some fences can on the contrary be completely covered; here it is important not to plant the climbers or wall shrubs against the posts for fear that supporting struts will be needed in due course; plant them *between* the uprights.

Although today new housing estates are often "landscaped" between the dwellings and the road, this does not seem to be very acceptable to the average Briton. We put a physical boundary round our plots and say "this is mine"; we also say to stray two-legged or four-legged creatures "keep out". But both thoughts can be said in a nice way. I will not go into the variety of walls and fences that can be erected because that would be entering into the realm of garden design, but they can be softened with plants, as intimated above.

HEDGES

When planting a hedge there are several important points for consideration. Perhaps when considered as a purely architectural feature, within or surrounding a garden, a dark green is best. First I should place English Yew and second the holly, either the common species raised from seed, or one of the broad-leafed kinds of uniform type raised from cuttings. The more formal the hedge is to be, the more important it is to have complete uniformity; seed-raised stock is usually cheaper than those raised from cuttings but all old yew hedges were undoubtedly raised from seed and along the line some variation of habit and colour is noticeable, likewise in Common Holly. Today some nurserymen are aware of this and raise approved types from cuttings even of species, whether beech, hornbeam, box, yew, holly or special types of cypresses. However, seed-raised yew is sufficiently uniform for most eyes. As to hollies I think I should choose one of the cultivars, raised from cuttings such as the extra sturdy dark green broad-leafed 'Hodginsii' (a male, it does not bear berries), or a free-berrying, moderately broad-leafed one such as 'J.C. Van Tol'.

Fallen holly leaves, however, are unpleasant when one is hand-weeding. Hollies are best not clipped but kept in shape by pruning with secateurs and thus present a less regular surface than yew which can be cut to a fine velvety finish. Holly is then undoubtedly the best choice as a background to other planting, or as an adjunct to a bright green lawn, or path. I may add here that, contrary to the general opinion, yew and holly are not slow growing; if the ground is well prepared and the young plants are given every encouragement in the way of water at dry times and an annual fertilizer in spring, they may be expected to put on a foot of growth every year after the first season.

Of brighter green than holly or yew is the Western Arborvitae, *Thuja plicata*; this in its excellent cultivar 'Atrovirens' is raised, uniform, from cuttings. Many people today plant the much-advertised, quickest growing hedge, the Leyland Cypress, but I think they will regret it later on because of the work in clipping. It is however of a good dark green. From cuttings also is grown 'Green Hedger', a form of the Lawson's Cypress (*Chamaecyparis lawsoniana*); this is rather slower than the species itself but of excellent uniform growth, and is much to be preferred to seed-raised Lawson's

Cypress which are extremely variable. There are many forms of Lawson's Cypress but those which have upright side shoots are not much use for hedging, hence my preference for 'Green Hedger'. It is unfortunate that these cypresses will not respond to hard pruning if they get too large, but of this more anon.

There are also some other conventional hedging plants: Common Beech and its coppery-purple variety; Hornbeam; Oval-leaf Privet, Box and *Lonicera nitida* in its more self-reliant forms. Privet and the *Lonicera* are well-known. People are apt to choose Beech in preference to Hornbeam, but the latter is more easily satisfied on any soil and its roots are not so close to the surface. On the other hand its dead winter foliage is not so warm a brown as that of beech. Beech moreover, is very slow to respond to reduction if it gets too high and wide and often suffers from aphides in summer.

Woking is a district full of nurseries and it is not surprising that a wide variety of hedging plants may be found. I have noted many less common kinds, such as Flowering Currant and *Cotoneaster simonsii* and *C. lacteus*, all achieving some 6 ft; among lesser plants are *Spiraea thunbergii*, *Mahonia aquifolium*, *Berberis thunbergii* and its variety 'Atropurpurea' and *Euonymus fortunei* 'Variegata'. The choice and possibilities are almost endless because practically any shrub that is of reasonably bushy growth will stand clipping or pruning. Thus we can choose from many to augment our schemes of colour.

For really dazzling brilliance we might choose Golden Privet as a background for a border devoted to flowers of red, scarlet and purple – but I should not want it in my own garden. 'Golden Queen' Holly would be another very gay plant for the job and of course Golden Yews are frequently employed, as at Ascott, a National Trust garden in Buckinghamshire. These, however, are bizarre ideas, only suitable for achieving vivid Victorian effects.

The Red Borders at Hidcote have a red "Japonica" on one side as a background; it is *Chaenomeles × superba* 'Rowallane'. It was chosen because there is a scarcity of red flowers early in the year and later on it makes a subdued green background; it is trained on wires. As a complete contrast *Prunus cerasifera* 'Nigra' is used with dramatic effect at Crathes Castle, Kincardineshire, a property of the National Trust for Scotland, as a background to the noted white borders. A border of soft colours might be given a greyish hedge; we should have to turn to conifers for this colour and a few that come to mind are *Chamaecyparis lawsoniana* 'Pembury Blue' or 'Triompf van Boskoop' – rather wide growing – or the Blue Cedar, *Cedrus atlantica* 'Glauca', which responds well to pruning.

There is also the "tapestry" hedge to be considered, but there is little to be

XXIV Purplish and grey foliage was used by Brenda Colvin at Filkins to create this soft effect. *Pyrus elaeagrifolia, Prunus spinosa* 'Purpurea', *Cotinus coggygria* 'Royal Purple', irises, hostas and *Rosa rugosa* 'Roseraie de l'Haÿ' are the principal ingredients.

XXV Every feature seems to be soft and rounded at Sezincote, Gloucestershire, echoing the shape of the great Weeping Hornbeam *(Carpinus betulus* 'Pendula'). The large central rock above the pool has been in place since the early years of the 19th century.

XXVI At Blickling Hall, Norfolk (National Trust), the old Oriental Plane in light green contrasts with Turkey Oak and Lime or Linden trees behind it. The flower parterre has four great squares of colour: the two nearest to the house are in pinks and mauves, surrounded by a border of crimson and pink roses ('Else Poulsen' and 'Kirsten Poulsen') surrounded by Catmint.

XXVII The two squares farther from the house are given to brighter colours – orange, yellow and red – surrounded by dwarf Polyantha roses 'Locarno' (crimson) and 'Gloria Mundi' (orange-red), also surrounded with Catmint. This view shows part of the great herbaceous border also.

XXVIII A corner given to white and yellow at Cedar House, Norfolk, to blend with the grey-blue of the garage doors. On the barn wall are *Hydrangea petiolaris* and *Pyracantha rogersiana*; in the border are roses, *Senecio* 'Sunshine' and Golden Elder (*Sambucus nigra* 'Aurea'). It is a good example of not attempting too much in a small space.

XXIX The warm, full-tinted stone of Tyninghame, Berwickshire, demanded that colours should be complementary, thus yellows and white roses are the principal plants on this side of the house, while rich purple lavenders and sages are added to the whites and yellows on the east side.

XXX The 'genius of the place' at Steadstone, Kirkcudbrightshire, was undoubtedly this giant outcrop of rock. All planting is subservient to it in placing, height and colour.

XXXI At Cliveden, Buckinghamshire (National Trust), the approach to the house is through a great walled and hedged court. The hedges of yew date from the 18th century. Against the wall, on each side, are herbaceous borders. This one, facing east, has flowers of soft colours, backed by light-coloured delphiniums, pink roses and pink and lavender–blue clematises.

XXXII In the Rose Garden at Sissinghurst Castle, Kent. Bearded Irises, *Kolkwitzia, Rosa glauca (R. rubrifolia),* aquilegias and other plants herald the opening of the roses.

XXXIII The border of strong colours at Cliveden, which is backed by red roses and purple clematises, and purple delphiniums. Note the stone flags along the front of the two borders which allow frontal plants to flop forward gracefully, without impeding the mower.

XXXIV The Azalea 'Coccinea Speciosa' takes the eye, with potentillas and tree lupins in the Sunk Garden at Mount Stewart, Northern Ireland (National Trust). It was designed with pergola and scalloped Bay hedges by Gertrude Jekyll.

XXXV The Italian garden at Mount Stewart, Northern Ireland (National Trust), is divided into two parterres; the east (above) is devoted to strong colours, red, orange and yellow with coppery foliage of *Cotinus*. At the time the photograph was taken the two middle foreground beds had just been planted with a dwarf hedge of *Thuja occidentalis* 'Rheingold'. Others are of dwarf purple-leaf *Berberis*.

XXXVI The west parterre has soft colours – pink, mauve, purple and white – and the beds are edged with grey-leafed plants: *Ruta graveolens* 'Jackman's Blue' and *Santolina chamaecyparissus*.

gained from such a planting unless the hedge is visible from top to bottom. If we call to mind what is perhaps the best example – that in the Fuchsia garden at Hidcote – it will be remembered that this has only very low beds of dwarf fuchsias in front of it. Thus the mixture of green and copper beech, green and variegated holly and green and variegated box is wholly at view.

When I came to work in Surrey early in the 1930s I was much intrigued by a boundary hedge at Knap Hill Nurseries. It was mainly a hedge of Hawthorn but at every 6 ft or so a holly had been planted among the thorns. In addition, in cycling past it in spring one caught a touch of glowing red from plants of "Japonica" (*Chaenomeles speciosa*) midway between the hollies. I have watched this hedge developing; it is now a dense holly hedge interspersed with thorn and quite impenetrable. The Japonicas have been choked out but this was I think owing to overgrowth and neglect through the years.

CLIPPING AND REDUCTION

This brings me to clipping and pruning. Although this is not a how-to-do-it book I must add that however closely a hedge is clipped or pruned annually – it is usual to do this in August – it will gradually get taller and wider. Some old hedges, owing to slack attention, may be 5 ft or more wide and clipping the tops is a real trial. Not only is the work tedious but the bulk of the hedge upsets the scale of the garden. It follows therefore that at some time most hedges will need severe reduction. Prior to reduction it is wise to get the hedge into a healthy and vigorous condition by clearing out ivy and weeds from the base and applying Growmore in spring. The normal procedure is to cut back all growth on one side to the main stems during one winter, bevelling the top as well, and, when the stems have put on good growth in 2–3 years' time, to reduce the rest of the top and the other side likewise. It takes a lot of courage to do this, but I have only known an occasional plant unresponsive in very old hedges. Feeding should be continued every spring and watering if necessary. Of the more usual species, the most responsive are privet, hornbeam, and yew, slower are Arborvitae, holly and box; beech is sometimes a failure, cypresses are never a success. The most difficult hedges to reduce in width effectively are those which have been planted in a "staggered" row – a double row alternately paired. Therefore always plant in a single row. The criterion of a good hedge is its denseness, not its width: it represents a wall in greenery.

PLACING THE HEDGE

The choice of a hedging plant is not an easy matter. Apart from the aesthetics of colour alluded to, there is the type of soil and position to be considered, and also the height required to be matched with the choice of the plant. Let us imagine an average plot around which perhaps runs a wire fence. The desire for privacy tempts the owner to plant a hedge. In front of the hedge must be left a space for clipping, and this means that the whole will take up at least three or four feet. This presumes that the neighbour will clip his own side. Does the size of the garden warrant giving up this considerable area to something that will cause a chore every August – clipping and clearing up – and will presumably be clipped with a level top thus accentuating the confines of the garden? If the wire fence is proof against intruders would it not be better to plant a selection of shrubs, augmenting the inner planting and providing a varied upper limit so that the garden appears to blend into the neighbour's shrubs and trees, thus creating an illusion of greater space? This is something that should be carefully considered by intending planters.

As intimated earlier, the background shrubs – used instead of a hedge – can be made to augment the summer colour of the garden or can provide spring colour in contrast. In an area devoted mainly to spring display the assembly of shrubs at the back could be designed for summer and autumn display. The possibilities are endless and refute the often repeated saying "I haven't room for shrubs in my garden".

FORMAL BOUNDARIES

I think we should now look at the subject of boundaries and their like from a new angle. Some of us are lucky enough to inherit a rectangular garden bounded by walls. This is the desire of many plantsmen; the walls provide the opportunity to grow climbing plants in a variety of situations. So far in this book I have stressed the theme of arranging the planting so that the garden appears to become more informal the farther away from the house one walks. Let us now visualize the art in planting a severely formal garden.

First, the planting can be informal or formal; about the former I think I have written enough. If we visualize a walled kitchen garden with its fruit trees and bushes, its vegetables and flower borders, we shall have before us the traditional form taken by the craft of gardening. It is not only nostalgia that makes us think of these areas where skill and hard work came first; the manuring, digging, sowing, and planting of vegetables in serried rows, the pruning and spraying, the clipping of the dwarf box edges and the attention to the long flower borders, dividing the whole area into perhaps four plots. I like to think that there are those among us who would, undaunted, develop and tend a garden thus along traditional lines if given the chance. The work today would be easier than of yore because of mechanical and chemical aids, coupled with the newer dwarfing stocks for fruit trees which would result in less pruning. And there would be fewer pricked fingers in gathering blackberries and loganberries owing to thornless varieties! Can you not anticipate the joy of walking down the flowery box-edged gravelled walks, now in the sun and now in the shade of recurring fruit trees or rose-covered arches?

In setting out the planting for such a garden I think formality is preferable; the fruit trees should be evenly spaced on walk and on wall and a certain amount of repetitiveness could be given to the flower planting, providing likewise a formal touch.

It may be that the area should be put down to the design of a formal ornamental garden. This brings me rather to the thought of designing than planting and I must be careful not to veer too much towards design. I will content myself therefore to making a few suggestions.

Probably some focal point would be desirable – a seat or summer-house, perhaps fronted by a pool with fountain. It would be a mistake however to leave the whole area open to view – there is nothing more boring. But if it is divided by hedges or dwarf cordon fruit trees with echoing plats of grass – perhaps each containing a fruit tree – and borders of flowers here and there, much can be made out of an uncompromising rectangle. If it is desired to avoid the use of ladders for gathering fruit, most of the trees – the apples and pears – can all be on dwarfing stock. The flower borders can be filled with short-growing hardy perennials which do not require staking.

A step further would take us into a different scheme, harking back to the seventeenth-century designs rather than the imitation of a walled kitchen garden. For this sort of thing we need long walks hedged on both sides with peep-holes to gain the view over a parterre; hedges-on-stilts as at Hidcote – and very much favoured by John Fowler – or pleached lime trees governing the views; strict canals of water complete with fountain or gushing mask in a wall.

Some of us yearn for formality, which gives a stabilizing effect, I think, to our peripatetic lives today, and there is no reason why we should not indulge ourselves. A long border for instance is all the better for recurring shrubs or wings of hedge. Colour or texture or both can be reiterated down the border's entire length. If it is a pair of borders the reiteration amounts to the feeling of an avenue. After all, avenue simply means a way of approach and does not have to be planted with trees. The double row of clipped box bushes at Tintinhull is as much an avenue as all the grandeur of the hundreds of limes in Clumber Park. Both are properties of the National Trust. Down a long pair of borders it certainly helps to have a reiteration of theme; and if only a few plants are selected to create this repetition they can be chosen to be at their most colourful at different times of the year, thus prolonging the display and interest.

A lot can be done with architectural tricks, such as a *trompe l'oeil* in a treillage flat on the wall at the end of the main vista, enticing the eye down an imaginary alley. Or, in the reiteration of the avenue scheme when clipped specimens are used, to decrease the size gradually towards the end, thus increasing the sense of perspective. Or, reverting to earlier chapters, to bring into play the colours and sizes of foliage to accentuate the distance.

It always surprises me how half-standard shrubs have gone out of fashion. It is understandable that roses should go because the average Hybrid Tea or Floribunda is much too vigorous to grow on a weak briar stem. There are a few new kinds being raised which it will perhaps be possible to buy as standards on the usual stems of about $3\frac{1}{2}$–4 ft and which are the very thing for planting on either side of a walk in a small garden. They take up no ground-room and will put up with any dwarf underplanting, economizing in space. But I also have in mind standard *Viburnum × juddii*, even more fragrant than roses in spring, where the flowers are, like the roses, lifted to nose level. The same is true of those superlative honeysuckles *Lonicera × americana* and the Late Dutch (*L. periclymenum* 'Serotina'), both of which can be made into neat, round, long-flowering heads of scented blossom; and a great boon to a small garden. Or the famous French idea of making big standards out of *Hibiscus syriacus* varieties, and treating them to hard pruning as one does for the Hybrid Tea roses. Thus treated they have at least a month's flowering period in the drier, sunnier parts of England.

THE PRODUCE-GARDEN

If we are planning, either in an old walled garden or in an open plot, a formal produce-garden – by which I mean a traditional kitchen or vegetable garden – there is much opportunity for artistry. There are few of us who do not enjoy seeing a well-kept area devoted to vegetables. The fresh green of parsley and carrots contrasts so well with glaucous leeks and the cabbage tribe, including the purple, and ornamental pink kales; the rows of onions, the giant decorativeness of Globe Artichokes and Cardoons, rows of peas, rows or tents of beans with white or scarlet flowers, all contribute to a delight in growing things and gustatory highlights. There are the waving masses of feathery green asparagus, beds of fragrant strawberries, mouth-watering rows of raspberries and currants and their kindred; screens or arches covered with thornless Loganberries, Boysenberries or Oregon Thornless Blackberry which is specially prolific. As suggested earlier all these can be in plots divided by fruit trees on dwarfing stock – cordons or espaliers, some perhaps to arch over the walks, with a narrow band of flowers or herbs on either side. To see how ornamental herbs can be we might go to Hardwick Hall, Derbyshire, where the National Trust has designed a large area specially for this class of plant.

Ornamental gardening today has moved far from the produce-garden but there is no denying the beauty and interest to be found in fruit trees of any size in flower or fruit. Pears, plums and cherries start the season in flower very early in the year, often before we are ready to linger in the garden for enjoyment. While they are all white in flower the apples give us flowers of joyous blush and pink, with a sweet scent. Some of the most colourful in flower are 'Sunset', 'Lord Derby', 'Arthur Turner', while – though of paler colouring – 'Upton Pyne' has very large flowers. By August 'Devonshire Quarrenden' will be showing its ripe dark red fruits, followed by numerous others of varying tints, while peaches and apricots delight us and plums offer, besides flavour, shape and size, that magical waxy "bloom" that adds so much to their appearance. Some pears like 'Durondeau' colour to a burnished red. Fruit trees are not noted for the autumn tints of their leaves but give much in other ways to the beauty of the garden and are due for re-appraisal by us all owing to the selection of dwarfing stocks which preclude the great old trees – so very beautiful and part of our heritage – which causes endless difficulty in spraying, pruning and gathering, although we might recall the words of William Lawson in 1618: "The very works of, and in an Orchard and Garden, are better than the ease and reste of and from other labours." So take heart!

The French have much to show us in the inclusion of art in practical matters. Some of their great gardens shine out to us as exemplary expositions. I remember particularly the charming radial planting in the garden of that old past-master of gardening, the Vicomte de Noailles at Fontainebleau. Truly there was art wedded to utility.

SCREENING

Lastly there is the art of screening. Any kind of shrub will do this in an informal way – so long as it will achieve 6 ft or so – and some of the loveliest surprises in a garden large or small are where a big shrub obscures part of a view. But sometimes there is not room for a 6 ft shrub (which will normally achieve the same or more in width) and we have to resort to a wall or fence or using climbing plants on some sort of support. Walls are expensive but final and complete in themselves and can be sited quite well within certain gardens; fences are seldom used other than as boundaries. Whatever the support it must be firm and long-lasting; nothing is more infuriating than, after achieving a good screen, to have the support collapse.

Perhaps for a support for climbing plants concrete posts and stout wires will prove the best and most long-lasting. One disadvantage of wires is found in cold districts; they are apt to harm all but the hardiest of plants in times of severe frost. Insulated wire is best. I think the most attractive screen for climbers is stout, rectangular wooden trellis. If this can be made of tanalized wood a long life is ensured.

When furnishing such a screen there is a great range of climbers and shrubs for selection. Evergreens of course are best, and I have a special weakness for the large-leafed fragrant Grecian Ivy, *Hedera colchica*, or its elegantly creamy-yellow and grey variegated form *H.c.* 'Dentata Variegata'. Either will make a complete and dense screen. The honeysuckle *Lonicera japonica* 'Halliana' is evergreen in all but severe winters and has the advantage of producing flowers of creamy-white from July until the frosts of autumn; it is very sweetly scented. To ensure the longest flowering period it is necessary to cut it back to the main stems in late March. Some roses are admirable, especially the nearly evergreen 'Albéric Barbier' and 'Félicité et Perpétue'. Pyracanthas of the newer kinds such as 'Orange Glow' and 'Shawnee' give a brilliant display of berries in autumn, besides being evergreen with flowers in June. The possibilities of variation and colour-scheming are almost endless. I will not go into further detail here except to append a short list for consideration: *Jasminum nudiflorum*, *Vitis vinifera* 'Purpurea', *Clematis tangutica* and *orientalis* 'Bill McKenzie', Rose 'Constance Spry', *Actinidia kolomikta* (for extra sunny positions). None of these is too vigorous for a screen 6–8 ft high.

Whereas shrubs can be trained horizontally at the base and so keep a screen solid to the ground, all climbers are apt to grow upwards with a result that they tend to be not only bare at the base but coarse and overpowering at the top. Here is surely the chance for something special in the way of colour combinations: a row of some dwarf shrub to fill in the lower part of the screen. It can just be a green companion, such as box or *Hebe rakaiensis*, or there is a choice of shrubs which will act as a contrast or complement to the climbing plant, to flower or produce its special foliage with those of the climbing plant or at a different season. I am only touching upon this subject here; it is worthy of much thought.

PLANTS IN CONTAINERS

We have wandered rather far into the realm of formal gardens with their rigid backgrounds and divisions but have neglected the immediate surrounds of the house. It is here that many of the fragrant plants in Chapter 14 will be the choice. And tucked away here and there around the patio or other sitting place is the spot for seasonal pot plants. Some of us are lucky enough to have a garden which includes a nursery corner, even frames or a greenhouse. Here plants in ordinary pots or ornamental containers can be nurtured, and placed according to their heights, colours and habits, to grace the sitting places or vantage points elsewhere. With ingenuity we can grow enough plants so that the grouping can be varied and adjusted during the season. Some perennials – the graceful large-leaf variegated Periwinkle for instance (*Vinca major* 'Variegata' or 'Elegantissima'), hardy fuchsias, hydrangeas, hostas, ferns, sedums and even sempervivums – will mingle well with shelter-bred geraniums, petunias and lilies. But some of the hardy plants, standing in their containers above ground during the winter, will need protection from frost. They need therefore plunging in soil or an ash bed, both for their well-being and to save the pots from cracking. Of course they entail frequent watering during the summer months but in my estimation this is worth the effort and the beauty achieved.

> . . . all walled gardens and compartments near a house; all warm, sheltered, sunny walks planted with fruit trees, are greatly to be wished for, and should be preserved, if possible, when once established.
>
> Sir Uvedale Price, *An essay on the Picturesque,* 1795

13

Water in gardens

And nearer to the river's trembling edge
    There grew broad flag-flowers, purple prank with white,
And starry river buds among the sedge,
    And floating water-lilies, broad and bright,
Which lit the oak that overhung the hedge
    With moonlight beams of their own water light;
And bulrushes, and reeds of such deep green
    As soothed the dazzled eye with sober sheen.

P.B. SHELLEY, 1792–1822

Water in gardens can be static, or gushing from spout or fountain, or can be made to appear as from nowhere to flow down an artificial stream. Sometimes of course a garden owner is fortunate enough to have natural, flowing water, but, also fortunately, there are means today of pumping water as desired and artificial means of containing it where required. All this is concerned with garden design and does not come within the scope of this book, but I must make one statement which I believe to be irrevocable and that is that water can be made to look natural only so long as it lies in, or makes its way to, the lowest part of the garden and that whenever water is needed on any other level it must be formally designed.

In these pages I just want to call attention to a few important rules in planting. We can leave aside the attraction that moving water always provides and consider the planting of static water. Most water plants in any case grow best in still water which will get warm in summer. This is a practical pointer to the fact that as much water as possible should be open to the sun's rays, and this fortunately goes hand in hand with the principal reason for having static water in the garden. It is to provide light and reflection from the sky. Water lilies are the perfect complement to a still pool but if the depth available is suited to the different needs of the different kinds they quickly spread and after a few seasons may cover too much water. A fair rule to apply is that at least two-thirds of the water surface should be free of growth.

94

To obtain this desired reflection of the sky the siting is important. If tall growth of shrubs or trees is to the south of the water the reflection will be lost. The angle of reflection must be considered.

Quite a small pool – and the term "small" is relative to the size of the garden – can be made to appear larger if the planting around it is suggestive of water. Grasses, rushes, rustling bamboos and the lithe, lax growth of willows all add up to this suggestion. A pond – whatever its size – does not need to have either a *Gunnera* or a weeping willow though these two plants are usually the first choice of anyone making a large water garden. Like many other projects of fair size today the creation of a lake in clay soil by means of a mechanical digger costs comparatively little. As little perhaps as engaging fifty men and carts at five shillings per week in the "good" old days – especially if no expensive lining is needed.

I was once asked to suggest some water-side planting around an artificial pool. All the trees and shrubs in the immediate vicinity were bamboos and willows, with poplars farther off. The whole area had a homogeneous planting with the exception of one lumpy dark Horse Chestnut, which to me spoilt everything. I asked for its removal and it went! One needs a large lake to take the majesty of a Horse Chestnut into its embrace.

The pond at Cliveden, a property of the National Trust in Buckinghamshire, has an intriguing pagoda brought from the Paris Exhibition of 1867. This gives the area a Japanese touch and we like to keep and to plant things with association with Japanese gardens around it – bamboos, wisterias, irises and azaleas. This is what we may term an association of ideas.

Whatever the choice of plants for the surrounding land or beds is, their reflection will double their impact. Since water is introduced in gardens because of its cool associations it is probably safest to continue this idea in the planting. Cool colours are therefore of great value – the blue *Pontederia*, the pink Flowering Rush or *Butomus*, white of *Calla*. Foliage of moisture-loving plants is almost without exception green and I feel that any variations towards purplish tones or grey are out of place – except the grey of the willow tribe: dwarf *Salix lanata* 'Stuartii', spreading *S. repens argentea* and the exquisitely silvery silkiness of *Salix exigua*. Apart from these and the broad blades of glaucous hostas, all glaucous, silvery, woolly or silky shrubs and plants prefer drier ground; in fact their leaf-covering is to combat the sun's heat and to prevent transpiration. So a water garden should mostly be given to greenery, and, I feel, cool colours, though no sooner is this written than images are conjured up in the imagination of banks of blazing azaleas and rhododendrons reflected in many a great pond or lake throughout the country.

14

Fragrance in the garden, month by month

I have loved flowers that fade,
Within whose magic tints
Rich hues have marriage made
With sweet unmemoried scents.

ROBERT BRIDGES, 1844–1930

Like the book itself, this chapter derives from a lecture given before the Royal Horticultural Society. It was printed in the *Journal* for July and August 1963. The subject has here been re-interpreted and adjusted.

Many of us are blessed with a keen sense of smell. At times it can be an embarrassment, even a disadvantage, but usually it adds to our enjoyment of all sorts of things. Most flavours are appreciated as much through the nose as through the mouth. We are not born with a keen sense of smell, but it comes with use and, I believe, can usually be sharpened by constant practice. Many of us, when passing plants that we may or may not know are distinctively fragrant, are apt to pick off a shoot, crush it and smell it. This is how our appreciation of the diverse aromas of plants becomes sharpened. All kinds of oaks, for instance, have a common likeness in the smell of a crushed leaf and certainly all species of the Walnut Family – *Juglandaceae* – have a very distinct redolence. Likewise the leaves and shoots of *Hedera colchica*, when crushed, at once reveal their difference from those of the common ivy, and the smell of a *Cupressus* is easily distinguishable from that of a *Thuja* – except *Thuja orientalis*. Even the seeds and roots of many plants are recognizable by the nose as anyone will know who has handled the seeds of *Valeriana* or *Penstemon*, or the roots of *Robinia pseudacacia* or *Fritillaria imperialis*. I often think that we do not give our sense of smell fair play in our classification of plants.

I am not sure that there is any really direct art in using fragrant plants in the garden, but feel that a chapter on the subject may well be considered an advantage in this book. I for one should find it impossible to suggest how fragrant plants should be arranged in the garden so that a sequence of the smells would enhance one another. In fact I am quite unable to classify smells in the mind or with words. I am totally lost in reading *Flower Scent* by F.A. Hampton so far as the classification of scent goes, apart from a recognition of lemon-fragrance and a few other very distinct odours, camphor, sandal-wood, tea, clove, and so on. The *Book of the Scented Garden* by F.W. Burbidge is also packed with interesting facts and details.

But I am not proposing to go into the classification of scents. It is quite beyond me. It might relate more closely to the title of this book and I feel that to suggest plants of sweet fragrance is hardly an art. However, the use of them in the garden certainly adds to our enjoyment. The beauties of shape, colour and texture are augmented by a delicious fragrance wafted towards us on the air, and this is the criterion I wish to set: to call attention to those plants whose fragrance – as Francis Bacon put it – is "free in the air".

In the old days before drains and other sanitary advantages were in common use, all manner of spices and fragrant leaves were treasured and were part of the everyday life of the richer households at least. Pomanders composed of spices and aromatic leaves were carried to allay noxious smells and were supposed to ward off diseases. Food, particularly meat, which quickly became stale, was disguised by spices, and the floors were strewn with Sweet Rush and other fragrant growths which when crushed by the feet give off a fragrance that helped to counteract the untoward smells of dogs and their uneaten food. Lotions, waters and pot-pourri together with powders and oils were in constant demand from the apothecaries. Practically all of them owed their fragrance to plant products. A brisk trade in such things was carried on with foreign countries.

Today we are very blessed. We have rifled the world for plants giving us all sorts of beauty and have within our call innumerable fragrant species and varieties for our gardens throughout the year.

If we could be sure in which direction the wind would blow during each month, we could plant our scented things where it would bring their aroma to us. But, apart from winds of an easterly direction in spring, it seems impossible – at least in Surrey – to say whence our prevailing winds come during the different seasons of the year. The evidence of tree shapes points to the fact that the south-west prevails, and as the scents are released more freely in what we call "growing weather" (i.e. warm and moist), we should plant most of our scented plants to the south-west of our walks, apart from the early spring flowerers which might be sited to the north-east. All this of course can be easily upset for obvious reasons in some garden designs and sites, but it is an idea worth considering at the very start of planting. "Awake, O north wind; and come thou south; blow upon my garden, that the spices thereof may flow out" (Song of Solomon).

It is amusing to read in Burbidge's book, mentioned above, that John Evelyn in 1661 made a reference to the prevailing winds and proposed that all low ground around London, especially east and south-west, should be divided into square plots of from twenty to forty acres, and separated from each other by plantations of fragrant shrubs, such as Sweetbriar, Jessamine, Syringa, Roses, and above all Rosemary. The last was specially to be included because its flowers, he observed, give their scent above thirty leagues from the coast of Spain. The square plots he recommended should be filled with Pinks, Gillyflowers, Cowslips, Lilies, Musk, Thyme, and Marjoram, and all those blooms "which upon the least cutting and pressure breathe out and betray their ravishing odours". By this means he thought the whole City would be improved for health, profit and beauty.

THE EARLY YEAR

During the first months of the year, if the weather be mild, several beautiful and valuable shrubs are in flower which are particularly fragrant. Extra valuable in their resistance to sharp frosts are Witch Hazels: all forms of *Hamamelis mollis* are sweetly and powerfully fragrant but I think *H.m.* 'Pallida' is not only the sweetest but the most telling tint in the garden. The forms and hybrids of *H. japonica* are also fragrant but less pleasingly so. *H.j.* 'Zucciniana' has a thin acid scent, like that of *Cornus mas* — which follows it in flower — and the much later *Euonymus sachalinensis*.

Lonicera × purpusii, a hybrid between *L. fragrantissima* and *L. standishii*, would be my choice of these three shrubs, with small but extremely sweet creamy flowers. The Fragrant Guelder, *Viburnum farreri* (*V. fragrans*), stands in front of all its close relatives for delicious fragrance and good habit, flowering from November onwards during mild spells like the loniceras. 'Dawn' (pink) and 'Deben' (white) are two good clones of *V. × bodnantense* which is a hybrid of *V. farreri*; their scent is not as sweet as that species, approaching more nearly to the other parent, *V. grandiflorum*, which has a strong aromatic scent. *V. foetidum* is white and very sweet; only its stems and foliage are foetid when crushed.

A splendid evergreen shrub, *Mahonia japonica*, provides its pale yellow flowers from November to April; on a warm day the scent from a large bush is amazingly potent, and the same may be said in the early year of the little evergreen bushes, related to the Box, the sarcococcas. I think *Sarcococca hookeriana digyna* is the most attractive but we scarcely notice their tiny flowers until assailed by their honeyed aroma. Among deciduous bushes the Winter Sweet (*Chimonanthus*) excels with a lovely spicy fragrance usually in January; in late February one may expect the pink or white flowers of *Daphne mezereum*.

When we consider the smaller winter flowering plants, like snowdrops, *Iris unguicularis* and *I. reticulata* and *Crocus tomasinianus* – all are sweetly fragrant – we must admit that the day has to be perfect and the quantities of flowers must be great for their scent to be noticed in the air. It is there, on good days, but our noses are seldom sufficiently trained. A little later the Grape Hyacinths may be noted, particularly *Muscari* (*Muscarimia*) *moschatum*, but who grows this delectable morsel with yellowish flowers by the hundred? And yet one flower-head will perfume a room for several days. With the coming of March, however, the violets start to flower, and when grown in generous patches the common white violet, *Viola alba*, or the purple *V. odorata*, gives off a powerful scent which will carry for a few yards.

March will usually find *Cornus mas* in flower with its sharp fragrance while that of the big, prickly *Berberis sargentiana* and its relatives are like honey. *Osmanthus × burkwoodii* (*Osmarea*) foreshadows the amazing sweetness of its parent *Osmanthus delavayi* in April, while its other parent *Osmanthus decorus* (*Phillyrea decora*) is less sweet, but powerful. A good broad-leafed evergreen is *O. serrulatus*; it has tiny creamy flowers with a pronounced fragrance and is of compact growth. I should not like to be without skimmias in March. All are fragrant but the males are best and none is so floriferous and fragrant as *Skimmia japonica* 'Rubella'; moreover its warm red-brown buds are an asset from autumn onwards.

The Japanese Apricot, *Prunus mume*, is perfectly hardy and flowers freely, but I usually give it some black cotton to defeat the birds before Christmas. The two varieties I know best, each of amazing sweetness, are of Japanese origin, 'Benichidori' – warm deep pink – and 'Omoinomama', creamy white. I find that almost alone among species of *Prunus* the buds of this one need to be well advanced, about to open, before picking for indoors. These are two of our most valuable winter flowers and some years the flowers open at Christmas.

Among the smaller plants of March we have the invaluable hyacinths; though these are gross and overfed when purchased, they settle down in the garden thereafter and flower yearly with graceful spikes, and their fragrance carries well. Before these are over the polyanthuses, primroses and auriculas are starting into flower with the wallflowers and early *Narcissi*. While daffodils do give off a little scent it is the short-cupped *Narcissi*, and in particular those descended from *N. ornatus*, *N. triandrus* and *N. jonquilla*, which are the most fragrant. Two very old fragrant favourites, still good for naturalizing, are 'Sir Watkin' and *N. barrii conspicuus*. *Hermodactylus* (*Iris*) *tuberosus*, the Little Widow, a fascinating study in green and black, will thrive in a warm corner, where *Helleborus lividus* may also be made at home. I have only been able to grow it in an alpine house where its fragrance was remarkable. I should give the benefit of shelter, too, to *Cyclamen repandum* whose flowers, usually of rich crimson-purple, make such a good contrast with primroses.

EARLY SPRING

Our spring weather is so fickle that it is impossible to say when spring begins. *Prunus yedoensis* is one of the larger things for this period, one of the earliest Japanese cherries and very sweetly scented; coupled with its beautiful blush flowers it brings a noteworthy graceful arching habit to our gardens.

Magnolias are all fragrant, but among the early hardy species particularly are *Magnolia stellata* and *M. heptapeta* (*M. denudata*, *M. conspicua*). The latter is a parent of the Soulangiana group and all of these shed fresh fragrance around. *M. kobus* and its form *borealis* and *M. salicifolia* are also delicious; in the Savill Garden one day I overheard the former being described as "smelling like champagne"!

The Currants give us special species worth noting; some may not approve of the scent of *Ribes sanguineum* and its varieties when brought indoors, but outside their offensiveness disappears and leaves a soft aroma. On the other hand *R. odoratum* (*R. aureum* of gardens) and the dwarf-growing *R. alpinum* – particularly the latter – are very sweet. The Tree Heaths, *Erica arborea* and *E.a. alpina*, both produce a honeyed scent.

SPRING IN ALL ITS BEAUTY

"All day in the sweet Box tree the bee for pleasure hummeth" is a delightful line of Robert Bridges which not only reminds us of an evergreen that gives off a sharp thin scent throughout the year, but which at flowering time is especially sweet. I do not think we plant enough box in our gardens today; in the past whole parterres were planted with it. Modern parterres, closely related to old patterns, have been laid out by the National Trust at Little Moreton Hall, Cheshire; Moseley Old Hall, Staffordshire; Ashdown House, Oxfordshire; and Clandon Park, Surrey.

Principal shrubs now in flower are the early lilacs: *Syringa* 'Lamartine', 'Buffon', *S, persica* and *S. × chinensis*. To walk through the *rond-point* at Hidcote when the Rouen Lilac is weeping to the ground with its lavish display is a delight to the senses. No less fragrant are *Viburnum carlesii* and *V.*

bitchiuense, but I usually plant 'Fulbrook', which is one of their hybrids; in growth and flower it is excellent and both it and another hybrid, *V. × juddii*, do not as a rule suffer from black fly, which is so prevalent in the first species. *Berberis* species are many and most are fragrant, but few excel the well-known *B. × stenophylla*. *Coronilla glauca*, which is often in flower from November onwards, gives a last spring rush of yellow blossom, richly fragrant, against a warm wall.

Turning to flowering trees, Japanese cherries are all somewhat fragrant, but among them I should choose *Prunus serrulata erecta* ('Ama-no-gawa') and the single white 'Jonioi'. The crabs are lavish with their fragrance. My choice would be *Malus baccata* and hybrids *M. spectabilis*, *M. floribunda* and 'Profusion' for early kinds, followed by still more fragrant species, *M. theifera*, the temperamental *M. ioensis* 'Plena' and its more vigorous but smaller-flowered relative *M. coronaria* 'Charlottae'. The last two are to be treasured for their fragrance of violets. Laburnums are all fragrant and also many willows, specially *Salix triandra* and *S. alba* 'Britzensis'.

Some other good shrubs for this period for warm gardens are the vanilla-scented *Azara microphylla* and several myrtles. *Daphne odora*, *D. blagayana* and *D. cneorum* 'Eximia' are a trio of low evergreens which I should not like to be without.

At this lavish time of the year the plants give wafts of fragrance for they are usually present in greater quantities than those which flower earlier. Many early flowering tulips are fragrant, particularly 'De Wet' and some orange and yellow varieties of the later Darwin and other strains. Among the species, *Tulipa sylvestris* and *T. clusiana* should be remembered. The last and most fragrant *Narcissi* flower at this time, notably *N. × gracilis* and *N. poeticus recurvus*. In shadier borders bluebells can be grown, together with Lily of the Valley, the common one for early flowering followed by 'Fortin's Giant'.

The dwarf Bearded Irises, the Intermediate and the taller kinds are mostly fragrant but among the taller ones those with *Iris pallida* parentage are reliable. For its scent and good foliage I always plant *I. pallida dalmatica*. There are several early fragrant species which are followed by all the splendid modern hybrid Bearded Irises most of which are freely fragrant. Though it does not float its scent away I feel I must mention *I. graminea* whose exquisite flowers, sunk among the leaves, smell like hot plum tart. I included a painting of this delectable gem in my book *Three Gardens*.

In cool corners in moist peaty soil I should like to have yards and yards of *Epigaea repens* – if it were not so difficult and scarce. I shall never forget seeing several square yards of it in the 1930s at Knap Hill Nurseries, happily naturalized in damp acid soil. Nowadays all we see are single plants cosseted in pots. *Hesperis matronalis*, the Sweet Rocket, in either the single or double form is a doubtful perennial of great sweetness. The double does best in the cooler north.

There are several good, scented shrubs which, being rather tender, are seen at their best in the south-west, such as *Pittosporum tobira*, *Cytisus × spachianus* (*C. racemosus* or *Genista fragrans* of gardens), *Drimys winteri* and the corokias. Particularly delicious are the trio of magnolias, *Magnolia sinensis*, *M. wilsonii* and *M. sieboldii*. It is always one of the highlights of the year to come across one of these in flower; the pure white, nodding, bowl-shaped blooms have dark crimson stamens in the centre more or less telling the nose where to sniff, if it were necessary. If *Pyracantha rogersiana* and its form *flava* were known as sweetly *fragrant* flowering shrubs of very high standing – as well as being autumn-fruiting shrubs – our gardens in May would be more blessed. *Cytisus × praecox* has a powerful aroma that I am never quite sure about; is it pleasant or not?

Species roses start to flower in late May as a general rule; *Rosa primula* is strongly redolent of incense in all its parts throughout the growing season. Of early hybrids we should have to go far to beat the sweetness exhaled from 'Frühlingsgold' and 'Frühlingsanfang', followed soon by the clove-fragrance of *R. rugosa* forms and the sweet 'Nevada'.

RHODODENDRONS

It is not generally realized, I think, what a very fragrant genus this is. Those who have weeded around or made cuttings of many of the little mountain species, particularly members of the Saluenense, Lapponicum and Glaucum Series – in fact almost all the 'Lepidotes' – will remember the rich pungent aroma from the leaves when bruised. In warm weather they give off a subtle richness without being bruised. Even in winter, on mild damp days, some of the Cinnabarinum Series are markedly fragrant; not only *Rhododendron cinnabarinum* itself, from which a delicate whiff of heliotrope can be detected, but also *R. concatenans* and *R. augustinii*.

So much for a brief review of those fragrant leaves. When it comes to fragrant flowers a remarkable similarity in fragrance and shape will be found to lilies. Whether so august a race as rhododendrons can be said to imitate lilies – one hears of 'plant mimicry' in other respects – I do not feel competent to decide; but the form and scent of lilies is so well known that we think of them instinctively when searching for what is an extraordinary resemblance. The trumpet-shaped flowers of certain rhododendrons are fashioned closely to those of *Lilium regale* and many have a similar fragrance, or like that of *L. speciosum*.

48 *Tamarix tetrandra* is noted for its "feathery" appearance, from its foliage all summer and from its pink flowers in May.

49 An old plant of *Acer palmatum* 'Linearilobum', one of the most "feathery" of slow-growing shrubs. There is also an 'Atropurpureum' form of it.

50 Furnishing the side of this glade at Hungerdown House, Wiltshire, are the cream-striped *Hosta fortunei hyacinthina*, *Iris foetidissima* 'Variegata', *Cornus alba* 'Elegantissima' and *Juniperus × media* 'Pfitzeriana'.

51 The Bamboo, *Arundinaria nitida*, is here strikingly contrasted by the upward thrusting dark green fronds of *Blechnum chilense* at Muncaster Castle, Cumbria.

52 Yellow-flushed leaves make a pool of sunlight in an enclosed London garden. *Catalpa bignonioides* 'Aurea' (left) and *Sambucus racemosa* 'Plumosa Aurea' (right).

53 Grey, silvery leaves in contrast at Salutation House, Kent. Left to right: *Artemisia* 'Powis Castle', *Stachys olympica* large form, *Ballota pseudodictamnus* and *Senecio leucostachys*.

54 A winter picture of the Heather Garden in Windsor Great Park. Heaths and junipers of all sizes contribute to this varied planting, in natural style.

55 By the waterfall at Sheffield Park Garden, where the hardy palms give an exotic touch. The area of water in relationship to its surrounds is small and thus water lilies would clutter the effect.

56 Steely grey-green of *Astelia nervosa*. Evergreen.

57 *Artemisia canescens*, silvery grey-green, for sunny positions.

58 A Weeping Ash at Cast-lewellan, County Down, grafted on a stem 20 feet high to achieve immediate height in an unnatural way.

59 A young Weeping Beech, *Fagus sylvatica* 'Pendula'.

60 The renowned Weeping Ash at Stourhead, Wiltshire (National Trust) grafted almost at ground level and achieving a more natural effect.

61 Young Weeping Birches, *Betula pendula* 'Youngii'.

FASTIGIATE TREES

62 Two unusual fastigiate deciduous trees, oak and birch; *Quercus petraea* 'Columnaris' and *Betula pendula* 'Fastigiata' on right.

THE HORIZONTAL LINE

63 One of the most elegant of white variegated shrubs, *Cornus controversa* 'Variegata'.

Some of the most beautiful of all rhododendrons are those tantalizingly in the Maddenii Series – tantalizing because only in the most favoured gardens of the west can they be grown outside. A lovely succession of delicious white or cream trumpets can be obtained in cold districts by bringing into a frost-proof glasshouse for the winter the following: *RR. bullatum* and *johnstoneanum* for very earlies; 'Fragrantissimum', 'Lady Alice Fitzwilliam', 'Countess of Haddington', 'White Wings', followed by *supranubium* and many others such as *edgworthii, cubitii, lindleyi, megacalyx* (a subtle nutmeg aroma), *nuttallii, tyermannii, dalhousiae, maddenii* and finally *crassum*. Apart from *R. bullatum* and *edgeworthii*, which are in the Edgeworthii Series, all of the above are species in the Maddenii Series or hybrids of them. A considerably hardier species in the same series is *R. ciliatum*.

The Fortunei series is, generally, considerably hardier, if given woodland conditions. Many are fragrant; quite early in the year comes *R. calophytum*, followed later by the hybrid *R*. Loderi in its many forms in May, all hybrids of *R. fortunei*; *R. fortunei* itself, hybrids such as 'Naomi' and 'Avocet'; also 'Angelo' and 'Kewense' which bring in *R. griffithianum*, another fragrant species; *R. decorum, R. discolor, R. vernicosum* and the hardy hybrid 'Mrs A.T. de la Mare'. *R. fortunei* has been a prolific parent and its scent has in the main been transmitted to its progeny. The latest of this series to flower is *R. diaprepes*, and late hybrids of *R. discolor* include 'Albatross' and 'Bonito'. 'Polar Bear', a giant rhododendron, combines *R. diaprepes* and *R. auriculatum* and these last bring us to July or even August and September.

Meanwhile the azaleas have flowered and gone; we do not need to be reminded of the common yellow Pontic azalea (*R. luteum*) which is naturalized in so many gardens in these islands. Forms of *Azalea mollis* – hybrids of *R. japonicum* (*sinensis*) – may not have fragrant flowers but their young foliage gives off an aroma rather like that of *Fritillaria imperialis*; the race known as "*Azalea occidentalis*" – mainly hybrids of *R. viscosum* and *molle* – are the queens of hybrid azaleas for fragrance, flowering abundantly with graceful growth and loose trusses of large delicately coloured flowers. Famous and unrivalled varieties are 'Delicatissima', 'Exquisita', 'Graciosa', 'Irene Koster', and 'Superba', and the older slightly smaller-flowered 'Viscosepala' and its lovely relative 'Daviesii'.

Almost all species of the Luteum group of the azaleas, to which *R. luteum* and *R. occidentale* belong, are exceptionally sweet. *RR. roseum, canescens* and *nudiflorum* flower more or less with these two well-known species, followed by *R. arborescens* and *atlanticum*; quite late in the azalea season, well into July and August, some of the very sweetest open, *RR. alabamense, oblongifolium*, and *viscosum* and its several varieties. They all have small dainty flowers with long stamens protruding and are exceedingly refined compared with the large-flowered hybrid strains; they resemble honeysuckle in shape and fragrance. Two splendid yellows related to *R. luteum* are 'Sir Christopher Wren' and 'Nancy Waterer'.

Lastly there are two azaleodendrons, *Azaleodendron* 'Fragrans' and *A.* 'Govenianum', probably hybrids between *R. viscosum* and *R. catawbiense*, producing sweet rosy mauve flowers in June.

FRAGRANT JUNE

We are much at the mercy of the weather in boisterous May, but we like to think that June will arrive and give us the first taste of summer. Very often it does, but only for a few days. The great volume of scents that reach our nostrils in June and July are not necessarily due to the plants that flower then being more fragrant than early ones, but because then, in good weather, everything is growing luxuriantly. When the air is warm and moist and a plant is growing well the scents are given off in greatest quantity. It is a wonderful thought that in the northern Temperate Regions at least, in those places where humans tend mostly to be at ease with the weather – not on mountain tops or in deserts but in more ordinary terrain – there, when the weather is right, the flowers are giving off most scent, delighting us all, and at the same time are fulfilling their function of securing the co-operation of insects in fertilization.

Great wafts of scent greet us in June. There are borders of pinks, old and new, but specially 'White Ladies' (the improved 'Mrs Sinkins'), *Dianthus fragrans* 'Plenus', a smaller flower which I have not seen for some years, and many single and double hardy garden pinks. The 'Highland' strain is a useful group of singles of all colours. Sweet Wivelsfield (*D. fimbriatus*) and Sweet Williams (*Dianthus barbatus*), close relatives, are all very free of scent.

The early Day Lilies appear, none more fragrant than *Hemerocallis flava* by day and *H. citrina* in the evening, with *H. middendorfiana* and *H. dumortieri* good runners-up.

Lupins, both the tree lupin *Lupinus arboreus* and many of the border hybrids, are very rich; I have not noticed any colour superior to another in fragrance. *Aquilegia fragrans*, *Paeonia lactiflora* (*P. albiflora*) and *P. emodi*, *Primula sikkimensis* and *P. alpicola* are all strong candidates for inclusion.

Among the shrubs for June, some late magnolias should be planted. *Magnolia virginiana* (*M. glauca*) and its hybrid *M. × thompsoniana* are each in flower for six or seven weeks and should be included in most gardens. *M. macrophylla* and *M. delavayi* are much larger; *M. obovata* and *M. × watsonii*

(M. × *wiezneri*), probably a hybrid of it, are in the forefront of "wafters", and even one flower can be detected some yards away on the right day.

Two early Mock Oranges are in bloom, *Philadelphus magdalenae* and *P. coronarius*. I have the golden-leafed form of the latter growing with *Lilium pyrenaicum* and the combination blows right across the garden and delights all comers, though the lily on its own or in close proximity is apt to be overpowering.

Genista cinerea is the first of the greater brooms to flower, shedding extreme fragrance from its thousands of canary-yellow small flowers. *Cytisus monspessulanus* and its hybrid 'Porlock' are suitable for sunny, warm, dry positions and follow quickly.

Of many tall trees none is more floriferous than *Robinia pseudacacia*, and a choice can be made between the great, prickly, common species and the pink hybrid *R.* × *ambigua* 'Decaisneana'. *R. viscosa* and *R.* × *hillieri* are fragrant to a lesser degree and are smaller trees.

ROSES

I have mentioned some very early flowering roses. While almost all roses are fragrant the vast majority are 'fast of their smell', or nearly so, and have to be sniffed to give up their inner delights. *R. rugosa* is one exception, and its near hybrids or forms, both singles and doubles, can carry for a few yards, particularly 'Blanc Double de Coubert'.

The fragrance of most roses is in the petals, which is the reason, of course, for the strong fragrance of many double-flowered roses. In the Musk group – the Synstylae – the fragrance is in the stamens, which thus accounts for some doubles of *R. arvensis* and *R. wichuraiana* derivation being scentless. The Musk Rose itself, *R. moschata*, is a rarity these days but once seen (and smelt) it is never forgotten and produces its sprays of white flowers from August until autumn.

By far the most powerful and free of their scent are the various species in the Musk group, medium to very great climbers, of which the strongest, *RR. mulliganii, brunonii, filipes* 'Kiftsgate', *helenae, rubus*, are all vast vigorous ramblers for hedgerows and trees. Rather smaller but equally fragrant are *R. soulieana* and *R. setigera*, while their relative with less showy flowers, *R. multiflora*, is exceptionally rich. Related to one or other of the above are garden hybrids like 'Wedding Day', 'Lykkefund', 'Kew Rambler', all equally fragrant. *R. wichuraiana*, another of the Musk group, does not flower until all of the above, except *R. setigera*, are over, and is the parent of many fragrant roses, the most powerful of all being 'Albertine', while the 'Albéric

Barbier' group embracing such as 'Gardenia', 'May Queen', 'François Juranville' and 'Paul Transon' are nearly as good.

Aromatic roses, whose leaves and other parts give off fragrance without being bruised, include the 'Sweet Brier' (*R. rubiginosa*), and to a lesser degree its hybrids the Penzance Briers; the 'Incense Rose', *R. primula*, mentioned earlier, and *R. serafinii*. To these we can add the little *R. glutinosa*, smelling of pines.

Owing most of their fragrance to *R. multiflora*, a long way back in their parentage, are the Hybrid Musks and principal among them is 'Cornelia', of amazing carrying power. Very good also are 'Penelope', 'Felicia', 'Buff Beauty', 'Pax' and 'Thisbe'. Though the big climbing species of Musk Rose flower only at mid-summer, the Hybrid Musks go on until the autumn.

The Gallicas, Damasks and Mosses give fragrance in the air on the right days. Many of the Hybrid Perpetuals such as 'Ulrich Brunner', 'Henry Nevard', 'Georg Arends', 'Prince Camille de Rohan'; Bourbons like 'Mme Isaac Pereire', 'Mme Ernst Calvat', 'Zéphirine Drouhin' and 'Kathleen Harrop' and many of the best Hybrid Teas will, when grown in bulk in beds, cast their scent on the air on suitable days; on other days one can walk past them without noticing them. To these may be added a few Floribundas like 'Masquerade' and 'Iceberg', and 'Fragrant Cloud' among the Hybrid Teas. Older modern roses which scored highly for scent are 'Étoile de Hollande' and 'Crimson Glory', 'Dame Edith Helen' and 'General MacArthur'. To lean out of a bedroom window over a curtain of blossom from climbing forms of such as these is a rich experience.

PLANTS FOR ANNUAL PLANTING

Many of the bedding flowers give us rich scent in the air. Memory is prodded by various scents through the year, and I never encounter the soft sweet scent of *Lobularia* (*Alyssum*) *maritimum* without my mind going back to a garden of my childhood. It increases through July and reaches its zenith in the still days of August and early September. Candytuft (*Iberis odorata*), Mignonette (*Reseda odorata*), stocks (*Matthiola spp.*) of various kinds, sweet peas (*Lathyrus odoratus*) (who has not met that lovely fresh odour from the massed trials at Wisley?), *Dianthus* 'Loveliness' and petunias (especially in the evening) are all delicious. Likewise the Heliotrope or Cherry Pie (*Heliotropium peruvianum*, *H. corymbosum* and their hybrids) is one of my principal summer joys; some varieties of very rich colouring are scarcely fragrant at all; 'Chatsworth' and 'Lord Roberts' are two of the very best. The strains of freesias which we can now plant to grow outdoors are well worth including.

Taller annuals include annual lupins (*Lupinus hartwegii* and others), and the

Tobacco flowers – of which I think the white *Nicotiana alata* 'Grandiflora' is the most powerful, when the flowers open in the evening – nasturtiums (*Tropaeolum majus* and *minus*), and balsams (*Impatiens balsamina*). The Night-scented Stock (*Matthiola bicornis*) is a joy in the evening, too, with Evening Primroses, *Oenothera biennis* (biennial).

JULY PERENNIALS

July is the month for lilies; *Lilium pyrenaicum* being in flower in June, *L. candidum* may take pride of place for July. *L.* × *testaceum*, *LL. brownii*, *centifolium*, *regale*, *auratum* and *speciosum* are among the most delicious, of good carrying power, but the last two do not flower until August and September.

Clematis recta, *Polygonum polystachyum* and the border phloxes are splendid from July to August, the phloxes lasting for weeks and casting the most heady perfume of those full summer days. All of the numerous varieties are good, but I sometimes think the white varieties excel in fragrance. This may be because phlox scent is particularly sweet at dusk onwards and white varieties are most noticeable then.

JULY SHRUBS

There is no lack of hard-wooded plants for full summer. The bulk of philadelphuses flower after June 30, following quickly those mentioned for June. Some have little fragrance, but among the best are *Philadelphus pubescens* and *P. microphyllus* – one of the largest growing species and the smallest. *P. microphyllus* and descendants of the creamy rather tender *P. mexicanus* (*P. coulteri* of gardens) gave us the numerous garden hybrids which are of medium height and exceedingly fragrant: 'Lemoinei Erectus', 'Bouquet Blanc', 'Belle Étoile', 'Sybille', 'Fantaisie', 'Nuage Rose', 'Beauclerk', and the exquisitely perfumed 'Purpureo maculatus'. They will carry right through the garden and with the Musk roses are the mainstay of mid-summer.

Other good sweet shrubs are *Clethra alnifolia* 'Paniculata', *Elaeagnus augustifolia*, *Spartium junceum*, *Romneya* species and hybrids, *Buddleia davidii* and *B. fallowiana* varieties and hybrids, *Aesculus parviflora*, *Jasminum humile wallichianum*, *Genista virgata* and *G. aetnensis*, *Styrax japonica* and *Ligustrum sinense*.

Lavenders are all fragrant but more so when bruised; the most free of its scent in my experience is 'Hidcote Giant', a dwarf plant with large heavy heads of bloom borne on long stout stalks.

Shrubs which give their fragrance freely from glands on the leaves are

Cistus ladaniferus and its hybrids; *Escallonia macrantha* and varieties, and the "curry plant", *Helichrysum angustifolium*.

July also finds most of the limes in flower. They saturate the air with their scent, and a succession may be obtained by planting the early flowering *Tilia platyphyllos*, mid-season *T. euchlora* and *T. oliveri*, and the latest *T. petiolaris* which in August smells like a red-clover field. All species of lime are very fragrant and a visit to Kew to see the extreme variations in height and habit and flowering periods is very instructive.

At the waterside the Bog Bean *Menyanthes trifoliata* is in flower and the 'brandy-bottles' (*Nuphar*) float on the water; these and *Nymphaea odorata* will delight us idling in a boat, with the Water Violet, *Hottonia palustris*, and Water Hawthorn, *Aponogeton distachyon*.

CLIMBING PLANTS

Few climbing plants flower early in the year, but in May *Clematis montana* and its varieties and hybrids such as *C. × vedrariensis* and *Wisteria sinensis* and *W. floribunda* (macrobotrys) 'Multijuga' and their forms are first class spreaders of perfumes. On warm sheltered walls the white and yellow single Banksian roses and the double white are very fragrant, but the usual double yellow is not so remarkably sweet, though a hardier and more productive plant. Later through the summer and into September *Clematis rehderiana* or *veitchiana* (they are very similar) are delicious, smelling of cowslips.

Meanwhile other favourite climbers have flowered: *Jasminum officinale* – more fragrant than the larger-flowered *J.o.* 'Grandiflorum'; and honeysuckles – *Lonicera caprifolium*, *L. periclymenum* 'Belgica', followed by *L.p.* 'Serotina', *L. × americana* and *L. etrusca* 'Superba' give us much richness during June and July. On warm walls *Trachelospermum jasminoides*, *Holboellia latifolia* and *Vitis vulpina* are exceedingly sweet.

Last but not least the great evergreen *Magnolia grandiflora*, whose big cream flowers appear for weeks on end with a rich lemon scent, lingering well into autumn; though not a climber, it is a frequent occupier of wall space in less favoured districts. 'Exmouth' is a named form frequently planted; 'Goliath' is equally fragrant but more compact. Those who cannot accommodate these big growers can take comfort in planting 'Maryland' and 'Freeman' instead; they are equally fragrant and flower when quite young. They are hybrids of *M. grandiflora* and *M. virginiana* (*M. glauca*).

AUTUMN

We come at length to September days, when the phloxes still linger, late lilies like *L. speciosum* and *L. auratum* are still with us, late Hybrid Musk roses, the lingering annuals and bedding plants and late clematises are still giving excellent value; all have been mentioned earlier in greater detail. Dahlias in the mass have a refreshing odour, one that I specially associate with early autumn, while the far more potentially fragrant chrysanthemums do not deliver their scent freely. *Crinum × powellii* and its relatives give a fresh sweet smell on warm days.

Several good shrubs flower in late September and October, *Hamamelis virginiana*, a sharp clear scent; *Osmanthus heterophyllus* (*O. ilicifolius*, *O. aquifolium*) and *Elaeagnus macrophyllus* and its hybrid *E. × ebbingei* (three of the sweetest things of the year), *Camellia sasanqua* and forms, and later on, 'November Pink' for sheltered corners; *Clerodendron trichotomum*, *C. fargesii* and *C. bungei* (*C. foetidum*), but take care to place these three well away from the path so that their leaves do not get bruised and give off their foetid odour; *Hebe × speciosa* and forms and hybrids; *Eupatorium ligustrinum* (*E. weinmann-ianum*), *Ligustrum quihoui*, and *Poliothyrsis sinensis*. On warm walls *Buddleia auriculata* (large bushes grow at Clevedon Court and Cliveden – both owned by the National Trust – and in other gardens with sheltered climates) will carry on into November, extremely fragrant. This tiny-flowered buddleia is the longest lasting thing I know for a fragrant buttonhole and remains fragrant when dead and dried. *Polygonum baldschuanicum* is fragrant on calm mild days.

But there are scents other than those from flowers for the autumn. There are the fallen ripening fruits of *Chaenomeles japonica* (*Cydonia maulei*) and – which should have been mentioned earlier – the ripening peaches, apricots and plums; the wild strawberry leaves dying off and the delicious odour like ripe strawberries given off by the early-falling foliage of *Cercidiphyllum japonicum*. The aroma is powerful and easily detected after the leaves have dropped onto damp ground. There is also the general scent of decaying leaves, especially the sharp tang of Walnut leaves (*Juglans regia*). A particular pleasure in November is of handling decaying raspberry leaves which give off a sweet tea-scent. One of the most remarkable whiffs which lasts through the winter is the heliotrope-scent from the foliage of *Rhododendron cinnabarinum*, while many of the aromatic species, together with *Cistus ladaniferus*, its hybrids and *Hebe cupressoides* and others, are with us through the year.

NOT FOR SENSITIVE NOSES

The following give off, to my nose, offensive smells and strangely enough members of the Rose Family are numerous: *Stranvaesia*, all species; *Pyracantha coccinea* varieties and *P. atalantioides* (*P. gibbsii*) (not *P. rogersiana*);

Cotoneaster, many species, but particularly *C. rotundifolia*; *Sorbus*, all species and varieties; *Pyrus*, all species and varieties (excluding *Malus* species); *Crataegus*, all species; *Escallonia illinita*, *Cupressus lawsoniana* and varieties; *Hypericum hircinum*; *H. androsaemum*; *Arum dracunculus*; *Salvia turkestanica*; *Viburnum opulus* – particularly in autumn – and a few other species; *Cleome spinosa*; *Symplocarpus foetidus*.

Many people object to elders (species of *Sambucus*), border phloxes, *Ligustrum vulgare* and *ovalifolium*; *Fritillaria imperialis*, *Codonopsis clematidea* and other species, and *Azalea mollis*, but I enjoy them, even the last three "foxy" odours. I like to let a few of the wild poisonous hemlock (*Conium maculatum*) seed themselves every year in my garden for they are extremely elegant, up to 7 feet or so, and like a giant Cow Parsley; when in flower I sometimes regret my leniency, as they smell like mice as one passes by.

AROMATIC FOLIAGE

It is not really within the scope of this book to mention all the numerous plants whose fragrant leaves give off a pleasant scent when bruised. They are all 'fast of their smell' like the many flowers I have excluded, though I have tried to think of all the exceptions, such as the Balsam Poplars and the Sweet Brier, cistuses and the Curry Plant.

There are, however, several shrubs and plants which can be *used* to produce fragrance. I recall an area of damp lawn in A.T. Johnson's garden in North Wales which was threaded by the creeping stems of *Mentha requienii*; as one stood about admiring the borders and trees the little mint gave off a delicious pungent scent. *Mentha pulegium* (Penny royal) is a larger version which is pleasant in the same way in paving, rock garden paths, shrub garden walks and the like. Lawns of camomile (*Anthemis nobilis*) give off a subtle scent when walked upon.

All the lavenders, the rosemaries, and the Lemon Verbena (*Lippia citriodora*) I like to grow close to where one walks daily, so that their scent is released in brushing past them. Along the kitchen garden path the various mints can be placed for the same reason with *Artemisia abrotanum*, together with Lemon Balm (*Melissa officinalis*), Marjoram (*Origanum vulgare* and *O. marjorana*) and sages (*Salvia officinalis* and varieties); dwarf hedges of Cotton Lavender (*Santolina spp.*), of Rue (*Ruta graveolens* – 'Jackman's Blue' is the best) are delicious when brushed by, though often considered too pungent to crush and sniff in the palm. In the bog or water garden the Sweet Gale (*Myrica gale*) and Sweet Rush (*Acorus calamus*) should be planted near the path also, and in the semi-woodland *Geranium macrorrhizum* and Sweet Cicely (*Myrrhis odorata*).

By seats set in a bank in sunny dry places various lavenders and rosemary, Sweet Bay (*Laurus nobilis*) and Myrtle (*Myrtus communis*) can be allowed to grow close, and the ground given to thymes, both the creeping varieties of *Thymus drucei* (*T. serpyllum*), the bushier Common and Lemon thymes (*T. vulgare* and *T. × citriodorus*) and the less hardy "seed-cake" or Caraway-scented species *T. herba-barona*. These also are excellent on rock garden ledges where one can sit, together with *Teucrium marum* and *Leontopodium aloysiodorum*. By woodland garden seats *Comptonia asplenifolia*, *Ledum* species, numerous small-growing rhododendron species and *Gaultheria procumbens* should be used. Let us beware however of *Umbellularia californica*, which looks like a Sweet Bay at first sight, and smells rather like one, but which gives headaches and creates a frenzy if inhaled repeatedly.

Seats in the flower border may have Bergamot (*Monarda didyma*) and Absinthe (*Artemisia absinthium*), and for the summer in pots and tubs and window boxes near at hand the large-leafed peppermint "geranium" (*Pelargonium tomentosum*) is invaluable, together with the smaller-leafed "oak-leafed" and other fragrant species such as *Pelargonium quercifolium*, *P. crispum*, *P. odoratissimum*, *P. papilionaceum* and *P. radula*.

EVENING SCENTS

I have referred here and there through this book to plants whose fragrance is good in the evening. It is true that the majority of flowers give off most scent in good growing weather during the early part of a warm day; during the heat of midday and the early afternoon in summer the scent lessens, to increase again later. Some plants are particularly potent in the evening and for the busy person, whose days are full, the following short list calls attention to some of the principal plants which excel at that time: *Daphne laureola*; *Gladiolus tristis* and near relatives; *Matthiola bicornis* (Night-scented Stock); petunias, bedding strains; *Dianthus* species (pink); *Saponaria officinalis*; *Hesperis matronalis*; *Oenothera biennis*, *O. marginata* and *O. caespitosa*; *Nicotiana alata* and others; *Hemerocallis*, such as *H. citrina*, together with some of its progeny with light yellow flowers which do not open until the evening; phloxes, tall border varieties (*P. paniculata* and *P. × hortorum*); *Magnolia grandiflora* and varieties, *M. × thompsoniana* and others; *Yucca filamentosa*, *flaccida* and others; *Lonicera* species, climbing honeysuckles.

THE GREENHOUSE

In the still, warm, damp atmosphere of a glass-covered structure scents are collected together and at times are overpowering to the senses; but to stand outside a greenhouse and let the concentrated fragrance pour past one's nose from the open vents is a wonderful experience. Fragrance is thereby unusually concentrated. A succession of rich lily-like fragrance can be obtained in spring from the scented rhododendrons mentioned in an earlier paragraph. Oranges (*Citrus* species), *Gardenia jasminoides, Stephanotis floribunda, Jasminum polyanthum, Gladiolus tristis* and related species and hybrids, *Cyclamen persicum* (the species and some new hybrids), *Datura cornigera* and *D. sauveolens, Buddleia asiatica* and *madagascariensis, Acokanthera (Toxicophlaea) spectabilis* and *A. venerata*, and some *Hibiscus* species are all deliciously fragrant and many others will come to mind. Some of these can be grown outside in warm districts together with *Heliotropium* species, *Cytisus* × *spachianus* (*C. racemosus* or *Genista fragrans* of gardens), *Hedychium gardnerianum* and others, and various acacias such as *Acacia dealbata, A. riceana* and *A. retinoides*. In the evening *Cestrum parqui*, the Tuberose (*Polianthes tuberosa*) and the Night-flowering cactus (*Selenicereus grandiflorus*) delight the nose.

Both in and out of the greenhouse *Humea elegans* provides one of the richest of aromas, like incense, floating in the air. The hand or nose that touches bloom or leaf is fragrant for hours, as it is from Moss Roses of midsummer. Many hothouse orchids are markedly scented and last in flower for a long time. Among them are species of *Epidendrum, Brassia, Vanilla, Gongora* and *Cattleya*.

OUTSIDE THE GARDEN

Most gardens today are too restricted to take the larger trees and I should perhaps have left the limes for inclusion in this paragraph accordingly, but they are frequently planted for their scent even in comparatively small gardens. One of the tallest growing conifers, the Douglas Fir (*Pseudotsuga taxifolia*), gives off a rich scent of ripe strawberries when the weather is warm. The full resinous odour from pines is similarly free in the air. While I have included *Chamaecyparis lawsoniana* among the outcasts for its sour turpentine smell, I should class *Thuja plicata* (*T. lobbii*) in the pleasant category as it has an odour of oranges, and I should certainly select this for a dense fragrant hedge.

The Balsam Poplars, of which *Populus trichocarpa* and *P. tacamahacca* are two of the most fragrant, are very pleasant in the spring air; a touch of the resinous buds on the nose will ensure the continuity of the fragrance after we get out of range! A small wood of birches (*Betula pendula*) and larches (*Larix decidua*) are valuable for the sweet scent of their unfolding leaves for about a fortnight in the spring.

Lastly we may remember how lucky they are who live surrounded by arable land, where fields of beans will alternate with mustard and clovers; or surrounded by commons where the gorse will shed its coconut fragrance in the air for many weeks; or living among the orchards of Worcestershire, Cambridgshire or Kent where plum will be succeeded by cherry and later by the sweetness of apple blossom, perhaps thick with bluebells beneath, themselves creating a delicate sweetness, all-pervading the air. Some of us, very few, live where thousands of roses or drifts of bulbs or seed-strains of annuals grow by the acre. Then it may be said that one's garden flows over the landscape while the wafts of scented air flow in towards us.

There is no doubt that the education of the nose is a rewarding occupation although at times one may regret it!

15

Garden idylls

Hyacinth, primrose fade from sight,
   Through dusk to darkness anthems thrill,
My garden rings with new delight
When blackbirds sing into the night.

ERIC PARKER, Sussex Woods, 1936

One of the reasons why gardens are so enchanting is that in this country we are so much at the mercy of the weather. A brilliant sunny day is such a contrast to what we often have to endure that when it comes – followed by a glowing evening and a gentle warm twilight – our cup is full; even daily workers can enjoy the light, the scents and the gradual emergence of the palest colours gleaming from the dusky background. It is at this sort of hour that evening entertainments are often arranged. We move out of the house onto the paved terrace and combine the beauties of fragrance of the garden with suitable refreshment and happy companionship. I think this *is* the time for companionship whereas otherwise I prefer wandering round and savouring the delights of a garden alone or with but one companion – a companion who knows when to keep quiet – to drink deeply of the spread of beauty that can occur in the smallest plots. All is quiet, and if there are close neighbours all *should* be quiet, and certainly the effluvium from a barbecue or smoke from a bonfire should not mar anyone's enjoyment.

Those who have lived or stayed in Cambridge will know that magical moment when, at the annual madrigal concert on the river, the singing of Wilbye's immortal *Draw on Sweet Night* begins, and its cadences for long reach our straining ears as the lantern-lit barge floats slowly down the river, accompanied by the quacking of ducks. Or on the lake at Winkworth Arboretum (the National Trust) when on a perfect evening the singing was in a way echoed by interludes of trumpet music of the same period from distant woodland across the water. But such evenings do not always materialize, drenching rain may upset everything; as like as not however the next evening may revert to summer's best. This I remember happened at The Vyne, another Trust property, where one hundred years separates the building of the house and the addition of the portico. During this period in history all the great madrigals and the trumpet music that were performed were composed.

Today floodlighting of gardens brings a new sort of awareness of the beauty of tree stems and all other features; *fêtes champêtres* are held at many National Trust properties, making preludes for the firework display after dark. In the old days we can imagine the host proclaiming to his guests after dinner that coffee would be served in boats on the lake at Claremont; candles would be lit in the spar-decorated niches in the grotto, and perhaps strings of many-coloured fairy lights would line the shores. Fairy lights, to me, are the ultimate in showing the garden and its design at dusk and later. Floodlighting is a different matter, to be enjoyed in a different way.

In addition to artificial lighting music can also play a great part. We should not need great imagination in our gardens in the gloaming to think we were enjoying a concert across the lake at Kenwood, provided the canned music reached us from among the shrubs, distantly sounding. But maybe a flautist might be persuaded to play gentle airs close at hand, in memory of Pan. Music and gardening, to me, go hand in hand as the perfect complement to one another. We can hang up those tinkling wind chimes that sound when the gentle airs of evening arouse their music. Richer notes tumble from church steeples, mellowed by distance.

These are, however, but man's efforts, adding a new perspective to the enjoyment of a garden. It is the early summer that gives the best of all music which comes from the paean of repetitive notes of the missel thrush on the topmost bough or gable, or the melodies of the blackbird which are so rich that they might almost be those of the nightingale. But these get past their singing season as the summer advances; then do the wood pigeons lift our hearts with their languorous cooing, repetitively, far and near, through the long days. Even as autumn advances do we take pleasure in the robin's always original sequence of sweet, sad notes, and these birds, the gardener's friends, will sing throughout the winter. But no other bird can surpass the volume and ecstatic piping of the wren, in spite of its diminutive size and a weight that does not exceed a third of an ounce.

Perhaps we do not all want sound other then birdsong in our gardens. Peaceful quietness may be counted even more valuable after a long day's work. Then all the sound we have is that of the humming bees. There is however one further delight that can be added to the enjoyment of a garden, and that is butterflies. Nothing else gives that touch of surprise and high pleasure as when a butterfly settles upon our arm or leg and gently suns itself, flexing and reflexing its gorgeous wings. There seems to be a general belief that butterflies are not as common as they used to be. This is more than likely to be true in this district because with every year more space is taken up by tiles, tarmac or concrete. Even in our smallest gardens we can provide flowers that butterflies enjoy. However rare the insects may be during the early summer, when the buddleias open they will be found sipping the nectar. Butterflies seem to prefer dense heads of small flowers and in addition to buddleias may almost always be found on the flat heads of sedums in August and September; many daisy flowers – erigerons, asters, Golden Rod as well as heleniums, Sea Holly and many more Compositae attract them. They are all in flower when the longest day is past. From the earlier Catmint, Valerian (*Centranthus*), Honesty (*Lunaria*) and Sweet Rocket (*Hesperis*) they are seldom absent. Lavenders are likewise favourites, and *Caryopteris*.

It is however one thing to provide the nectar-bearing flowers and another thing to allow a large group of stinging nettles to grow, which will guarantee good meals for the caterpillars of Red Admiral, Peacock and Tortoiseshell butterflies. It was with surprise that I noted in an otherwise well-kept garden, open to the public, a nettle with several stems some four feet high, left in full view in a border. Afterwards I realized the reason. Occasionally a stinging nettle crops up that does not sting; these should be treasured!

For further reading about encouraging butterflies, see my book *Perennial Garden Plants*, where I paid due note to that pioneer in these matters, L.H. Newman and his *Create a Butterfly Garden*. I do not see how the cuckoo is to be attracted to this built-up part of Surrey again, but we can all do something about providing the necessities of life for butterflies. The majority have only a few days of life and it behoves us to make their stay as enjoyable as possible. But, with all their own great beauty of colour those more common glories mentioned above seem insensitive to colour scheming, for they often settle on blue-pink flowers!

16

For students of all ages

I hold that everything that is beautiful should be sought for and
studied in a garden.

FRANK GALSWORTHY

in *Flower Grouping* by M. Waterfield, 1907

If a hundred people were given identical plots for garden-making each plot
would develop differently from the next. As I stressed earlier in the book, in
addition to environment and soil, taste and fashion dictate what we do in our
gardens. And how very fortunate this is. A garden has been described as "the
greatest refreshment to the spirits of man" (Bacon) but this claim could not
be upheld if garden schemes were repetitive. They would become boring.
From this it might be thought that to make a "different" garden would be
easy, but it is not.

We are all beginners and students; we do not live long enough – nor, as a
rule do we start gardening when sufficiently young – to realize to the full the
majesty of the trees we plant; shrubs may give of their best in ten years and
herbaceous and bulbous plants take less time for their maturing. This is
however only half the battle. We have to spend many years in learning how
to use the plants to their own best advantage and to our own tastes.

There are many ways other than trial and error of achieving some
expertise, taste and ability, but it is not easy to say how we should start. Here
again the personal taste comes into the picture and whether we are making
our garden for our own pleasure, or becoming a student of horticulture in
order to earn a living making gardens for other people. I started by getting to
know plants; later came the study of garden art and its history. Whatever our
motive we cannot start too soon and there is no doubt that visiting gardens is
not only one of the best ways of learning, but also one of the most enjoyable.
Today it is comparatively easy with numerous gardens deliberately open to
the public and cars of some sort to be had comparatively cheaply. It was very
different fifty or more years ago when it was a day's trek by train and 'bus to
such meccas as Kew and Wisley. Cycling, though so enjoyable in those days
of car-scarcity, is today also a different matter when the roads are crowded

with so much traffic. But whatever the difficulties, do visit gardens – anywhere, and of any size. There is something to be learned in even the tiniest gardens. There are the plants themselves and how they are used in relationship to the garden design; with this for study you cannot but profit from observation.

To become conversant with plants, in order to be able to use them to the best advantage, we need to know their approximate height and spread, mode of growth, style of foliage and season of flower – to say nothing of the colours of all of their parts. Today in many of our excellent training places for budding horticulturists much stress is placed on the *science* and *craft* of horticulture, at the expense of art. Art cannot be taught if art is not latent in the student, but all can be *educated* to some extent if there is even a spark of awareness of beauty in them – as is usual. It is not enough to grasp the botanical side of plant identification if you wish to make a beautiful garden. Almost every plant can be recognized, with practice, *at a distance*; this single fact is at the bottom of all the plant knowledge that is needed to evaluate plants, so that each one can play its part in garden design and planting. There is no other matter of such importance in horticulture. It is something that each one of us can develop within ourselves; it is not something we can cull from a reference book or take from a shelf, ready made.

Keeping a diary – whether we are a professional student or only trying to get the best out of our own plot – is an admirable help. Notes of plants in gardens visited, and the date, are a tremendous help in later thoughts for planting.

I think the great movement of flower arranging has done a lot for us. The dedicated artists in the National Association of Flower Arrangement Societies have worked hard for years to educate us to the beauties that can be brought out of groupings of colour and shape, and much of their artistry can be translated into garden planting. While this may be the *detail* of the picture, the use of mass and void, in contrast in garden design, can be perceived on the canvases of great painters like Constable and Richard Wilson.

If we are too much aware of the ultimate size to which a tree or shrub may grow we are in danger of making a garden which might be described as petty. Often in visiting larger gardens we shall come across an overgrown shrub which is – though out of scale – the dominant note, and it is these odd specimens which give character to the planting, though obviously size cannot be completely neglected in the scheme of things. This is one of the reasons why I always try to think in an upward scale of size when selecting a shrub for a given spot. A very useful exercise is to note some magnificent planting for, say, contrast of shapes, in a large garden and to work out similar contrasts for

XXXVII Lavender-blue and white *Campanula latiloba, Nepeta sibirica, Hemerocallis* 'Thelma Perry', *Philadelphus* 'Monster', Martagon lilies, *Hydrangea arborescens* 'Grandiflora', Rose 'Madame Hardy' and glaucous foliage contribute to the colouring in the author's garden.

XXXVIII The herbaceous border at Killerton, Devon (National Trust), is given height by buddleias – to combat the winds from Dartmoor – and spring flowering, grey-foliaged plants along the rocky verge.

XXXIX In the Mairi Garden, Mount Stewart, the flower colours are kept to white, blue and purple throughout the season. To go with the quotation round the pool, the garden includes 'silver bells, cockle shells and Pretty Maids' (*Saxifraga granulata* 'Plena'), but not in a row!

XL A portion of the circular herbaceous garden at Lanhydrock, Cornwall (National Trust), where a general mixture of colours is to be found, supplemented by the tall grey *Aruncus donax, Canna iridiflora*, crocosmias, fuchsias and *Agapanthus campanulatus*.

XLI The blue and yellow border at Clare College, Cambridge.

XLII The red and orange borders at Clare College, Cambridge.

XLIII One quarter of the formal garden, surrounding a hedged, formal pool, at Crathes Castle, Kincardineshire (National Trust for Scotland). The coppery purple of *Cotinus coggygria* 'Royal Purple' unites the rich colours of thyme, *Papaver commutatum*, Gallica roses and other disparate plants in a highly successful way.

XLIV Grey and yellow variegated foliage with *Philadelphus* 'Beauclerk' lead the eye to the garden shelter at Eyford House, Gloucestershire.

XLV Purple, crimson, dark pink and coppery foliage warm the grey stone of Eyford House on the south front terrace, augmented by a hedge of purple 'Hidcote' lavender. Rose 'Marlena', *Fuchsia magellanica* 'Gracilis Versicolor', verbenas and *Sedum* 'Autumn Joy' contribute in September.

XLVI At Barrington Court, Somerset (National Trust), the brick wall and path are of the same soft colouring. Brown and yellow heleniums, *Macleaya* and *Hypericum* 'Hidcote' are lightened by pale yellow and white.

XLVII The Red Borders at Hidcote are justly famed for the colour provided from July onwards, by means of scarlet *Lobelia,* roses, cannas, dahlias, augmented by coppery purple foliage of shrubs and plants, purple delphiniums and recurring clumps of *Hemerocallis fulva* 'Kwanso Flore Pleno'.

XLVIII The long, August border at Wallington, Northumberland (National Trust), created on the site of the old carriage drive, is quite moist at the lower end. Here are grouped ligularias in orange and yellow, scarlet phloxes and roses. Strangely, Day Lilies did not thrive. The upper part of the border contains soft and rich tinted phloxes and fuchsias, *Hydrangea villosa* and *Cornus alba* 'Elegantissima'.

XLIX The orangery terrace at Powis Castle, Powys (National Trust), was made in the early 18th century. From strong colours at the east end, the western reaches are devoted to pinks and mauves, including phloxes, monardas and *Lavatera albia* 'Rosea'. The large old specimen of *Acer palmatum* 'Atropurpureum' in dark reddish brown makes a strong contrast in summer. The tall, distant tree in full flower is *Tilia cordata*.

gardens of ever lessening size. The same exercise could be done not only with shape but with colour, or with shape, colour and texture all combined. I referred to this earlier on page 42. It is a fascinating exercise for students of all ages to practise, no matter what their objectives may be, and will reveal many weaknesses. Take as an example the age-old contrast of rounded pine and slim cypress, present in so many old landscape pictures of Italy: how should we achieve the same dramatic contrast in a garden only fifty feet square? Or, seeing the rich green of laurel or Pontic *Rhododendron* under a weeping willow or upright poplar, how should we repeat this in our limited gardens of today? The exercises are endless in their variety and I often think some such poser as one of these might be a very useful extra for the horticultural examination papers of today.

Whether you look upon gardening as a hobby, a science or an art, the fundamental point returns again and again: that we garden because of the beauty of plants. This should never be forgotten.

> You never enjoy the world aright, till the sea itself floweth in your veins, till you are clothed with the heavens, and crowned with the stars . . . yet further, and you never enjoy the world aright, till you so love the beauty of enjoying it that you are covetous and earnest to persuade others to enjoy it.
>
> Thomas Traherne, d. 1674

Part IV

Lists of plants for special purposes

Lists of plants for special purposes

All the wars of the world, all the Caesars, have not the staying power of a lily in a cottage border. . . . The immortality of marbles and of miseries is a vain, small thing compared to the immortality of a flower that blooms and is dead by dusk.

REGINALD FARRER, *The Rainbow Bridge*, 1921

The following lists call attention to plants which play a principal part in whatever area they are used. Except where a great assembly of any of the groups is being made, one is enough to add a definite character to any planting. Plants of colour other than green, and plants whose shape is out of the usual, or leafage which is exceptional should not be overdone. "A green thought in a green shade" is the best background for almost all flowers, but surprising contrasts of floral and leaf colour will, when used with circumspection, lift a planting out of the ordinary.

Sizes:	The figures given are only approximate; climate and soil will obviously affect growth and make nonsense of any definite measurements. The height is followed by the width apart for planting.
Leaf shape:	One or two words to indicate the main character.

Deciduous or *Evergreen* are indicated by D or E.

Colour:	Usually only one word of flower colour is included, and also one for the colour of the fruits, if any.
Season:	I feel it useless to give a month for flowering because what may flower in March in Cornwall may not open until May in Northumberland or Scotland. Hence the terms Early Summer, Late Summer, etc.

122

Habit:	To save space I have had to limit myself to only a word or two in this column; the word chosen does, however, refer to the plant's salient character or mode of growth.
Special conditions:	W = needs shelter or a warm climate. M = needs moisture. S = needs shade.
Propagation:	C = propagated by cuttings. L = propagated by layering. D = propagated by division. S = propagated by seeds. G = propagated by grafting or budding. R = propagated by root-cuttings.

Group 1
Large-leafed plants

TREES AND SHRUBS

We speak in a very comparative way when describing or listing large-leafed plants. We use the term "broad-leafed" trees to distinguish them from conifers with tiny or very narrow leaves, but shrubs with large leaves are generally termed "with bold foliage". A Plane tree at perhaps a height of 100 feet will have leaves which are only in proportion to its size, while a lesser tree, such as a *Paulownia* or *Catalpa*, which scarcely exceeds a third of the height of the Plane, has leaves just as large and so creates a more striking effect. An even greater contrast in size is a shrub perhaps 6 feet high with leaves a foot across such as *Fatsia japonica*. But the ultimate occurs with herbaceous plants: a *Gunnera manicata*, achieving 8 feet in height, may have leaves as much as 6 feet across. And so it goes down the scale to plants like *Bergenia*, less than a foot high with leaves three quarters as wide; or *Galax* whose leaves are smaller for less height, and the creeping Bugle or *Ajuga*.

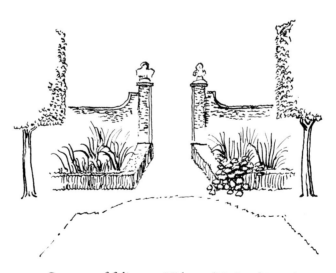

Contrast of foliage at Hidcote (National Trust)

I think that intending planters, anxious to create a dramatic effect, have more recourse to large leaves than to any other leaf-shape, or to the habit of plants. Therefore I have listed this category first and in spite of the dry statistics in the following lists I think a cursory glance through them may be helpful. In all sections I will take the largest first, picking out the rounded and lobed leaves before looking at the deeply divided or pinnate leaves.

LARGE-LEAFED TREES

So we start with our biggest trees, the London Plane (*Platanus × hispanica*) and the Oriental (*Platanus orientalis*). No tree in the southern half of this country can equal the majesty of the former, but for something rather less large and more elegant I should choose the Oriental species. Gardeners curse the lobed, long-lasting, fallen leaves in autumn! Still large trees are *Acer macrophyllum*, so brilliant in autumn colour, and *A. velutinum vanvolxemii*; both have very big, lobed leaves. We might next take some trees noted for their flowers; spring-flowering Paulownias and late summer-flowering Catalpas. They all require the sun of our warmer counties to encourage growth and flowers; the flowers of all are in upright spikes like those of a Horse Chestnut, the Paulownias resemble lilac-blue foxgloves and the Catalpas are mostly white with orange and other tints in the throat. Rather taller in maturity, and without colourful flowers are two Poplars: *Populus lasiocarpa*, and *P. wilsonii* with blue-green leaves. In *Idesia polycarpa* the female produces strings of scarlet berries in autumn. *Quercus dentata* and *Q. pontica* are two oaks with large, long leaves; they are of more shrubby growth. For sheltered gardens there is the immense-leafed *Magnolia macrophylla*, probably the largest-leafed deciduous woody plant that we can grow; *M. tripetala* is a close second, and *M. obovata* a good third in size of leaf, but a taller grower. All three have superb creamy flowers. *Magnolia grandiflora* is often grown on a wall to encourage flowers even in our sunnier counties, but will make a huge shrubby tree in the open, witness the great clump at Wisley. Other magnolias are fragrant but this is supreme. For sheltered corners in the south and west are *Magnolia delavayi* which excels in leaf but not in flower, and the Loquat, *Eriobotrya japonica*. With leaves of a greyish tint is the fine *Sorbus mitchellii* ('John Mitchell'); the parent tree at Westonbirt is over 60 feet.

LARGE-LEAFED SHRUBS

We come now to shrubs with large leaves, such as the rare *Rhamnus imeretina*, which thrives in the damp and shade; *Hydrangea sargentiana* and the (probably hybrid) plant known as *H. aspera macrophylla* in gardens, both with velvety or hairy leaves and magnificent flower heads in late summer: both will thrive in chalky or other soil in sheltered cool conditions, whereas for the similar sheltered, cool woodlands in the south and west will be found the rhododendrons of the Grande Series, such as *Rhododendron grande*, *R. sinograde*, and also *R. falconeri*. I should certainly give *Viburnum rhytidophyllum* some shelter from wind; otherwise it is tough and hardy, with fine corrugated foliage, likewise two lesser species with, in proportion, large leaves, *V. cinnamomifolium* and the lowly *V. davidii*. Both have blue berries on female plants if both sexes are planted.

LOBED OR PINNATE LEAVES

The Horse Chestnut (*Aesculus hippocastanum*) is the yardstick before which all others are decidedly smaller in growth, even the June-flowering pink *A. indica*, an excellent tree away from frost pockets, and the extra large-leafed *A. turbinata*. Some large trees with large pinnate leaves are *Juglans cinerea*, *Ailanthus altissima* – which is prone to produce suckers freely – and several species of Ash, *Fraxinus*. One would scarcely plant the Common Ash in gardens, handsome though an old tree may be, but from *F. latifolia* (*F. oregona*), *F. pennsylvanica*, coming down the scale to the attractively flowering *F. ornus* and *F. spaethiana* there is a range of good trees. Choicer are *Gymocladus dioicus* and *Meliosma veitchiorum* with notably divided leaves. For wet conditions one could select nothing better than *Pterocarya* species. These sucker freely, making a dense thicket. *Aralia elata*, *A. chinensis* and *A. spinosa*, all with prickly suckering stems and handsome doubly pinnate leaves, have frothy cream flowers and nearly black berries. They are elegant and sparse in growth, but the pinnate sorbarias make huge suckering mounds, typified by *Sorbaria arborea*. In July we have the additional beauty of large sprays of tiny creamy flowers. The most popular of all the large pinnate-leafed plants is undoubtedly *Rhus typhina*, the Stag-horn Sumach. Even more beautiful is *R. glabra*, a very close relative. Both have 'Laciniata' variants with lacy leaves of great beauty; they are all prone to suckering. Those who garden in Cornwall and in sheltered spots in like climates can plant *Gevuina avellana* whose dark green, glittering doubly pinnate leaves are remarkable. Also needing some shelter is *Fatsia japonica*, another very remarkable evergreen. *Melianthus major* brings us down to lesser shrubs; it is by no means hardy but the beauty of its grey-green, pinnate leaves makes up for its unpleasant smell when bruised. But I have left out the hardy palm *Trachycarpus fortunei* whose gaunt stems and great fan-like leaves may be seen in gardens in the south. Two suckering shrubs with fine large palmate leaves are the white-flowered *Rubus parviflorus* (*R. nutkanus*) and the pink-flowered *R. odoratus*, while the fruiting fig, *Ficus carica*, which is usually grown on a wall to hasten the ripening of its fruits, will make a characterful large shrub on its own, as may be seen in St James's Park, London. Of the many varieties 'Brown Turkey' is perhaps the most handsome in leaf. Two bamboos have extra large leaves but highly invasive roots: *Sasa palmata* in plain green, while *S. tessellata* is green edged with creamy fawn. There is one variety of the Common Laurel, *Prunus laurocerasus*, which qualifies for inclusion, that is *P.l.* 'Magnoliifolia' which reaches its greatest size in thin woodland. I will finish with a large-leafed elder *Sambucus canadensis* 'Maxima' and the well-known mahonias. *Mahonia × media* 'Charity' and its close relatives will reach a gaunt 10 feet or so, but respond well to reduction, and flower before Christmas; to follow them is *M. japonica*, an ornament wherever it is grown.

CLIMBERS

There are several good large rounded leaves among climbers, the most noted being *Vitis coignetiae*, whose leaves turn to such brilliant colour in autumn; *V. davidii* is somewhat smaller, while *V. amurensis* is deeply lobed, which takes us a step nearer to *Ampelopsis megalophylla* with bipinnate leaves. This is surprisingly rare; it is of extreme beauty and quite hardy.

PERENNIALS

Turning now to herbaceous perennials we have first the giant gunneras, *Gunnera manicata* with leaves sometimes exceeding 6 feet in diameter, and *G. chilensis (G. scabra)* only slightly smaller. They both demand really moist soil. It is somewhat of a step down to the next largest, the ornamental rhubarbs. Their only disadvantage is that they lose their beauty in late summer, being early risers. The medicinal species *Rheum officinale* has tall cream spikes of flowers, while *R. palmatum*, whose jagged leaves may be richly tinted especially beneath, has flower spikes of white or pink, or crimson in 'Atrosanguineum'. They all need rich moist soil. Rodgersias may be completely rounded as in *R. tabularis*, or deeply lobed in *R. aesculifolia*, *R. podophylla* and others. They all have attractive spires of creamy flowers, while rather smaller in leaf is *R. pinnata*, whose 'Superba' form is a brilliant pink in flower. Of a similar size, with the rounded leaves of *R. tabularis*, is *Peltiphyllum peltatum* whose heads of pink flowers appear before the leaves. Both this and the rodgersias need rich moist soil, which is also appreciated by the several species of *Ligularia*, while both species of *Lysichitum* require a wet boggy site. Their leaves are very large and long.

Herbaceous plants are rich in a variety of leaves and nothing could make a more striking contrast to any of the above than the dry-soil plants *Cynara scolymus*, the Globe Artichoke, and *C. cardunculus*, the Cardoon. Silvery grey, the leaves are pinnate and it is not until their giant stems of violet-blue thistle flowers appear that one realizes how difficult they are to place. The Giant Parsnip, as it is sometimes called (*Heracleum mantegazzianum*), is only for moist semi-wild conditions and will reach 10 feet in height; the leaves are green and deeply divided. It seeds itself alarmingly. The leaves of various species of *Acanthus* are of polished dark green tint and they have a stoloniferous habit. Not so the giant spiraea, *Aruncus dioicus*, whose elegant bipinnate leaves and creamy flower plumes will be produced in moist or fairly dry soils. *Aralia cachemirica* is of similar size and requirements. The giant lily, *Cardiocrinum giganteum*, is perhaps not fully qualified for inclusion; though its leaves are very large and handsome, the bulbs after flowering split into small ones and thus it is two or three years before the majesty is again repeated; they need deep, rich soil. The very tall *Filipendula palmata* and the shorter *F. purpurea* have fine heads of flowers and handsome vine-like leaves; they need moist conditions, likewise *Cimicifuga cordifolia*. For spring and early summer effects the various species of *Veratrum* are valuable, but to remain long in beauty they need shelter from winds and sun. There are several somewhat tuberous rooted plants for inclusion, the near-hardy *Sauromatum venosum (S. guttatum)* with deeply divided leaves; *Arisaema candidissimum; Canna iridiflora* for warm gardens, and the nearly hardy Arum, *Zantedeschia aethopica* 'Crowborough', podophyllums, peonies in general, and hellebores.

But I have omitted a few taller plants: the elegant macleayas, spreading *M. microcarpa* (the best is 'Coral Plume') and the less rampageous *M. cordata;* another spreader *Buphthalmum speciosum*, with elegant orange-yellow daisy flowers; the perennial *Verbascum vernale* with large dark green basal leaves and tall spikes of yellow flowers; the giant Seakale-relative, *Crambe cordifolia* with leaves large enough for inclusion in the first paragraph and clouds of tiny white flowers in early summer, and those infamous spreaders the huge-leafed *Petasites japonicus* and the Winter Heliotrope *P. fragrans*.

We are now down to hosta-sized plants. There are the species, varieties of forms of *Hosta* themselves, all best in shade or part shade except *H. plantaginea; Trachystemon orientale* with similar but hairy leaves, for sun or shade, dry soil or moist, somewhat a spreader; the valuable evergreen bergenias of which the largest-leafed are 'Ballawley' and *B. cordifolia* 'Purpurea'; the hairy *B. ciliata* and its variety are not evergreen but very handsome. *Brunnera macrophylla, Phlomis russeliana*, the Japanese Anemones, *Geranium psilostemon, Kirengeshoma* for moist shade, the Lungworts for shade (the largest green-leafed species is *Pulmonaria mollis*) and *Alchemilla mollis* bring us down to comparatively small plants. *Astilbe* species and hybrids are moisture lovers with plentiful bipinnate leaves and are dense clump-formers apart from the tall, wandering *A. rivularis*.

A gardener's dodge for producing gigantic foliage is by planting a *Paulownia* or a *Catalpa* and cutting it to the ground every winter, and feeding it well. Erect, thick shoots arise and will achieve above 6 feet by late summer every year when the plants are fully established. *Ailanthus* will do the same but cutting this down will increase its propensity for producing suckers, which is an undesirable trait.

TREES	Country of origin	Height/ Width	Leaf shape
ACER　Maple			
macrophyllum	Western N. America	60–80 ft	Palmate
AESCULUS			
hippocastanum　Horse Chestnut	S.E.Europe	60–100 ft	Palmate, divided
indica　Indian Horse Chestnut	N.W.Himalaya	50–80 ft	,,
turbinata　Japanese Horse Chestnut	Japan	,,	,,
AILANTHUS			
altissima　Tree of Heaven	N.China	60–80 ft	Pinnate
ARALIA			
chinensis　Chinese Angelica Tree	N.E.Asia	10–25 ft	Bipinnate
elata　Japanese Angelica Tree	Japan	,,	,,
spinosa　Devil's Walking Stick	N.America	10–15 ft	,,
CATALPA			
bignonioides　Indian Bean Tree	E.USA	30–50 ft	Broad, rounded
×*erubescens*	Hybrid	50–60 ft	,,
fargesii	China	30–50 ft	,,
ovata	,,	20–30 ft	,,
speciosa	Central USA	40–70 ft	,,
ERIOBOTRYA			
japonica　Loquat	China, Japan	10–20 ft	Broad
FRAXINUS　Ash			
latifolia (F. oregona)	N.America	60–80 ft	Pinnate
ornus　Flowering Ash	S.Europe, Asia Minor	40–50 ft	,,

Deciduous or Evergreen	Colour of flower	Period of flower	Habit	Special conditions	Propagation
D	Yellow; fruits reddish	Spring	Rounded		S
D	White; fruits green	L.Spring	Widespread		S
D	,,	E.Summer	,,		S
D	Pink, fruits green	L.Spring	,,		S
D	Yellowish; fruits reddish on female trees	Summer	Open head		S Suckers
D	Cream; fruits black	L.Summer	Gaunt		S Suckers
D	,,	,,	,,		Suckers
D	,,	Summer	,,		Suckers Suckers
D	White; purple marks	L.Summer	Widespread		S
D	,,	,,	,,		C
D	Pink	Summer	Open head		S
D	White; yellow marks	E.Autumn	,,		S
D	White; purple marks	Summer	,,		S
E	White	Autumn	Erect shrubby	W	C
D	Inconspicuous; 'keys' green	Summer	Open		S
D	Green white	,,	Dense rounded		S

TREES (cont.)	Country of origin	Height/ Width	Leaf shape
FRAXINUS (cont.)			
spaethiana	Japan	30–40 ft	Pinnate
GEVUINA			
avellana	S.Chile	10–20 ft	Bipinnate
GYMNOCLADUS			
dioicus Kentucky Coffee Tree	E. & Central USA	30–50 ft	Bipinnate, superb
IDESIA			
polycarpa	Japan, China	,,	Broad, rounded
JUGLANS Walnut			
cinerea Butternut	Eastern N.America	60–80 ft	Pinnate
LIRIODENDRON			
tulipifera Tulip Tree	N.America	80–110 ft	Broad, rounded
MAGNOLIA			
hypoleuca (M. obovata)	Japan	30–80 ft	Broad, long
macrophylla (needs shelter)	S.E.USA	10–25 ft	Extra broad, and long
tripetala Umbrella Tree	E.USA	20–30 ft	Broad, long
MELIOSMA			
veitchiorum	W.China	,,	Pinnate, very large
PAULOWNIA (shelter)			
fargesii (preferable to P. tomentosa)	,,	30–50 ft	Broad, rounded
tomentosa (P. imperialis)	China	25–30 ft	Broad
PLATANUS Plane			
× *hispanica (P. acerifolia)* London Plane	Hybrid	90–120 ft	Palmate
orientalis Oriental Plane	S.E.Europe	80–100 ft	,,
POPULUS Poplar			
lasiocarpa	Central China	30–50 ft	Broad, rounded
wilsonii	Central & W.China	,,	Broad, blue-green, rounded

Deciduous or Evergreen	Colour of flower	Period of flower	Habit	Special conditions	Propagation
D	White; 'keys' green	Summer	Open		S
E	White	L.Summer	Bushy	W	SC
D	White; females best	Summer	Open, slow	W	S
D	Yellowish; berries red	,,	Open		S
D	Large green nuts	,,	,,		S
D	Yellowish	,,	,,		S
D	Cream	E.Summer	,,		S
D	,,	,,	Open		S
D	,,	,,	Open, shrubby		S
D	Cream; fruits violet	L.Spring	Gaunt, slow	W	S
D	Lilac blue	Spring	Open		S
D	,,	,,	,,		S
D	Greenish brown	,,	,,		C
D	,,	,,	,,		CS
D	Green catkins; white fluffy seeds	,,	,,		CGS
D	,,	,,	,,		CGS

TREES (cont.)	Country of origin	Height/ Width	Leaf shape
PTEROCARYA			
fraxinifolia	Caucasus to N.Persia	80–100 ft	Pinnate
QUERCUS Oak			
dentata Daimyo Oak (needs shelter)	Far East	20–40 ft	Large, broadly lobed
frainetto (*Q. conferta*) Hungarian Oak	S.E.Europe	90–100 ft	,,
pontica Armenian Oak	Armenia, Caucasus	15–20 ft	,,
SORBUS Whitebeam			
mitchellii ('John Mitchell')		50–70 ft	Broad, rounded
TRACHYCARPUS			
fortunei Chusan Palm	Central China	10–20 ft	Broad, deeply divided

SHRUBS

FATSIA			
japonica	Japan	8 ft × 8 ft	Broad, deeply lobed
HYDRANGEA			
aspera macrophylla (of gardens)	Hybrid?	9 ft × 9 ft	Broad, velvety
quercifolia	S.E.USA	4 ft × 4 ft	Broad, lobed
sargentiana	China	8 ft × 6 ft	Broad, velvety
MAGNOLIA			
delavayi	China	25 ft × 15 ft +	Large, broad
grandiflora	S.E.USA	40 ft × 20 ft	,,

— 'Exmouth' and 'Goliath' are recommended varieties

MAHONIA			
japonica	China	7 ft × 7 ft	Pinnate, prickly
× *media*	Hybrid	15 ft × 8 ft	,,

'Charity', 'Lionel Fortescue' and other varieties

Deciduous or Evergreen	Colour of flower	Period of flower	Habit	Special conditions	Propagation
D	Green catkins; fruits green	Spring	Open		S Suckers
D	Catkins, acorns	,,	Open, shrubby		S
D	,,	,,	Wide spreading		S
D	,,	Spring	Open, bushy		S
D	White; fruits red	E.Summer	Compact		G
E	Cream	Summer	Gaunt, slow	W	S
E	Cream	Autumn	Open	W	S
D	Lilac/white	L.Summer	Bushy		C Suckers
D	White	Summer	Lax	W	CLS
D	Lilac/white	L.Summer	Gaunt	W	CS Suckers
E	Cream	Summer	Bushy	W	CL
E	,,	L.Summer/ Autumn	,,	W	CL
E	Yellow; fruits bluish	Winter	Lax		C
E	Yellow	L.Autumn	Gaunt		C

SHRUBS (cont.)	Country of origin	Height/ Width	Leaf shape
MELIANTHUS			
major	S.Africa	7 ft × 7 ft	Pinnate, glaucous
PHLOMIS			
fruticosa	Mediterranean Region	4 ft × 4 ft	Broad
RHAMNUS			
imeretina	W.Caucasus	8 ft × 10 ft	Large, broad
RHODODENDRON			
falconeri & relatives	Himalaya etc	20 ft × 30 ft	,,
grande & relatives	,,	20 ft × 15 ft	,,
RHUS			
glabra Smooth Sumach	Eastern N.America	10 ft × 10 ft	Pinnate
typhina Stag Horn Sumach	,,	,,	,,

—Both above species have 'Laciniata' varieties, with extra elegant leaves

RUBUS			
odoratus	Eastern N.America	6 ft × 3 ft	Palmate
parviflorus (R. nutkanus)	Western N.America	5 ft × 3 ft	,,
SAMBUCUS Elder			
canadensis 'Maxima' American Elderberry	Eastern N.America	8 ft × 8 ft	Pinnate
SORBARIA			
arborea and relatives	China	12 ft × 15 ft	,,
VIBURNUM			
cinnamomifolium	,,	6 ft × 5 ft	Broad, glossy
davidii	W.China	3 ft × 6 ft	,,
rhytidophyllum	China	10 ft × 10 ft	Broad, corrugated
— 'Roseum' (pink flowers)			

Deciduous or Evergreen	Colour of flower	Period of flower	Habit	Special conditions	Propagation
D	Reddish; fruits reddish	L.Summer	Lax	W.	CS
E	Yellow	E.Summer	Dense	W	CS
D	Inconspicuous		Spreading		CLS
E	Yellowish	Spring	Bushy	W	LS
E	,,	,,	,,	W	LS
D	Yellowish; fruits red	Summer	Open		S Suckers
D	,,	,,	,,		S Suckers
D	Pink; fruits red	Summer/ Autumn	Erect		D Suckers
D	White; fruits red	E.Summer	,,		D Suckers
D	White; fruits maroon	L.Summer	Open		C
D	White; fruits green	,,	Arching		C Suckers
E	White; fruits bluish	Summer	Dense	W	CLS
E	,,	Spring	,,		CLS
E	White: fruits red/black	,,	,,		CLS

CLIMBERS	Country of origin	Height/ Width	Leaf shape
ACTINIDIA *chinensis*	China	30 ft × 20 ft	Rounded
AMPELOPSIS *megalophylla*	W.China	,,	Bipinnate
ARISTOLOCHIA *macrophylla (A. sipho)* Dutchman's Pipe	E.USA	20 ft × 15 ft	Rounded
HEDERA Ivy *colchica* 'Dentata'	Caucasus etc	20 ft × 20 ft	,,
RUBUS *irenaeus*	Central & W.China	8 ft × 8 ft	Rounded, felted beneath
VITIS Vine *amurensis*	Manchuria etc	30 ft × 20 ft	Rounded
coignetiae	Far East	,,	,,
davidii (V. armata)	China	,,	,,

BAMBOOS

SASA *palmata (Bambusa palmata)*	Japan	5 ft spreading	Long, broad
tessellata *(Arundinaria ragamowskii)*	China	4 ft spreading	,,

Deciduous or Evergreen	Colour of flower	Period of flower	Habit	Special conditions	Propagation
D	White	E. Summer	Twiner		CS
D	Inconspicuous; fruits black		Tendrils		CS
D	Greenish brown	,,	Twining		CS
E.	Yellowish, inconspicuous	Autumn	Self-clinging		CL
E	Small, cream	Summer	Sprawling		CLS
D	Yellowish, inconspicuous		Tendrils		CLS
D	,,		,,		CLS
D	,,		,,		CLS
E	—	—	Rampageous	M	D
E	—	—	,,	M	D

PERENNIALS	Country of origin	Height/Width	Leaf shape
ACANTHUS			
mollis latifolius	Portugal	5 ft × 3 ft	Dark shining green, broadly lobed, arching
spinosus	S.Europe	,,	Dark shining green, deeply cut, arching
ALCHEMILLA Lady's Mantle			
mollis	Asia Minor	2 ft × 2 ft	Rounded, velvety
ANEMONE			
× *hybrida* Japanese Anemones	Hybrids	4 ft × 2 ft	Deeply divided
tomentosa (*A. vitifolia* of Tibet gardens)		,,	,,
ARALIA			
cachemerica (*A. macrophylla*)	Kashmir	6 ft × 6 ft	,,
ARISAEMA			
candidissimum	W.China	1 ft × 18 ins	Three-lobed
ARUNCUS			
dioicus (*Spiraea aruncus*)	N.Hemisphere	7 ft × 4 ft	Bipinnate
ASTILBE			
rivularis	Nepal, W.China	6 ft × 4 ft	,,
BERGENIA (*Megasea*)			
various	Asia & Hybrids	1–2 ft × 1–2 ft	Rounded
BRUNNERA			
macrophylla	W.Caucasus	2 ft × 2 ft	,,
BUPHTHALMUM			
speciosum	S.E.Europe	5 ft × 3 ft	,,
CANNA			
iridiflora	Peru	,,	Broad
CARDIOCRINUM Lily			
giganteum	W.China	8 ft × 4 ft	,,

Deciduous or Evergreen	Colour of flower	Period of flower	Habit	Special conditions	Propagation
D	Spikes of mauve	L.Summer	Spreader		D
D	,,	,,	,,		D
D	Clouds of greeny yellow stars	E.Summer	Clump		DS
D	White or pink	L.Summer/ Autumn	Spreaders		DR
D	Pink	L.Summer	Spreader		DR
D	Green	,,	Clump		DS
D	Pink and white	Summer	Tuber		DS
D	Cream	E.Summer	Clump		DS
D	Greenish	L.Summer	Spreader		D
E	Pink	Spring	Clump		D
D	Blue	,,	Clump, spreader		D
D	Yellow	Summer	Spreader		D
D	Dark pink	L.Summer	Clump	W	D
D	White	Summer	Bulb		DS

PERENNIALS (cont.)	Country of origin	Height/ Width	Leaf shape
CEPHALARIA *gigantea (C. tatarica)*	Siberia	6 ft × 4 ft	Bipinnate
CIMICIFUGA *cordifolia*	N.America	5 ft × 2 ft	Deeply divided
CLEMATIS *heracliifolia*	China	3 ft × 4 ft	Pinnate, broad
CRAMBE *cordifolia*	Caucasus	6 ft × 4 ft	Deeply lobed
DRACUNCULUS *vulgaris*	Mediterranean Region	3 ft × 18 ins	Divided
FILIPENDULA *palmata (Spiraea camtschatica) (Spiraea gigantea of gardens)*	Kamtchatka	4 ft × 2 ft	Broad, lobed
purpurea (Spiraea palmata)	Japan	,,	,,
rubra Queen of the Prairies	E.USA	7 ft × 3 ft	,,
GERANIUM *psilostemon (G. armentum)*	Armenia	3 ft × 4 ft	Divided
GUNNERA (shelter) *chilensis (G. scabra)*	Chile	5 ft × 7 ft	Rounded, lobed
manicata	S.Brazil	6 ft × 8 ft	,,
HELLEBORUS *various*	Europe, Asia Minor	1–2 ft × 1–2 ft	Deeply lobed
HERACLEUM *mantegazzianum*	Caucasus	10 ft × 8 ft	,,
HOSTA *various*	Japan, China	1½–2 ft × 1½–2 ft	Broad
KIRENGESHOMA *palmata*	Japan	4 ft × 3 ft	,,
LIGULARIA (Senecio) *dentata S. clivorum*	China	4 ft × 2 ft	Rounded
veitchiana and others	,,	5 ft × 3 ft	,,

Deciduous or Evergreen	Colour of flower	Period of flower	Habit	Special conditions	Propagation
D	Pale yellow	E.Summer	Clump		DS
D	Cream	L.Summer	,,		DS
D	Blue	,,	,,		DS
D	White	E.Summer	,,		DRS
D	Maroon, stinking	,,	Clump		DS
D	Pink	Summer	,,	M	D
D	Cerise	,,	,,	M	D
D	White/pink	,,	,,	M	D
D	Magenta	E.Summer	,,		D
D	Greenish	,,	,,	M	D
D	,,	,,	,,	M	D
E	Various	Winter/ Spring	,,	S	DS
D	White	Summer	,,	M	S
D	Lilac/white	L.Summer	,,	S	D
D	Yellow	Autumn	,,	SM	CDS
D	Orange	L.Summer	,,	M	DS
D	Yellow	,,	,,	M	DS

PERENNIALS (cont.)	Country of origin	Height/ Width	Leaf shape
LYSICHITUM			
americanum	Western N.America	4 ft × 4 ft	Broad
camtchatcense	N.E.Asia	3 ft × 4 ft	,,
MACLEAYA			
cordata	China, Japan	7 ft × 2 ft	Rounded, lobed
microcarpa (*Bocconia cordata* of gardens)	China	7 ft × 3 ft	,,
PAEONIA			
various	Europe, Asia	2–4 ft × 2–3 ft	Deeply lobed
PELTIPHYLLUM			
peltatum (*Saxifraga peltata*)	California	4 ft × 2 ft	Rounded
PHLOMIS			
russeliana (*P. samia* of gardens)	Syria	3 ft × 2 ft	Broad
PODOPHYLLUM			
peltatum and others	N.America	18 ins × 1 ft	Lobed
RHEUM			
officinale	Tibet	8 ft × 6 ft	Broad
palmatum	China	6 ft × 6 ft	Broad, divided
— 'Atrosanguineum'		,,	Broad, divided, red beneath
RODGERSIA			
aesculifolia	,,	4 ft × 3 ft	Deeply lobed
pinnata 'Superba'	,,	,,	,,
podophylla	Japan	,,	,,
tabularis (*Astilboides tabularis*)	China	5 ft × 3 ft	Rounded
SAUROMATUM			
venosum (*S. guttatum*)	Himalaya etc	2 ft × 2 ft	Deeply divided
SYMPLOCARPUS			
foetidus	N.E.Asia, N.E.America	18 ins × 18 ins	Broad

Deciduous or Evergreen	Colour of flower	Period of flower	Habit	Special conditions	Propagation
D	Yellow	Spring	Clump	M	S
D	White	,,	,,	M	S
D	White	L.Summer	,,		DRS
D	Fawn	,,	Spreader		DRS
D	Various	Spring/ E.Summer	Clump		DRS
D	Pink	E.Spring	Creeping rhizomes		D
E	Yellow	Summer	Clump		DS
D	White; fruits pink	,,	Clump, spreading		DS
D	White	E.Summer	Clump	M	DS
D	White/pink	,,	,,	M	DS
D	Crimson	,,	,,	M	D
D	Creamy	Summer	,,	M	DS
D	Pink	,,	,,	M	D
D	White	,,	,,	M	DS
D	,,	,,	,,	M	DS
D	Purplish	Spring	,,	W	D
D	Purplish, dwarf	E.Spring	,,	M	D

PERENNIALS (cont.)	Country of origin	Height/ Width	Leaf shape
TRACHYSTEMON			
orientale	Asia Minor, Caucasus etc	18 ins × 2 ft	Broad, hairy
VERATRUM			
album	Europe, Siberia	6 ft × 2 ft	Broad, pleated
nigrum	,,	,,	,,
viride	N.America	4 ft × 2 ft	,,
VERBASCUM			
vernale, of gardens		6 ft × 3 ft	Broad
ZANTEDESCHIA			
aethiopica	S.Africa	4 ft × 2 ft	,,
'Crowborough' and 'White Sail'			

Deciduous or Evergreen	Colour of flower	Period of flower	Habit	Special conditions	Propagation
D	Blue	E.Spring	Spreader		D
D	White	L.Summer	Clump	M	DS
D	Maroon	,,	,,	MS	DS
D	Green	,,	,,	MS	DS
D	Yellow	Summer	,,		DR
D	White	,,	,,		D

Group 2

Sword-like leaves

SHRUBS

This is a rather mixed bag. To start with, it is unbalanced because there are really no hardy trees with the required foliage, and I have left the grasses themselves to their own chapter. But a garden is lost without some grassy, strap-shaped or sword-like leaves; they add a leavening and variety of line provided by nothing else. It is sad that practically all of the splendid newer hybrids of Bearded Irises are so poor in foliage after July; to hide their dying leaves I like to grow them behind plants which will shield them from later view.

In the south-west and along the coastal towns in our warmer counties the so-called Cabbage Palm (*Cordyline*) may be seen making quite large branching trees. Their stems are crowned with drooping strap-shaped evergreen leaves. The purplish forms are even less hardy. Yuccas are classed as shrubs, especially *Yucca gloriosa* and *Y. recurvifolia* which in part compensate for the lack of hardiness in cordylines; they will make large trunks which in time flop over with their own weight. Needing full sun, all of them, they will thrive in dry positions but need good soil to encourage their flowering. And what a flowering it is! Creamy bells, lemon scented in the evening (they are pollinated by moths in Mexico), borne on tall spikes, occasionally on the two big ones mentioned above, but freely in *Y. filamentosa* and *Y. flaccida* whose rosettes only take about three years to produce flowers. Thus a selection of rosettes of different ages is helpful. 'Ivory' has the same admirable character and the great red-budded 'Vittorio Emmanuele' is not far behind. Other evergreens, much smaller, are found in *Libertia*, *Iris foetidissima* and the *Liriope*.

Phormium tenax is undoubtedly the most striking of all the sword leaves. It gets killed to the ground in Surrey in severe winters, also its beautiful variegated forms. Even small plants give an exotic and unique effect in our gardens, while to see great clumps in Cornwall is to realize what they must be like in their native country, New Zealand.

148

PERENNIALS

The giant *Eryngium decaisneana* is not reliably hardy in Surrey, but is an astonishing sight when in flower in early autumn and its prickly narrow leaves are the longest of the species listed; *E. agavifolium* and *E. eburneum* are progressively smaller, but they are all evergreen.

No deciduous plant has such fine sword-like foliage as *Curtonus paniculatus*; next would come *Iris orientalis* and its hybrids, and *I. sibirica*, *I. spuria*, *I. graminea* in a descending scale. The flowers of the first three irises are held well aloft, while those of *I. graminea* are hidden low among the foliage; their rich fragrance is their redeeming feature, to say nothing of their exquisitely varied colours, all in the one flower. Day Lilies (*Hemerocallis*) need no introduction from the flower point of view, but I would stress the garden value of the lighter colours as opposed to the dusky browns, and the clear yellows usually have the best scent. It is unfortunate that so many of the grandiflora hybrids of today have coarse foliage and do not always hold their flowers well above the clump of valuable leaves which remain in beauty until the autumn. Some, descended in part from *H. fulva*, delight us with bright pale green in spring.

For grasses see Group 3.

SHRUBS	Country of origin	Height/ Width	Brief description
CORDYLINE			
australis	New Zealand	12 ft Single stem at first	Long, drooping, green, narrow
— 'Atropurpurea'		,,	Long, drooping, purplish narrow
PHORMIUM			
cookianum	,,	4 ft × 2 ft	Sword-like from ground level
(P. colensoi)			
tenax	,,	7 ft × 4 ft	,,
(for hybrids with variously coloured leaves, see Groups 5 and 9)			
YUCCA			
filamentosa	S.E.USA	5 ft × 2 ft	Narrow, greyish in rosettes, 2 ft
flaccida	,,	,,	Narrow, lax, greyish in rosettes, 2 ft
gloriosa	,,	7 ft × 4 ft	Narrow, dark green in rosettes, 3–5 ft
'Ivory'	Hybrid	4 ft × 2 ft	Narrow, greyish in rosettes, 2 ft
recurvifolia	S.E.USA	7 ft × 4 ft	Narrow, lax, dark green, in rosettes, 3–5 ft
'Vittorio Emmanuele'	Hybrid	6 ft × 3 ft	Narrow, dark green in rosettes, 3 ft

PERENNIALS

	Country of origin	Height/ Width	Brief description
ASTELIA			
nervosa	New Zealand	18 ins × 3 ft	Grey-green
CROCOSMIA S.Africa			
× *crocosmiiflora*	Hybrid	2½ ft × 1 ft	Narrow, fresh green, 2 ft
many sizes and colour forms			

Deciduous or Evergreen	Colour of flower	Period of flower	Habit	Special conditions	Propagation
E	White, tiny, in sprays; fragrant	E.Summer	Erect	W	CS
E	,,	,,	,,	W	C
E	Yellowish	L.Summer	,,		DS
E	Reddish brackets on very tall stems	,,	,,	W	DS
E	Cream	,,	,,		DR
E	,,	,,	,,		DR
E	,,	Autumn	,,		DR
E	,,	Summer	,,		DR
E	,,	L.Summer	,,		DR
E	,,	,,	,,		DR
E	Inconspicuous		Arching	W	DS
D	Yellow and orange	L.Summer	Erect		D

PERENNIALS (cont.)	Country of origin	Height/ Width	Brief description
CROCOSMIA (cont.)			
pottsii	S.Africa	3 ft × 1 ft	Narrow, fresh green, 2 ft
— × CURTONUS			
'Lucifer'	Hybrid	5 ft × 2 ft	,, 4 ft
CURTONUS			
paniculatus	S.Africa	4 ft × 2 ft	,, 4 ft
DIERAMA			
pulcherrimum	,,	5 ft × 2 ft	Narrow, dark green, 2 ft
ERYNGIUM			
agavifolium	Argentina	6 ft × 2 ft	Narrow, toothed 2 ft
decaisneanum (E. pandanifolium)	,,	9 ft × 3 ft	,, 4 ft
eburneum	,,	5 ft × 3 ft	Narrow, toothed 2 ft
HEMEROCALLIS			
many	Europe, Asia	1 ft–4 ft	Narrow, arching
IRIS, most species qualify for this Group			
foetidissima Gladwyn or Stinking Iris	Europe	2 ft × 1 ft	Narrow, arching dark shining green
— 'Citrina' has better flowers			
— 'Variegata', see Group 7			
graminea	,,	18 ins × 9 ins	Very narrow, dark green
orientalis (I. ochroleuca of gardens)	Asia Minor	4 ft × 15 ins	Narrow
pallida dalmatica	Europe	3 ft × 1 ft	Sword-like
spuria	S.E.Europe etc	3 ft × 15 ins	Narrow

Deciduous or Evergreen	Colour of flower	Period of flower	Habit	Special conditions	Propagation
D	Red	L.Summer	Erect		D
D	Orange-red	,,	,,		D
D	,,	,,	,,		D
D	White, pink, purple etc., drooping sprays	Summer	Arching	W	DS
E	Greenish white in branching heads	L.Summer	Erect		DS
E	Chocolate-purple, tiny in large branching heads	Autumn	,,	W	DS
E	Greenish white in branching sprays	Summer	,,	W	DS
D	Yellow, orange, red, purplish	Mostly Summer	,,		D
E	Inconspicuous; fruits red	Spring	,,		DS
D	Purplish	E.Summer	,,		D
D	White	,,	,,		D
E	Lavender-blue	,,	,,		D
D	,,	,,	,,		D

PERENNIALS (cont.)	Country of origin	Height/ Width	Brief description
IRIS (cont.)			
sibirica	Europe, N.Asia	3 ft × 1 ft	Narrow, 2 ft
many garden forms and hybrids			
LIBERTIA			
formosa	Chile	3 ft × 2 ft	Narrow, dark green arching
LIRIOPE			
muscari	E.Asia	1 ft × 1 ft	Narrow, dark green
SISYRINCHIUM			
striatum	Chile	2 ft × 9 ins	Narrow, greyish

Deciduous or Evergreen	Colour of flower	Period of flower	Habit	Special conditions	Propagation
D	Various, white to purple	E.Summer	Erect		D
E	White	,,	,,		DS
E	Violet	Autumn	,,		D
E	Pale yellow	E.Summer	,,		S

Group 3
Grassy leaves

We must start with Bamboos, being far larger than any hardy grasses, and I only intend mentioning those kinds which are graceful and do not spread unduly at the root. The most plumose and graceful of all is *Arundinaria anceps* but it is a rampageous spreader. I have noted a few flowering shoots in Cornwall of late years and this could be the beginning of general flowering, after which species of all kinds of Bamboos are prone to die. *A. fastuosa* so flowered some years ago; this is one of the tallest and might well have been included in Group 13. Two charmers of less height and small-leafed grace are *A. nitida*, about 9 feet high, and *A. murieliae*, about the same. Unique among the Bamboos generally cultivated, the latter's older leaves turn to clear yellow in autumn. But apart from this latter my choice would always be the species of *Phyllostachys* distinguished from *Arundinaria* mainly by their grooved, not round, culms (stems). Among the species more often seen, the largest is the wide and tall, arching *P. viridi-glaucescens*. The leaves like those of the arundinarias mentioned and the other species of *Phyllostachys* are comparatively small and the breeze brings to delightful life all kinds, causing them to wave and rustle. I should give top marks after considering all Bamboos to *P. nigra henonis*; just that bit better in every way than *P. nigra* (in spite of the latter's blackish culms), this is the ultimate in grace and fresh greenery, a greenery which remains unbruised throughout the winter, which is unusual among other species unless we garden in the sheltered coombes of Cornwall. *P. flexuosa* is a smaller edition of *P. viridi-glaucescens*, while a step further down still in size is *P. aurea*. There are many more species in both genera, but I am confident that none of the above will disappoint. Broad-leafed bamboos are treated in Group 1.

The most magnificent of tall grasses is undoubtedly *Arundo donax*. It is sometimes 12 feet high. The trick is to cut out all 2-year-old stems every winter and thus the 1-year-old stems (except in severe winters) will have a start on the new ones. The leaves are long, drooping and glaucous. Often advocated as a windscreen for the summer months the tallest *Miscanthus*, *M. sacchariflorus*, is a huge landscape plant, spreading steadily at the root like the *Arundo*. *M. sinensis* and its varieties are of a size for the average garden. It is wise to cut down all the stems in winter to avoid the tiresome job of picking up dead leaves from all over the garden.

Of the Pampas Grasses, the tallest is the pink form, *Cortaderia selloana* 'Rendatleri'; ordinary white forms are nearly as tall, with 'Pumila' a useful compact form. 'Sunningdale Silver' is much sought by lovers of these things, but is less graceful and plumose than 'Monstrosa'. I find *C. fulvida* from New Zealand rather tender. It is a rare plant, the only garden where I have seen it apart from the Chelsea Physic Garden is Kiftsgate Court, Gloucestershire. Its value is in its summer (not autumn) flowering. *C. richardii* is tough, graceful and hardy. But it must be admitted that all of these are grown for their fine plumes of flowers rather than for their arching foliage, which except in 'Pumila' and the New Zealand species is a bit of a nuisance.

Calamagrostis acutiflorus gives not only grassy foliage but a vertical line. The glaucous clump-forming *Helictotrichon sempervirens* is a great beauty; while the same may be said of the even more glaucous *Elymus arenarius*, it must be admitted that it has the questing tendencies of a coarse couch grass, and is not to be trusted, in spite of Miss Jekyll's powers of persuasion. Two beautiful variegated grasses are *Glyceria maxima* 'Variegata' for damp ground where it will quickly spread, and the Gardeners' Garters, *Phalaris arundinacea* 'Picta', also a spreader. A lesser, variegated, clump-former of distinction is *Molinia caerulea* 'Variegata'; a form of the Purple Moor Grass, which flowers prettily in early autumn. But there are many more grasses of excellence which are slowly becoming more popular, and I will refer you to the pretty exhaustive list in *Perennial Garden Plants* which also includes such lovely Sedges as *Carex riparia* 'Variegata', Bowles' Golden Sedge, which is a form of *C. stricta* and not to be confused with Bowles' Golden Grass (*Milium effusum* 'Aureum') – and the splendid arching *Carex pendula*. All these are worthy garden plants imparting a lightness to the scene which no other plants can give.

Among the herbaceous plants, of similar value to the grasses, are many of the kinds in Group 2, while other grasses and sedges are grown in gardens only in their variegated forms and thus will be found in Groups 5, 6 and 7; glaucous ones are in Group 8.

Many other grasses are fully described in my *Perennial Garden Plants*.

BAMBOOS	Country of origin	Height/ Width	Brief description
ARUNDINARIA Bamboo			
fastuosa	Japan	18 ft × 8 ft	Small, bright green
murieliae	China	9 ft × 6 ft	Small, bright green, yellow autumn colour
nitida	,,	,,	Small, dark green
PHYLLOSTACHYS Bamboo			
aurea	,,	8 ft × 6 ft	,,
flexuosa	,,	,,	Soft green, small
nigra	,,	10 ft × 8 ft	Small, dark green, black stems
— *henonis*	,,	,,	Small, dark green
viridi-glaucescens	,,	15 ft × 15 ft	Small, light green

GRASSES

ARUNDO			
donax	S.Europe	8 ft × 3 ft	Glaucous arching leaves
CALAMAGROSTIS			
× *acutiflorus*	Europe, Russia	6 ft × 2 ft	Narrow
CAREX			
pendula	Europe, N.Africa, Britain	4 ft × 3 ft	Narrow, arching
CORTADERIA			
fulvida	New Zealand	7 ft × 4 ft	,,
richardii	,,	8 ft × 6 ft	,,
selloana Pampas Grass	S.America	8 ft × 5 ft	,,
— 'Monstrosa'		7 ft × 5 ft	,,
— 'Pumila'		5 ft × 4 ft	,,
— 'Rendatleri'		9 ft × 6 ft	,,
— 'Sunningdale Silver'		7 ft × 5 ft	,,

Deciduous or Evergreen	Colour of flower	Period of flower	Habit	Special conditions	Propagation
E			Erect	M	D
E			Arching		D
E			,,	M	D
E			Erect	M	D
E			Arching	M	D
E			,,	M	D
E			,,	M	D
E			Widely arching	M	D
D			Erect		D
D	Brown	Summer	,,		D
E	Green	,,	Arching	M	DS
D	Flesh	,,	,,	W	DS
D	Cream	,,	,,		DS
D	White	Autumn	Erect		DS
D	,,	,,	,,		D
D	,,	,,	,,		D
D	Rosy lilac	,,	,,		D
D	White	,,	,,		D

GRASSES (cont.)	Country of origin	Height/ Width	Brief description
ELYMUS			
arenarius	N.Hemisphere, Britain	4 ft × 3 ft (rampageous)	Narrow, glaucous
GLYCERIA			
aquatica 'Variegata'	Britain, Europe, Asia	4 ft × 2 ft	Narrow, cream striped
HELICTOTRICHON			
sempervirens	S.W.Europe	4 ft × 1 ft	Narrow, glaucous
MISCANTHUS (Eulalia)			
sacchariflorus	E.Asia	9 ft × 3 ft	Arching
sinensis	China, Japan	6 ft × 3 ft	,,
PHALARIS			
arundinacea — 'Picta'	N.Hemisphere	3 ft × 2 ft	Narrow, arching

Deciduous or Evergreen	Colour of flower	Period of flower	Habit	Special conditions	Propagation
E	Grey	Summer	Arching		D
D	Creamy	,,	,,		D
D	Grey	,,	,,		DS
D	Green		Erect		D
D	Fawn	Autumn	,,		D
D	Creamy	Summer	Arching		D

Group 4

Plants of feathery effect

TREES AND SHRUBS

This group has caused a lot of hesitation on my part. I am not sure that it is worth including, but at times I have felt the need of soft feathery plants as a foil to those of more decisive outline. The selection is of course prompted by ferns and the more graceful bamboos. Even ferns at times, with their regular shuttlecock shapes, do not provide quite what is needed. The plants chosen have small or tiny leaves coupled usually with graceful growth but there is little uniformity and my brief cataloguing can only act as a spur for inspection and further examination.

Salix exigua occurs again in Group 8 and is a slender and very graceful silvery plant. Of taller trees we have the fine filigree of the *Alnus*, *Fraxinus*, *Gleditsia*, *Robinia* and *Sophora*. The last two are the largest in growth, and considering the lateness of its flowering period and the ease with which it can be raised from seeds it is surprising that the *Sophora* is not more often grown. The big tree at Kew, near the rock garden, is a great sight every late summer or early autumn.

But I think the need for this softness for which we are seeking is felt more among shrubs and plants than among trees. The plumose effect of *Juniperus* × *media* 'Pfitzeriana' and *J. virginiana* 'Grey Owl' and their relatives might have warranted their inclusion, but in the *Azara* (rather tender) and the *Escallonia* we have two evergreens of tiny foliage and pretty growth. *Cassinia fulvida* is a more dense evergreen with tiny leaves but for all its beauty of foliage is somewhat demoted on account of the dead flowers which hang on the plant. *Caesalpinia* needs a warm wall and few plants can equal the beauty of its feather-like leaves and in a hot summer the flowers are remarkable.

The several Spiraeas qualify in their small leaves and graceful arching growth; species of *Indigofera*, so difficult to separate and recognize, are of open feathery foliage, but not graceful growth, nor are the little-known *Amorpha* species. Grace and small foliage are found in *Kerria* (but not the erect double-flowered kind which normally does duty for the species). All species of *Tamarix* have the desired feathery foliage but the stronger growing ones have awkward open growth. Those which flower on the summer's shoots can be hard-pruned in spring and thus produce tall feathery sprays bearing plumes of minute pink flowers in late summer. For this treatment they need good soil, though they will exist in sand. I have singled out *Tamarix pentandra* which is available in select colour forms – all pink – and whose foliage is pleasingly greyish in complement.

For a large area one could do worse than choosing *Salix purpurea* 'Pendula' grown from a cutting. Though termed a Weeping Willow its growth is scarcely drooping and it makes a confused tangle of shoots with tiny dark green leaves. For tumbling over a sunny bank *Lespedeza thunbergii* is very useful. It dies to the ground in winter, but is a good, graceful foliage plant. It should have in the foreground a carpet of silver foliage over which its large branching sprays of tiny crimson-purple pea-flowers will astonish in autumn.

Rosa multiflora is included for the sake of its graceful growth – it will climb into trees and hang out of them, flooding the air with sweet fragrance; the other species, especially *R. elegantula*, have tiny leaves. Two more favourites are the White Portuguese Broom, *Cytisus albus*, and *Stephanandra tanakae*. The latter has many assets: graceful arching growth, small to medium-sized leaves, dainty blooms, autumn colour and bright brown bark for winter. It is a strangely neglected shrub.

The Japanese Maples are well known and the cut-leafed forms of *Acer palmatum*, 'Dissectum' and 'Dissectum Atropurpureum', and some newer darker forms are among the most feathery of shrubs. They are susceptible to spring frosts, but a rare little shrub could be used in frost-pockets to create the same effect as the green 'Dissectum': it is *Sambucus racemosa* 'Tenuifolia'.

Ferns are fully treated in my *Perennial Garden Plants* so I will not duplicate the information here.

This list is by no means exhaustive; there are many more feathery-leafed plants among smaller perennials and sub-shrubby plants such as *Artemisia*.

TREES	Country of origin	Height/ Width	Leaf shape
ALNUS			
glutinosa Common Alder	Europe etc	15 ft × 10 ft	Finely cut, dark
— 'Imperialis'			green
FRAXINUS Ash			
angustifolia			
— *lentiscifolia*	Europe etc	50 ft × 30 ft	Pinnate, small
GLEDITSIA			
triacanthos	Eastern USA	80 ft × 40 ft	Bipinnate, small
— 'Elegantissima'		10 ft × 10 ft	,,
— 'Sunburst', see Group 6			
ROBINIA False Acacia			
pseudacacia 'Rozynskyana'	Eastern USA	20 ft × 15 ft	Pinnate, small
			drooping
SOPHORA			
japonica Pagoda Tree	China	50 ft × 40 ft	Pinnate, small

SHRUBS

ACER			
palmatum Japan			
— 'Dissectum' and its varieties		6 ft × 6 ft	Finely cut, green
			or purplish
AMORPHA			
canescens Lead Plant	N. America	4 ft × 4 ft	Pinnate, greyish
fruticosa False Indigo	Southern USA	6 ft × 6 ft	Pinnate
ARTEMISIA			
'Powis Castle'	Hybrid	3 ft × 4 ft	Finely cut, silvery
AZARA			
microphylla	Chile	10 ft × 7 ft	Tiny dark green
CAESALPINIA			
japonica	Argentina	10 ft × 10 ft	Bipinnate
CASSINIA			
fulvida (Diplopappus	S.America	4 ft × 4 ft	Tiny, yellowish
chrysophyllus)			

Deciduous or Evergreen	Colour of flower	Period of flower	Habit	Special conditions	Propagation
D	Purplish catkins	Spring	Open		GL
D	Inconspicuous		,,		GL
D	,,		Open		S
D	,,		Bushy		CG
D	White	E.Summer	Open		G
D	White	L.Summer	,,		S
D	Inconspicuous	Spring	Rounded		G
D	Violet	E.Autumn	Open		S
D	,,	Summer	,,		S
D/E	Seldom produced	Summer	Rounded	W	CL
E	Yellow, tiny, fragrant	Spring	Open	W	C
D	Yellow	E.Summer	,,	W	S
E	Dull white	Summer	Dense		C

SHRUBS (cont.)	Country of origin	Height/ Width	Leaf shape
CYTISUS, many species but particularly *multiflorus (C. albus)*	Spain, etc	8 ft × 4 ft	Minute, green, green twigs
DANAË *racemosa*	S.W.Asia	3 ft × 3 ft	Small, shining, dark green
ESCALLONIA 'Edinensis'	Hybrid	6 ft × 8 ft	Small green
INDIGOFERA *heterantha (I. gerardiana)* other species have similar value and colour	N.W.Himalaya	10 ft × 7 ft	Pinnate, tiny
KERRIA *japonica* — 'Variegata', see Group 7	China, Japan	5 ft × 6 ft	Light green
LESPEDEZA *thunbergii* (*L. sieboldii*) (*Desmodium penduliflorum*)	Japan, China	5 ft × 7 ft	Three-lobed, small
LEUCOTHOË *fontanesiana* (*L. catesbaei* of gardens)	N.America, Japan	4 ft × 4 ft	Medium, shining
ROSA *elegantula (R. farreri)* — 'Persetosa'	W.China	4 ft × 6 ft	Tiny, pinnate
multiflora	Japan, Korea	6 ft × 12 ft	Small, pinnate
webbiana	Asia	5 ft × 8 ft	Tiny, pinnate
willmottiae	N.W.China	6 ft × 10 ft	,,
SALIX *exigua*, see Group 8 *purpurea* 'Pendula' (when grown as a bush)	Europe	8 ft × 15 ft	Narrow, small, dark green

Deciduous or Evergreen	Colour of flower	Period of flower	Habit	Special conditions	Propagation
D	White	E.Summer	Open		S
E	Insignificant		Open arching	S	DS
E	Pink	Summer	,,		C
D	Mauve-pink	Summer/ Autumn	Open		CS
D	Orange	Spring	,,		CD
D	Crimson-purple	Autumn	Open, arching		DS
E	White, tiny	Spring	,,		CS
D	Pink, small; fruits red	Summer	,,		CS
D	White, small; fruits small, red	,,	,,		CS
D	Pink, small; fruits red	,,	,,		CS
D	,,	,,	,,		CS
D	Catkins	Spring	,,		C

SHRUBS (cont.)	Country of origin	Height/ Width	Leaf shape
SAMBUCUS			
Common Elder			
nigra	Europe etc		
— 'Laciniata'		7 ft × 7 ft	Deeply cut leaves
Fern-leafed Elder			
racemosa Red Berried Elder			
— 'Tenuifolium'	Europe, W.Asia	3 ft × 3 ft	Finely cut, green
SPIRAEA			
× *arguta*	Hybrid	6 ft × 5 ft	Tiny
canescens	Himalaya	7 ft × 8 ft	,,
cantoniensis	China	6 ft × 6 ft	Small
henryi	,,	9 ft × 12 ft	,,
STEPHANANDRA			
tanakae	Japan	5 ft × 8 ft	Medium, stems bright brown
TAMARIX			
pentandra	Asia	5 ft × 4 ft	Minute, greyish

many other species of stronger growth, some flowering in spring, others later

Deciduous or Evergreen	Colour of flower	Period of flower	Habit	Special conditions	Propagation
D	White; fruits black	Summer	Open		CS
D	White; fruits red	,,	Rounded		CG
D	White	Spring	Open		C
D	,,	Summer	Open, arching		C
D	,,	E.Summer	,,		C
D	,,	Summer	,,		C
D	Blush white	,,	,,		C
D	Pink, tiny in feathery sprays	,,	Open		C

Group 5
Yellow-variegated foliage

Usually called "golden" varieties – as if "gold" can add any brilliance to "yellow" – these varied plants give of their brightest when grown in full sun. If grown in shade the yellow is dimmed to a yellowish green in most plants; where yellow foliage is required in shade it is better to choose a yellow-flushed deciduous plant, such as those starred in Group 6.

Any sort of variegation tends to produce a bizarre effect and they should all be used with great circumspection; the planting of all sorts of variegation is not to be recommended. On the other hand a deliberate repetitive planting of any one kind, with due selection of plants which will in flower-colour subdue or bolster the general effect, can be salutary. However, it has to be a very large garden that can accommodate a yellow-variegated tree.

TREES AND SHRUBS

The most spectacular large tree with this sort of leaf colour is the *Liriodendron*, of which a fine young specimen at Stourhead, Wiltshire, dominates everything in late spring and early summer. Considerably smaller is the form of *Acer negundo*, so ridiculously termed Box Elder; it has no connection with box or elder. Seldom seen because it is apt to revert to green and is of slow growth, *Castanea sativa* 'Aureomarginata' is spectacular in early summer. The *Ligustrum* is a revelation to most people; though comparatively slow in growth it is attractive from a young state, and excels among the privets in achieving the size and port of a small tree in warm counties.

There is no lack of yellow-variegated evergreen shrubs. The invaluable aucubas and elaeagnuses will remain brilliant even in shade. They and the hollies – which are best in full sun – are amongst our staple diet for evergreens, and the hollies are well-loved, and with a little pruning and staking of the leader when young can be encouraged to make superlative, glittering specimens. To see a 'Golden King' with its magnificent foliage interspersed with red berries is a heart-warming sight in autumn. It is obvious that the blackbirds hold their Christmas feast earlier than we do! The Golden Privet, the ivies for walls of any aspect (but preferably not too hot) or for tree-trunks and fences, and the useful forms of *Euonymus* scale us down to the gay little Periwinkle. So much for a brief look at the evergreens.

Without doubt the *Aralia* when fully established, showing its thick branching stems and wide canopy of foliage, is the outstanding deciduous shrub. It is strange that its yellow colouring fades to cream by late summer, at which stage, in full flower or fruit, I prefer it. The elder is not to be despised, especially when in flower, for dark positions by a north facing wall; the *Syringa* is not spectacularly marked with yellow, but rather with yellowish green. The most frequently planted is *Cornus alba* 'Spaethii', a shrub of many attractions and unbeatable for a choice of brilliant early summer colour – retained in great part until autumn – when it turns to a pinkish tint before dropping its leaves and revealing its plum-crimson thicket of twigs. *Cornus mas* 'Aurea Elegantissima' is a larger shrub, bright and open, and particularly a shrub to conjure with when studded with its scarlet fruits in summer. The *Weigela* is good in summer and until autumn, but when in flower (pink) its colour scheme is upsetting; I prefer *W. praecox* 'Variegata' in Group 7. On warm walls the *Abutilon* is certainly a shrub full of character, its yellow-splashed leaves vying with the yellow-and-red pendant blooms which are produced for many weeks. I think I prefer the green-leafed type.

This brings us down to our smallest shrub, *Symphoricarpos orbiculatus* 'Variegatus', a dense bushy plant whose tiny flowers scarcely spoil the general effect.

PERENNIALS

Phormiums are sometimes classed with shrubs and sometimes with herbaceous plants. They are not shrubs and they are not herbaceous, coming between the two with their spectacular, evergreen sword-like foliage. They are further treated in Groups 2 and 9. The old *Phormium tenax* 'Variegatum' is variable but of great importance. To see it at Glendurgan, Cornwall, is to realize what it can achieve: the leaves reach to 7 feet or so, overtopped by the bloomy-plum coloured flowering stems, set with red-brown flowers on side brackets. Neither this species nor the hardier, smaller *R. cookianum* is reliably hardy in Surrey and I fear the same must be admitted about the numerous new hybrids from New Zealand, such as the beautiful 'Cream Delight' and brighter 'Yellow Wave'. After these splendid spectacular plants the yellow-variegated form of *Iris pallida* can only be described as a "come down". I do not find the yellow stripes on the grey leaves attractive and prefer the form in Group 7 which tones in better, too, with the flowers. Neither of these forms is specially good in flower, being derived from a poor sort of *I. pallida* and not from the excellent *I.p. dalmatica*. Very much smaller are *Carex morrowi* 'Variegata' and *Hakonechloa macra* 'Aureola'.

There is no doubt that the forms of *Hosta* reign supreme in this little list. Chelsea Show could hardly be held without *H. fortunei* 'Albopicta', though its short-lived brilliance turns to green in summer, like that of the wholly yellow 'Aurea' (Group 6). *H.f.* 'Obscura Marginata' is a fairly good plant margined with yellow, but cannot compare with *H. ventricosa* 'Variegata', whose yellow leaf-edges turn to cream at its purple flowering time. There is no doubt that the form of *H. sieboldiana* called 'Frances Williams' (there are others very similar) is outstanding in its huge blue-grey leaves broadly banded with dark yellow until one contemplates a comparatively new form of *H. elata* from Japan. In this the dark green shiny blades are broadly edged – even particoloured – with clear yellow. I hope it will become available commercially before long.

Those whose soil and conditions are not conducive to good growth of hostas can take comfort in *Symphytum × uplandicum* 'Variegatum'. Let it flower, by all means, though the stems are lanky and wayward, but then cut it down and the reward will be new foliage as good as that of spring and a rival to the best of hostas. It unfortunately reverts to green occasionally, which shoots must be removed from below soil level. In the same botanical family, the borages, is the *Brunnera* with subdued creamy yellow edge to the leaf, for a semi-shady place. This leaves us with two ardent sun-lovers the *Sedum* and the *Salvia*; the colour scheme of the second is preferable to that of the first, though the sedum's pink is inoffensive.

Although some conifers are actually variegated, the effect of the tiny striped leaves is due to their mass rather than to individuals, so I have left them for Group 6.

TREES	Country of origin	Height/ Width	Brief description
ACER			
negundo	N.America		
— 'Elegans'		30 ft × 20 ft	Pinnate, yellow edge
CASTANEA	S.Europe etc		
sativa 'Aureomarginata'		25 ft × 15 ft	Broad, yellow edge
LIGUSTRUM			
lucidum	China		
— 'Excelsum Superbum'		20 ft × 10 ft	Small, splashed yellow and white
LIRIODENDRON　　Tulip Tree			
tulipifera	N.America		
— 'Aureomarginatum'		50 ft × 40 ft	Broad, yellow splashed

SHRUBS

ABUTILON			
megapotanicum	Brazil		
— 'Variegatum'		6 ft × 6 ft on wall	Small, yellow splashed
ARALIA			
elata	Japan		
—'Aureovariegata'		8 ft × 8 ft	Bipinnate, large; yellow splashed, white later
AUCUBA			
japonica			
—'Crotonifolia'	,,	,,	Medium, yellow splashed
— 'Gold Dust'		,,	Yellow splashed
— 'Sulphurea'		,,	Creamy yellow edged
— 'Variegata'		,,	Spotted yellow

Deciduous or Evergreen	Colour of flower	Period of flower	Habit	Special conditions	Propagation
D	Inconspicuous	Spring	Open		G
D	White	Summer	Open, slow growing		G
E	,,	L.Summer/ Autumn	Dense		CG
D	Yellowish	Summer	Open		G
D	Yellow/red	Summer/ Autumn	Lax	W	C
D	White, fruits maroon	L.Summer	Open, stout		G
E	Maroon (male)	Spring	Dense		CL
E	Maroon; fruits red in spring	,,	,,		CL
E	,,	,,	,,		CL
E	,,	,,	,,		CL

SHRUBS (cont.)	Country or origin	Height/ Width	Brief description
CORNUS Dogwood			
alba 'Spaethii'	N.E.Asia	6 ft × 8 ft	Small, edged yellow
mas 'Aurea			
Elegantissima'	Europe	8 ft × 8 ft	Small, yellow edged, flushed pink
ELAEAGNUS			
× *ebbingei* 'Gilt Edge'	Hybrid	8 ft × 10 ft	Small, edged yellow
pungens	Japan		
— 'Dicksonii'		8 ft × 5 ft	,,
— 'Maculata'		9 ft × 12 ft	Small, yellow centre
— 'Variegata'		8 ft × 8 ft	Small, thin yellow edge
EUONYMUS			
fortunei	China		
—'Emerald 'n Gold'		2 ft × 3 ft	Small, yellow variegated, reddish flush
japonicus	Japan		
—'Auteopictus'		8 ft × 5 ft	Small, yellow centre
— 'Ovatus Aureus'		6 ft × 5 ft	Small, yellow edged
ILEX			
aquifolium	S.Europe/ China	20 ft × 12 ft	Holly leaf

some of the most attractive yellow variegated cultivars are 'Golden Milkboy' (male), 'Golden Queen' (male), 'Golden Van Tol' (female), 'Madame Briot' (female), 'Myrtifolia Aureomaculata' (male), 'Ovata Aurea' (male); 'Watereriana' (male) is slow and compact

× *altaclerensis*   Hybrid   25 ft × 12 ft
— 'Camelliifolia Variegata' (female), 'Golden King' (female), 'Lawsoniana' (female), 'Maderensis Variegata' (male) are some good varieties; 'Silver Sentinel' is paler in variegation

LIGUSTRUM
ovalifolium   Japan
— 'Aureum'   8 ft × 8 ft   Small, yellow edged

Deciduous or Evergreen	Colour of flower	Period of flower	Habit	Special conditions	Propagation
D	White; fruits blush white	Spring	Dense		CL
D	Yellow	Late Winter	,,		CL
E	White	Autumn	,,		CL
E	,,	,,	Upright		CL
E	,,	,,	Dense		CL
E	,,	,,	,,		CL
E			Dense or will climb		C
E			Dense, erect	W	C
E			Dense	W	C
E	,,	Spring	Dense, erect		C
E	,,	,,	,,		C
E	,,	L.Summer	Dense		CL

SHRUBS (cont.)	Country of origin	Height/ Width	Brief description
SALVIA Sage			
officinalis	S.Europe		
— *icterina*		18 ins × 2 ft	Edged creamy yellow
SAMBUCUS			
nigra	Europe etc		
— 'Aureomarginata'		10 ft × 9 ft	Pinnate, yellow edged
SYMPHORICARPOS			
orbiculatus	E.USA		
— 'Variegatus'		4 ft × 4 ft	Tiny, yellow edged
SYRINGA			
emodi	Himalaya		
—'Aureovariegata'		8 ft × 8 ft	Broad, yellow edged
VINCA			
minor Lesser Periwinkle	Europe, W.Asia		
— 'Aureovariegata'		1 ft × 2 ft	Small, yellow blotches
WEIGELA			
florida	Far East		
— 'Variegata'		6 ft × 6 ft	Small, yellow edged

CLIMBERS

HEDERA Persian Ivy			
— *colchica* 'Variegata'		Climber	Large, yellow margins
— 'Sulphur Heart' ('Paddy's Pride')		Climber	Large, yellow centre
helix Common Ivy	Europe, Asia Minor etc		
— 'Gold Heart'		Climber	Small, yellow centre
JASMINUM Sweet Jessamine			
officinale	Sino-Himalaya		
— 'Aureovariegatum'		Twiner	Yellow splashed
LONICERA Honeysuckle			
japonica	Japan		
— 'Aureoreticulata'		Twiner	Yellow veined

Deciduous or Evergreen	Colour of flower	Period of flower	Habit	Special conditions	Propagation
E	Violet	E.Summer	Clump		CDL
D	White; fruits maroon	,,	Open		C
D	Inconspicuous	Summer	Dense		CD
D	Lilac–white	,,	,,		CL
E	Lavender blue	Spring	Carpeter		CL
D	Pink	E.Summer	Dense		CL
E	Yellowish	Autumn	Dense		CL
E	,,	,,	,,		CL
E	,,	,,	,,		CL
D	White	Summer/ Autumn	,,		CL
E			,,		CL

PERENNIALS	Country of origin	Height/ Width	Brief description
ASTRANTIA			
major	Austria		
— 'Sunningdale Variegated'		2 ft × 18 ins	Edged creamy yellow
BRUNNERA			
macrophylla	W.Caucasus		
— 'Hadspen Cream'		18 ins × 2 ft	Rounded, edged creamy yellow
CAREX			
morrowi 'Variegata'	Japan	1 ft × 2 ft	Narrow, arching; dark green, centre yellow
HAKONECHLOA			
macra 'Aureola'	Japan	1 ft × 2 ft	Narrow, arching; mainly yellow
HOSTA			
fortunei	Hybrid		
— 'Albopicta'		2 ft × 2 ft	Broad; yellow centre, turning green
— 'Obscura Marginata'		,,	Broad, yellow edge
sieboldiana	Japan		
— 'Frances Williams'		2 ft × 3 ft	Broad, grey-green edged yellow
ventricosa	Japan		
— 'Aureomaculata'		3 ft × 2 ft	Broad; centre yellow
— 'Variegata'		,,	Broad; edged yellow
IRIS			
pallida	Europe		
— 'Aureovariegata'		3 ft × 1 ft	Grey leaves, edged yellow
PHORMIUM			
— *tenax*	New Zealand		
— 'Variegatum'		9 ft × 3 ft	Sword leaves, edged yellow
— 'Yellow Wave', 'Cream Delight' are two new cultivars of less size, for sheltered positions			
SEDUM			
alboroseum	Far East		
— 'Variegatum'		1 ft × 2 ft	Grey-green splashed yellow

Deciduous or Evergreen	Colour of flower	Period of flower	Habit	Special conditions	Propagation
D	Pinky-white	Summer	Clump		D
D	Blue	Spring	,,	S	D
E	Creamy	Summer	,,		D
D	Yellowish	L.Summer	,,		D
D	Lilac	Summer	,,	S	D
D	,,	,,	,,	S	D
D	Lilac-white	,,	,,	S	D
D	Dark lilac	L.Summer	,,	S	D
D	,,	,,	,,	S	D
E	Lilac	E.Summer	,,		D
E	Reddish	Summer	,,	W	D
D	Pink	L.Summer	,,		D

PERENNIALS (cont.)	Country of origin	Height/ Width	Brief description
SYMPHYTUM			
× *uplandicum*	Hybrid		
— 'Variegatum'		4 ft × 3 ft	Particoloured creamy yellow

Deciduous or Evergreen	Colour of flower	Period of flower	Habit	Special conditions	Propagation
D	Bluish	E.Summer	Clump		D

Group 6
Yellow-flushed foliage

In a general way these are more valuable to me in planting than are the yellow variegated plants; their colouring is less bizarre but just as telling. As with the other groups I will start with the largest first and there is no doubt where the choice lies – with the yellow Black Italian Poplar, *Populus × canadensis* 'Serotina Aurea'. It is light and yet majestic and of a pleasing cool tint. On the other hand the *Catalpa* is a great bully, taking command of any situation; it needs very careful placing. The large leaves open in June and just as one is getting used to their overpowering splendour, it produces its pinky-white flowers. Time was when one could count on the brilliant yellow-leafed Wych Elm as a third strong competitor, but the elm disease has put a stop to that. There is no lack of trees of medium size however: no less than three good Acers, all of great brilliance; the exquisite lacy golden-greenery of the 'Sunburst' *Gleditsia*, slow-growing *Quercus* and *Fagus*, and the pretty, weak tree *Populus alba* 'Richardii'. One seldom sees big trees of any of these but the silvery undersides of the Poplar's leaves give it a special quality which outweighs its lack of vigour. (This lack of vigour is of course due in all these trees to lack of chlorophyll and the same is true of plants in Groups 5 and 7.) This same mixture of colours is found in the more sturdy *Sorbus aria* 'Chrysophylla', while the all-yellow of *Sorbus aucuparia* 'Dirkenii' is good in the early year. For an all-yellow effect I know of nothing more telling for early June than the *Laburnum*, while the *Alnus* enchants us not only with yellowish leaves, but orange-red winter catkins.

Through this long paragraph I have been shrinking from discussing *Robinia pseudacacia* 'Frisia'. It is becoming so popular, and is dotted about many gardens in suburbia, and also in some greater gardens, often without much thought. It is fortunate that its late leafing does not allow it to show colour until the 'Kanzan' cherries are well over! It gets more strident every month until autumn when it goes out in a yellow flame. All of these vivid trees need similar, but more gentle, tones to lead up to them rather than just putting in a sudden appearance here and there; but such a scheme with shrubs and trees needs a large garden. Given such, with an area set aside for a grouping not within the main vista, much can be done, linked perhaps for the most bizarre contrast with plants in Group 9. This would get about as far away from the sublime greenery as one could.

Among the shrubs there are also some very brilliant things. The *Weigela*, *Philadelphus*, Brocklebank's *Ribes* and *Sambucus racemosa* 'Plumosa Aurea' can be overpowering. Both the *Sambucus* and *Philadelphus* have the good taste to provide white flowers, the latter with a far-reaching and delicious scent, and the same may be said about the much larger growing *Ptelea*. The *Corylus* and *Viburnum* have their uses too. As to the yellow form of the Common Elder, I find it just the thing to use to lighten dark corners even under yews, where its sick yellow turns to a gentle lime green and its white flowers, when produced, add to the lightness. The two little shrubs *Ribes alpinum* 'Aureum' and the *Berberis* have fragrant but inconspicuous flowers. It must be admitted that this whole brilliant group suffers from leaf scorch when growing in full sun. It is best to afford them part shade, at least for the hottest part of the day; in cooler positions their yellow is muted. Where yellow is needed in full sun it is wisest to choose variegated shrubs. We are left with the slow growing and quite exquisite colour and shape of leaf and beautiful habit of the Japanese *Acer*. After a hundred years one may expect it to achieve 10 feet or so.

Then there are a few evergreens: the ivies, both spectacular 'Buttercup' – which again burns in hot sun – and the more resistant, stronger growing 'Angularis Aurea', whose growth may be green or, with wayward recurrence even from green shoots, will put forth growths of pure yellow, or green veined with yellow. The scorching of the leaves by the sun does not occur in this and in the other three valuable evergreens. They are the very large growing *Laurus* or Sweet Bay, the vigorous privet called 'Vicaryi' and *Lonicera* 'Baggesen's Gold'. With all of these the sunny side of the bush is the most brilliant. This applies also to cultivars of *Calluna* of which there are many today, but not to cultivars of *Erica* which are inclined to scorch. I have not included them as they mostly lack vigour. Among the callunas I have been at pains only to recommend two with white flowers; I fail to visualize a colour scheme which could tolerate the long-lasting pinky-mauve flowers of the several others. Fortunately the pink flowers of the Brocklebank *Ribes* and the *Weigela* which I have included are of short duration. These evergreens lead us straight into the conifers, which give us many yellow variants. Adrian Bloom, at Bressingham, Diss, Norfolk, has a most impressive collection which well repays a visit. Many also are growing in the Valley Garden, Windsor Great Park. In clear, dry air and full exposure to sun and wind both yellow and glaucous forms achieve the utmost brilliance. They deserve a whole chapter to themselves, containing as they do these widely differing tints as well as tones of green and growth habits from the completely prostrate to the narrowly vertical with every possible variant in between. Together with certain heathers (mainly *Calluna*) they create a completely new conception in labour-saving gardening with year-long colour. I have included a few well-tried favourites in this group and Group 8.

PERENNIALS

For early summer no climber can compete with the yellow leaves of the Golden Hop, *Humulus*. It is a rapid annual climber and therefore is included among the herbaceous plants. Its perennial roots spread far and wide. Otherwise we are short of yellow-flushed herbaceous plants. I find the Valerian is ideal for associating with purple crocuses and blue scillas; after the spring its foliage turns to green and its flowers are of no consequence. The Meadow Sweet is a pretty enough plant for the early year, but loses its colour, as do so many deciduous yellow-flushed plants; the *Hosta* on the other hand is only a spring glory and turns to mid green by the middle of June, but, as it would normally be best suited for a shady place along with others of its genus, it will carry the gaiety of spring into the darkest corners. Some newer kinds, typified by *Hosta* 'Wogon', keep their yellow colouring until autumn.

TREES	Country of origin	Height/ Width	Brief description
ACER			
cappadocicum Maple	Asia		
— 'Aureum'		40 ft × 40 ft	Palmate
negundo	N.America		
— 'Auratum'		30 ft × 20 ft	Pinnate
pseudoplatanus Sycamore	Europe,		
— 'Worleei'	W.Asia	40 ft × 30 ft	Lobed
ALNUS			
incana	Europe,		
— 'Aurea'	E.N.America	20 ft × 10 ft	Rounded, small
CATALPA			
bignonioides	E.USA		
— 'Aurea'		20 ft × 20 ft	Large, rounded
FAGUS			
sylvatica	Europe		
— 'Zlatia'		Very slow	Small
GLEDITSIA			
triacanthos	USA		
— 'Sunburst'		30 ft? × 15 ft?	Tiny, pinnate
LABURNUM			
anagyroides	Europe		
— 'Aureum'		10 ft × 10 ft	Small, trifoliate
LAURUS			
nobilis	Mediterranean		
— 'Aurea'	Region	30 ft × 20 ft	Small
POPULUS			
alba	Europe, Asia		
— 'Richardii'		20 ft × 10 ft	Small, white beneath
× *canadensis* 'Serotina		80 ft × 40 ft	Small
Aurea' ('Van Geertii')			
QUERCUS			
robur	Europe etc		
— 'Concordia'		15 ft × 10 ft	Small, lobed

Deciduous or Evergreen	Colour of flower	Period of flower	Habit	Special conditions	Propagation
D	Yellow, reddish 'keys'	Spring	Dense head		G
D	Inconspicuous	,,	Open		G
D	Yellow	,,	Dense		G
D	Catkins red	,,	Slender		GL
D	Pinky-white	L.Summer	Open		CG
D			Dense		G
D	Green; brown fruits	Summer	Open		G
D	Yellow; fruits green	E.Summer	,,		G
E	Cream	,,	Dense	W	C
D	Green catkins	Spring	Open		CL
D	Reddish catkins	,,	,,		CL
D	Green	,,	Dense		G

TREES (cont.)	Country of origin	Height/ Width	Brief description
ROBINIA			
pseudacacia False Acacia	E.USA		
— 'Frisia'		50 ft × 30 ft	Pinnate
SORBUS			
aria Whitebeam	Europe		
— 'Chrysophylla'		50 ft × 30 ft	Small, yellow above, grey beneath
aucuparia Rowan	,,		
— 'Dirkenii'		30 ft × 15 ft	Pinnate, yellow when young
ULMUS			
glabra Wych Elm	Europe, Asia		
— 'Lutescens'		40 ft × 40 ft	Small, yellow when young

CLIMBERS

	Country of origin	Height/ Width	Brief description
HEDERA			
helix Common Ivy	Europe to		
— 'Buttercup'	N.Persia	Climber	Small, yellow, part shade
— 'Angularis Aurea'	,,	,,	Medium, some yellow, some green

CONIFERS

Conifers with yellow foliage (where exposed to sunlight) are:

Cedrus atlantica 'Aurea'; *C. deodara* 'Aurea', both open and slow growing; *C.d.* 'Aurea Pendula', semi-weeping.

Chamaecyparis lawsoniana 'Erecta Aurea', slow, narrow, best in part shade; 'Hillieri', 'Lanei', 'Lutea', 'Stewartii', 'Winston Churchill' are all excellent yellow forms; 'Stewartii' is the broadest in growth.

Chamaecyparis obtusa (less vigorous and tall than the best *C. lawsoniana* cultivars) 'Crippsii' is of considerable splendour; *C.o.* 'Tetragona Aurea' is more of a bush.

Chamaecyparis pisifera 'Filifera Aurea', a pyramid of drooping twigs, brilliant yellow; 'Squarrosa Sulphurea', feathery sulphur-green.

Deciduous or Evergreen	Colour of flower	Period of flower	Habit	Special conditions	Propagation
D	White	Summer	Compact but brittle		G
D	White; fruits red	E.Summer	Compact		G
D	White; fruits red	,,	Open		G
D			,,		G
E	Yellowish	Autumn	Dense, slow		CL
E	,,	,,	Vigorous		CL

CONIFERS (cont.)

Cupressus macrocarpa 'Lutea', hardy, greenish yellow; 'Donard Gold' and 'Gold Crest' are brighter but less hardy. Rapid growth.

Juniperus chinensis 'Aurea', sulphur yellow, feathery, narrowly conical, slow.

— *communis* 'Depressa Aurea', carpeting plant, foliage yellow in spring, bronze later.

— × *media* 'Pfitzeriana Aurea', wide plumose spreader, flushed yellow in sun; 'Plumosa Aurea' ('Japonica Aurea') open, long-branched, dark yellowish bronze, semi-erect.

Picea abies 'Aurea', yellow in spring, green later, small growth; *P.a.* 'Aurea Magnifica' is green but young growth is yellow; vigorous.

— *orientalis* 'Aurea', young shoots yellow, green later, fine compact tree.

Pinus sylvestris 'Aurea'. Young leaves pale green, turning to yellow in winter. Slow.

Taxus baccata 'Elegantissima', bright yellow in summer, straw-tinted in winter; 'Semperaurea' is a richer colour.

— 'Fastigiata Aurea'. The Golden Irish Yew; columnar.

— 'Dovastonii Aurea'. Wide spreading branches, of good colour.

Thuja occidentalis 'Ellwangeriana' and 'Rheingold'. Two brilliant orange-yellows, compact, feathery pyramids. 'Wareana Lutescens' is a dense khaki-sulphur tint.

— *orientalis* 'Elegantissima'. Dense, erect, bright yellow passing to bronze; slow. 'Semperaurea' is wider in growth.

— *plicata* 'Zebrina'. Foliage speckled with creamy yellow giving an overall yellow effect. Vigorous.

SHRUBS	Country of origin	Height/ Width	Brief description
ACER			
japonicum	Japan		
— 'Aureum'		12 ft × 6 ft	Small, rounded, lobed
BERBERIS			
thunbergii	,,		
— 'Aurea'		3 ft × 3 ft	Tiny; green later
CALLUNA			
vulgaris Heather, Ling	Europe,		
— 'Gold Haze'	Asia Minor	8 ins × 1 ft	Minute; yellow all the year
— 'Serlei Aurea'		2 ft × 2 ft	,,
CORYLUS			
avellana Hazel	Europe etc		
— 'Aurea'		6 ft × 6 ft	Rounded; yellowish green

Deciduous or Evergreen	Colour of flower	Period of flower	Habit	Special conditions	Propagation
D	Red; fruits reddish	Spring	Compact; very slow		G
D	Yellow; fruits red	,,	Compact		C
E	White	L.Summer	,,		C
E	,,	,,	,,		C
D	Catkins		Open		CL

SHRUBS (cont.)	Country of origin	Height/ Width	Brief description
LIGUSTRUM			
ovalifolium Oval-leaf Privet	Japan		
— 'Vicaryi'		8 ft × 6 ft	Small; yellowish green
LONICERA			
nitida	W.China		
— 'Baggesen's Gold'		4 ft × 4 ft	Tiny; yellow where exposed
PHILADELPHUS			
coronarius Mock Orange	Europe		
— 'Aureus'		6 ft × 6 ft	Small, bright yellow
PHLOMIS			
chrysophylla	Lebanon	3 ft × 3 ft	Broad, khaki-green
PTELIA			
trifoliata Hop Tree	Eastern N.America		
— 'Aurea'		15 ft × 15 ft	Three-lobed; yellowish
RIBES			
alpinum Alpine Currant	Europe		
— 'Aureum'		3 ft × 4 ft	Small yellowish
sanguineum Flowering Currant	Western N.America		
— 'Brocklebankii'		6 ft × 6 ft	Bright yellow
SAMBUCUS			
nigra Common Elder	Europe etc		
— 'Aurea'		8 ft × 8 ft	Yellowish green, brightest in sun
racemosa Red-berried Elder	,,		
— 'Plumosa Aurea'		8 ft × 7 ft	Laciniate; bright yellow
VIBURNUM			
opulus Guelder Rose	Europe, Asia etc		
— 'Aureum'		9 ft × 9 ft	Lobed; yellowish; part shade

Deciduous or Evergreen	Colour of flower	Period of flower	Habit	Special conditions	Propagation
E	White; fruits black	L.Summer	Dense		CL
E	Inconspicuous		,,		CL
D	White, fragrant	Summer	,,	S	CL
E	Yellow	E.Summer	,,	W	CS
D	Small, yellowish, fragrant; fruits green	Summer	Open		CL
D	Inconspicuous; fragrant	Spring	Dense		CL
D	Pink	,,	,,	S	CL
D	White; fruits maroon	Summer	Open		CL
D	Cream; fruits red	,,	,,	S	CL
D	White; fruits red	E.Summer	Dense		CL

SHRUBS (cont.)	Country of origin	Height/ Width	Brief description
WEIGELA 'Looymansii Aurea'	Hybrid	7 ft × 8 ft	Broad; bright yellow; part shade

PERENNIALS

	Country of origin	Height/ Width	Brief description
FILIPENDULA *ulmaria* Meadow Sweet — 'Aurea'	Europe, Asia	2 ft × 1 ft	Pinnate; yellow, part shade
HOSTA *fortunei* — 'Aurea'	Hybrid	2 ft × 2 ft	Broad; green later
'Wogon'	Japan	18 ins × 1 ft	Broad; yellow
HUMULUS *lupulus* Hop Deciduous Twiner 'Aurea'	N.Hemisphere	20 ft × 20 ft	Lobed; bright yellow, green later
MILIUM *effusum* — 'Aureum'	Europe, Britain	2 ft × 1 ft	Narrow; yellow
VALERIANA *phu* — 'Aurea'	Europe, Caucasus	3 ft × 1 ft	Lobed; yellow, green later

Deciduous or Evergreen	Colour of flower	Period of flower	Habit	Special conditions	Propagation
D	Pink	Summer	Dense	S	CL
D	White	Summer	Spreader	S	D
D	Lilac	L.Summer	Clump	S	D
D	,,	,,	,,	S	D
D	Inconspicuous	Summer	Invasive		DR
D	Yellowish	E.Summer	Clump seeds itself	S	DS
D	White	,,	Clump		D

Group 7

White or cream variegated foliage

It is extraordinary that the variegated Plane has not achieved a greater popularity among the trees of this group. I can think of some city squares which, when the fullness of summer's greenery has sunk upon them, would be lightened considerably by this spectacular cream-variegated tree. The variegation is patchy in the leaf which thereby lacks a uniformity over the tree, but it brings a ray of sunshine with it when seen from a distance. Now that we no longer see the cool grey-white greenery of the pretty variegated Elm we must have recourse to another large tree, the variegated Sycamore. This is a very old cultivar, sometimes occurring from seed, and was used in the eighteenth century. It can be very splendid and at a distance takes on the appearance of a pale-leafed tree, the variegation merging into the general tone. The white-edged Sweet Chestnut is rather slow growing, and is prone to reversion to the green; I have yet to see a large tree on which the variegation is not at once apparent. It is left to two Maples to give us the most noticeable variegation: the boldly marked *Acer platanoides* 'Drummondii' and the much quieter tone of the *Acer negundo* form. Both are apt to revert to green. In winter the green twigs of the latter contrast well with the masses of parchment-coloured "keys" which last until spring.

There is no lack of shrubs in this group and their number grows yearly. I think we must give pride of place to the *Aralia* as we did in Group 5. Nothing can compare with a luxuriating specimen, whether just in foliage or with the bounty of flower or fruit. The most popular of white variegated shrubs is undoubtedly the *Cornus*; when the leaves have turned to pink in autumn and have fallen we have a bounty here too, of the plum-crimson twigs. But *Cornus* gives us three others of note, *Cornus mas* 'Variegata', *C. alternifolia* 'Argentea', a fairly dense, tiered bush of fine tinting and, much more dramatic in shape and foliage, *C. controversa* 'Variegata'. The cooler Irish climate seems to suit this best. It may be seen 18 feet high with tier upon tier of flat branches (arranged like those of a prim *Abies*) of half the width. It is rare, costly, and slow as a youngster, and just as we have despaired of the top tablecloth of branches ever making a new leader, one will occur to make the next tier. At times a little help must be given with cane and string; the reason being that this plant is produced by grafting, using side shoots, not leaders.

The *Philadelphus* is best in shade. In fact, as I have intimated elsewhere, all deciduous shrubs produce the greatest amount of white in shade. The *Weigela* is creamy yellow to start with, turning to nearly white; both its growth and colour are preferable to the cultivar in Group 5 and I like it particularly as the pink flowers open from crimson buds in June. A similarly satisfying contrast is found in the *Buddleia* whose rich cream-edged leaves accentuate the crimson-purple flower spikes. For the sake of its lilac-tinted flowers the neat cream-edged *Hibiscus* must be grown in sun. Some lesser plants are the pretty, cool greyish *Kerria* with soft orange flowers in spring: the creeping Blackberry (*Rubus*) is effective in fruit; the much taller *Acanthopanax* has much beauty, especially when bearing its black fruits; the white-edged *Fuchsia* brings some leavening to the usual sober greens of this genus, and is highly attractive when in flower. The form of *Cotoneaster* listed appeals to me very much, particularly when its leaves turn to pink in autumn; so far I have not seen it bearing berries. This leaves us with the white-edged Elder, which is not of great consequence until hung with maroon berries – and then we are worried at the thought of the seedlings which will accrue; they are not likely to perpetuate the variegation.

Pride of place among evergreens must be given to the Hollies; for the sake of its beautiful foliage, elegant growth and red berries *Ilex aquifolium* 'Argenteomarginata' comes first with me, and the weeping variety a close second. They grow happily in sun or shade, though I would give the *Rhamnus* a sheltered position in sun. Its leaf effect is excellent and it has great vigour; the fruits are tiny and seldom of much consequence. It is by no means wind-firm and requires a stout stake or metal pipe for support. Much more tender is the dainty *Azara*. *Pieris japonica* 'Variegata' has pinkish young foliage and flower buds and is a slow grower for lime-free soil, while the variegated *Laurustinus* will thrive even on chalk if in a sheltered position. Next in decreasing size comes the varieties of *Buxus*, *Euonymus* and *Hebe*. The first are excellent in shade, in fact *Buxus sempervirens* 'Argentea' lightens many a dark old-fashioned shrubbery. 'Elegantissima' shows much more variegation but the plant is dense and slow and in this echoes the smallest *Euonymus japonicus* 'Microphyllus Variegatus', an erect, surprising little bush, best suited to our warmer and maritime districts, like the parent species. *E.j.* 'Macrophyllus Albus' is a real beauty for a warm wall, with comparatively large, rounded leaves. The forms of *E. fortunei* are good as short and spreading shrubs but they will also ascend walls and are more or less self-clinging. The large-leafed forms sometimes delight us with intriguing and colourful fruits in autumn.

Hebe × *andersonii* 'Variegata' is by no means hardy; *H.* × *franciscana* 'Variegata' is a little more tolerant of the cold; both have great beauty when producing their spikes of bloom from summer until autumn. It is rather disappointing that the variegated *Pachysandra* is nothing like such a vigorous, colonizing ground-cover as its species in green. We could do with the variegation in sheets under dark shrubs and trees where the normal species is so successful. The variegated Periwinkles *are* vigorous however and charming in spring when decorated with their lilac-blue flowers.

PERENNIALS

Among the herbaceous plants the two beautiful *Phlox* varieties stand out, in sun or shade, and their variegation assorts well with their flower colours. But, though of lesser growth, the several Hostas are extremely valuable and their preference for shade results in superb growth wherever they can be grown, in moist, not wet, soil. I think there is no doubt that *Hosta fortunei* 'Marginato Alba' leads the cultivars; its greyish green leaves, broadly edged with white and grey beneath, are nothing if not spectacular. *H. crispula* – for sheltered places in non-windy gardens – is a splendid plant too, but less of a "good doer" in more exposed gardens than 'Thomas Hogg'. *H. decorata* carries its variegation noticeably down its wide-flanged leaf stalks and is quicker of increase than the others owing to a somewhat stoloniferous rootstock. *H. albomarginata* is very colourful in flower and good with its narrow leaves. The two forms of *H. undulata* bring up the rear, so to speak, with smaller, attractively convoluted leaves and conspicuous cream splashes in the centre; the more variegation, the slower of increase, in fact several forms have been separately named.

Like *Hosta crispula*, *Brunnera macrophylla* 'Variegata' needs shelter otherwise the white areas of the leaves become bruised or browned. It is unusual for a herbaceous plant to put up its fresh leaves in autumn but this is what the *Arum* does. They remain in their arrowhead-shaped creamy-grey striped beauty until the spring when their pale green flowers (Lords and Ladies) appear, followed in summer by spikes of bright orange-red berries. Another excellent plant for winter effect (truly evergreen) is the variegated Gladwin Iris; it likes some shade and looks well with *Tellima grandiflora* 'Purpurea'. Not so *Iris pallida* 'Variegata Alba' which with the *Sisyrinchium* needs sunshine. Their white variegation on grey-green leaves makes a delicate contrast. The *Sisyrinchium* is named after Mrs May Amory in whose garden near Tiverton it originated; it is unfortunately sometimes named simply 'Variegata'. This catalogue will finish with the two variegated Solomon's Seal varieties, of which I prefer that of *Polygonatum falcatum* (often labelled *P. japonicum*), and finally with the moisture lover *Scrophularia aquatica* 'Variegata'. This is a form of a common ditch weed, the Figwort, whose tiny brown flowers, if not picked off, may result in an unwanted crop of green-leafed seedlings.

TREES	Country of origin	Height/ Width	Brief description
ACER			
negundo	N.America		
— 'Variegatum'		30 ft × 20 ft	Pinnate; white edges. Apt to revert if pruned
platanoides Norwegian Maple	Europe, Caucasus		
— 'Drummondii'		50 ft × 20 ft	Palmate; white edges. Apt to revert to green
pseudoplatanus Sycamore	Europe, W.Asia		
— 'Variegatum'		90 ft × 40 ft	Palmate; splashed creamy white
— 'Leopoldii' is similar, leaves flushed pink.			
CASTANEA			
sativa Sweet or Spanish Chestnut	S.Europe		
— 'Albomarginata'		70 ft × 40 ft	Broad, white edges. Apt to revert
LIGUSTRUM			
lucidum	China		
— 'Tricolor'		20 ft × 10 ft	Narrow; edged white, pink when young
PLATANUS			
× *hispanica* London Plane	Hybrid		
— 'Suttneri'		60 ft × 40 ft	Palmate, heavily splashed cream
ULMUS			
procera English Elm			
— 'Argenteo-variegata'		70 ft × 40 ft	Small; white splashed

SHRUBS

ACANTHOPANAX			
sieboldianus	China		
— 'Variegatus'		7 ft × 6 ft	Small, five-lobed; white edges

Deciduous or Evergreen	Colour of flower	Period of flower	Habit	Special conditions	Propagation
D	Inconspicuous; fruits creamy grey	Spring	Open		G
D	Yellow; fruits green	,,	,,		G
D	Yellow; fruits green/red	,,	Dense		GS
D	White; green, spiny fruits	Summer	Open		G
E	White	L.Summer/ Autumn	Dense		CG
D			Open		CG
D			,,		CGS
D	Greenish; fruits black	Summer	Open		CG

SHRUBS (cont.)	Country of origin	Height/ Width	Brief description
ARALIA			
elata	Japan		
— 'Variegata'		8 ft × 8 ft	Bipinnate, large; white edges
AZARA			
microphylla	Chile		
— 'Variegata'		8 ft × 5 ft	Tiny, cream variegated
BUDDLEIA			
davidii	China		
— 'Harlequin'		9 ft × 7 ft	Narrow; cream edges
BUXUS			
sempervirens Box	Europe etc		
— 'Argentea'		6 ft × 6 ft	Tiny; white edges
— 'Elegantissima'		4 ft × 4 ft	Tiny; creamy edges
CLEYERA			
fortunei	Japan	5 ft × 5 ft	Medium, edged cream, touched pink
CORNUS			
alba Red Dogwood	N.E.Asia		
— 'Elegantissima'		8 ft × 10 ft	Medium; irregular white edges. 'Variegata' is inferior
alternifolia	Eastern		
— 'Argentea'	N.America	8 ft × 7 ft	Small; white edges
controversa	Japan,		
— 'Variegata'	China	18 ft × 12 ft	Medium; conspicuously variegated cream
mas Cornelian Cherry	Central & South-		
— 'Variegata'	ern Europe	8 ft × 8 ft	Small; white edges

Deciduous or Evergreen	Colour of flower	Period of flower	Habit	Special conditions	Propagation
D	White; fruits maroon	L.Summer	Open, stout		G
E	Tiny yellow; fragrant	Spring	Open	W	C
D	Spikes of red-violet fragrant	L.Summer	,,		C
E	Inconspicuous; fragrant	Spring	Bushy		CL
E	,,	,,	Very dense, slow		CL
E	Pale yellow; small	L.Summer	Bushy	W	CL
D	White; fruits blue-white	Spring	,,		CL
D	Inconspicuous white	Summer	Dense		CL
D	Cream; fruits black	,,	Striking horizontal branching habit		GL
D	Small, yellow; fruits red	Winter	Dense		CL

SHRUBS (cont.)	Country of origin	Height/ Width	Brief description
COTONEASTER			
horizontalis	W.China		
— 'Variegatus'		2 ft × 8 ft	Tiny; white edges, pink in autumn
EUONYMUS			
fortunei	China		
— 'Emerald Gaiety'		2 ft × 3 ft	Small, grey-green; thin white edges
— 'Silver Queen'		4 ft × 4 ft	Conspicuous cream variegation
— 'Variegatus'		2 ft × 3 ft	Small; irregularly and effectively edged white
japonicus	Japan		
— 'Macrophyllus Albus' ('Latifolius Albomarginatus')		4 ft × 4 ft	Broad; white margins
— 'Microphyllus Variegatus'		3 ft × 2 ft	Tiny; white edges
FUCHSIA			
magellanica	S.America		
— 'Sharpitor'		4 ft × 2 ft	Small; white edges
— 'Variegata'		2 ft × 2 ft	,,
HEBE			
× *andersonii*	Hybrid		
— 'Variegata'		4 ft × 4 ft	Narrow; white edges
× *franciscana*	,,		
— 'Variegata'		3 ft × 3 ft	Narrow; cream edges
HEDERA			
helix 'Little Diamond'		9 ins × 18 ins	**White variegated**
HIBISCUS			
syriacus	E.Asia		
— 'Meehanii'		7 ft × 6 ft	Lobed; white edges

Deciduous or Evergreen	Colour of flower	Period of flower	Habit	Special conditions	Propagation
D	Pinky-white	E.Summer	Fish-bone growth		CL
E	Inconspicuous		Bushy, or will climb		CL
E	Inconspicuous; fruits cream, orange seeds		,,		CL
E	Inconspicuous		,,		CL
E	,,		Lax	W	CL
E	,,		Dense, slow	W	C
D	Blush-white	Summer/ Autumn	Bushy		C
D	Crimson	,,	,,		C
E	Lavender, fading	,,	,,	W	C
E	Lavender-blue	Summer/ Autumn	,,	W	C
E			Dense, ground-cover		CL
D	Lavender	L.Summer	Erect, bushy		C

SHRUBS (cont.)	Country of origin	Height/ Width	Brief description
ILEX			
aquifolium Common Holly	Europe to China		

— 'Argenteomarginata' (broad leaf silver) (female) and its weeping form 'Pendula'; 'Elegantissima' (male), 'Ferox Argentea' (male), 'Handsworth New Silver' (female), 'Silver Milkboy' (male) and 'Silver Queen' (male) are good cultivars

KERRIA			
japonica	China,		
— 'Variegata'	Japan	4 ft × 4 ft	Small; grey green, white edges
PACHYSANDRA			
terminalis	Japan		
— 'Variegata'		1 ft × 1 ft	Small; white edges
PHILADELPHUS			
coronarius	S.E.Europe		
— 'Variegatus'		7 ft × 5 ft	Medium; conspicuous white edges
PIERIS			
japonica	Japan		
— 'Variegata'		4 ft × 3 ft	Small; edged white, pinkish when young
RHAMNUS			
alaternus	Mediterranean		
— 'Argenteovariegata'	Region	10 ft × 9 ft	Small; white edges
RUBUS			
microphyllus A blackberry	Japan		
— 'Variegatus'		2 ft × 5 ft	Pinnate; white edges

Deciduous or Evergreen	Colour of flower	Period of flower	Habit	Special conditions	Propagation
D	Orange	Spring	Bushy		CDL
E	White	,,	Suckering carpeter	S	CD
D	White, fragrant	Summer	Dense	S	C
E	White	Spring	,,	S	CL
E	Inconspicuous; small red fruits		Dense, vigorous	W	CL
D	Pink; black-berries	Summer	Sprawling suckers		CL

SHRUBS (cont.)	Country of origin	Height/ Width	Brief description
SAMBUCUS			
nigra Common Elder	Europe etc		
— 'Albovariegata'		7 ft × 7 ft	Pinnate; white edges
VIBURNUM			
tinus Laurustinus	S.Europe		
— 'Variegatum'	etc	6 ft × 6 ft	Medium; cream variegation
VINCA			
major Periwinkle	Mediterranean Region		
— 'Variegata' ('Elegantissima')		2 ft × 3 ft	Medium; cream edges
minor Lesser Periwinkle	Europe,		
— 'Variegata'	W.Asia	1 ft × 2 ft	Small; white edges
WEIGELA			
praecox	Far East		
— 'Variegata'		6 ft × 6 ft	Narrow; cream edges

CLIMBERS

HEDERA Ivy			
canariensis	Canary		
— 'Variegata'	Islands	Climber	White variegated, large and broad
helix	Europe, Asia Minor etc		

many varieties with white variegation, vigorous climbers

CONIFERS

Although there are several forms with a flecking of white here and there, they do not have much garden value.

Sequoia sempervirens 'Adpressa' ('Albo-spica') has pleasing white tipped shoots and is slow growing; *Chamaecyparis lawsoniana* 'Pygmaea Argentea' slowly makes a dense bulky cone-shaped bush and looks as though a bowl of cream has been poured over it.

Deciduous or Evergreen	Colour of flower	Period of flower	Habit	Special conditions	Propagation
D	White; fruits maroon	Summer	Bushy		C
E	White	Spring	,,	W	CL
E	Lilac	,,	Sprawling		CL
E	White or lavender-blue	,,	,,		CL
D	Pink	Summer	Dense		CL
E	Creamy	Autumn	Vigorous	W	CL

PERENNIALS	Country of origin	Height/ Width	Brief description
ACORUS			
calamus Sweet Flag	Europe		
— 'Variegatus'		3 ft × 1 ft	Grassy; white striped
ARUM			
italicum Lords and Ladies	Europe etc		
— 'Pictum' (of gardens)		18 ins × 1 ft	Hastate; marbled with grey
BRUNNERA			
macrophylla	W.Caucasus		
— 'Langtrees'		18 ins × 2 ft	Rounded; spotted with silver
— 'Variegata'		18 ins × 2 ft	Rounded; particoloured with white
HOSTA			
albomarginata	Japan	20 ins × 15 ins	Narrow; edged cream
crispula	,,	2½ ft × 2 ft	Broad; edges white, wavy
decorata	,,	2 ft × 18 ins	Broad; white edge
fortunei	,,		
— 'Marginata Alba'		2½ ft × 2 ft	Broad; grey green; broad white edges
helonioides	,,		
— 'Albo Picta'		18 ins × 1 ft	Narrow; white edged
'Thomas Hogg'		2 ft × 20 ins	Broad; white edges
undulata	,,	18 ins × 1 ft	Curly; white striped
— *univittata*		2 ft × 18 ins	Curly; white central stripe
IRIS			
foetidissima Gladwin, Stinking Iris	W.Europe		
— 'Variegata'		2 ft × 18 ins	White striped
pallida	Europe		
— 'Variegata Alba'		2½ ft × 1 ft	Grey; white striped
PHLOX			
paniculata	Eastern N.America		
— 'Harlequin'		4 ft × 2 ft	Narrow; white edges
— 'Norah Leigh'		3 ft × 2 ft	,,

Deciduous or Evergreen	Colour of flower	Period of flower	Habit	Special conditions	Propagation
D	Inconspicuous		Waterside 'rush'	M	D
D	Pale green; fruits red	Spring	Clump		D
D	Blue	,,	,,	S	D
D	,,	,,	,,	S	D
D	Lilac	L.Summer	,,	S	D
D	Pale lilac	Summer	,,	S	D
D	Dark lilac	,,	,,	S	D
D	Lilac	L.Summer	,,	S	D
D	Lilac	,,	,,	S	D
D	,,	,,	,,	S	D
D	,,	,,	,,	S	D
D	,,	,,	,,	S	D
E	Seldom produced		,,	S	D
D	Lavender-blue	E.Summer	,,		D
D	Purple	L.Summer	,,		D
D	Pale lilac	,,	,,		D

PERENNIALS (cont.)	Country of origin	Height/ Width	Brief description
POLYGONATUM			
falcatum (P. *japonicum* of gardens)	Japan		
— 'Variegatum'		3 ft × 2 ft	Leaves finely edged pink and white
× *hybridum* Solomon's Seal			
— 'Variegatum'		2 ft × 18 ins	Striped with cream
SCROPHULARIA			
aquatica	Europe		
— 'Variegata'		3 ft × 2 ft	Medium; heavily variegated cream
SISYRINCHIUM			
striatum	Chile		
— 'Aunt May'		2 ft × 1 ft	Grey; striped white

Deciduous or Evergreen	Colour of flower	Period of flower	Habit	Special conditions	Propagation
D	White	E.Summer	Clump	S	D
D	,,	,,	,,	S	D
D	Brown; pick off seed stems	Summer	,,	M	CD
E	Straw colour; fruits green	,,	,,		D

Group 8

Grey and glaucous leaves

TREES AND SHRUBS

Without exception all these plants give their best colouring in full sun. This is understandable from the fact that surfaces of leaves are covered with pubescence (woolliness or silkiness) or wax (glaucous) as a shield against the sun's rays. This means that for a light effect in shade we must turn to white variegated plants and *Rosa glauca*, which see below and in Group 9. In the garden the value of glaucous foliage is different from the downy or pubescent; though they will both augment pastel-tinted groupings, I find glaucous leaves give a generally more blue effect, and the pubescent ones – silvery, silky, woolly – tend to verge towards grey or even white in strong light during a dry summer. In addition to all these plants loving sun, they will thrive in dry positions and all appreciate well-drained soil. I make it a rule not to plant or transplant woolly or grey foliage plants until the spring. For a dry rooty position in full sun in front of a tree they have no equal for general furnishing.

There are few trees of this tint. The brightest in bark and foliage for really warm parts of the country is *Eucalyptus coccifera*. With the light shining on it the hardier and much bigger *E. gunnii* is useful but unless pollarded – to get plenty of young leaves – it is a dull blue green rather than conspicuously grey, except at the tips of the shoots. The White Poplar is another big tree with conspicuous white undersurfaces to the leaves, revealed by the breeze. The Weeping Silver Pear is discussed in Group 12; its relative *Pyrus elaeagrifolia* is much less well known, taller, less grey and useful where a tree of middle height is needed. Leaving *Salix exigua* until we come to the shrubs, this leaves *S. alba* 'Sericea', which again is of medium height and silvery silky – a delight.

Most of the grey shrubs are small in growth. A few larger ones include *Buddleia fallowiana* and its invaluable white variety; unfortunately both are liable to be killed to the ground in cold districts, but the flowers, continuously borne from summer to autumn, raise them well above other buddleias. One of the largest glaucous shrubs is *Berberis temolaica*; the pale yellow flowers make a delightful contrast against the comparatively large leaves. *B. dictyophylla* combines grey leaves with grey twigs and when both leaves and berries turn to red in autumn it is a remarkable sight. Of very large size is the grey-white *Elaeagnus angustifolia*; while *E. commutata (E. argentea)* is a low glaucous shrub. I always think that when it is in the full beauty of its scaly-silvery young foliage, *E. macrophylla* is a superlative evergreen, but it does not thrive in cold heavy soils and is not above suspicion in hardiness. Of considerable height, too, is the Sea Buckthorn (*Hippophaë*) which seems to be successful in any soil and situation. One male bush is needed to fertilize six or so females which are very showy in autumn from the orange berries thickly studding the shoots among the grey leaves. The sexes can be distinguished in the winter from the shape of the flower buds; the males are knobbly and large, the females slim and small.

Salix exigua will make a small tree but it is of suckering habit and I think is best kept to about eye-level when the silvery silky, very narrow foliage glints in the sun. It is a remarkable plant and is not dependent upon a moist soil for its wellbeing. Of the other willows I have selected I specially recommend the *S. lanata* 'Stuartii' for its bold rounded foliage and compact low habit, and *S. repens argentea* for its graceful, nearly prostrate growth. With rather the metallic grey of *Elaeagnus commutata* is *Atriplex halimus*, a neglected shrub for poor soils, while for warm gardens there is *Leptospermum lanigerum*, combining white flowers with silvery leafage.

It would be too space-taking to browse through all the remaining short-growing shrubs in the Group. *Senecio* 'Sunshine' (better known, though erroneously, as *S. greyi* or *S. laxifolius*) needs no introduction from me, nor the admirable glaucous dwarf hebes; the santolinas and lavenders, helianthemums, salvias and potentillas. Less well known is the near-hardy *Artemisia* 'Powis Castle'; the tender *Cistus albidus* and *Teucrium*; warmth-loving species of *Caryopteris*; *Halimium* species, *Ruta*; olearias, *Helichrysum* and the like which give so much for so little trouble. For lime-free soil *Erica tetralix* 'Alba Mollis' and the two variants of *Calluna* give a new note to the heather garden.

There are some superlative glaucous-leafed rhododendrons, the best being in the Cinnabarina Subsection, headed by *R. cinnabarinum* itself. The most strikingly glaucous is *R. concatenans*, a species with orange-yellow tubular flowers; in part shade or full exposure its foliage in summer will astonish with its pale blue-grey. The little low-growing *R. lepidostylum* has narrow leaves edged with conspicuous hairs. The leaves are of glaucous pale green contrasting charmingly with the small pale yellow flowers. Quite startling in its young foliage is Hooker's form of *R. campanulatum aeruginosum*; in this the young foliage is of a brilliant verdigris-blue. The flowers are lilac. These are all hardy types but need woodland conditions.

Mentioned above was *Rosa glauca*, so long known to us gardeners as *R. rubrifolia*. This species has the special value of having grey leaves in shade, but if it is grown in the sun qualifies for Group 9. The other roses give a lovely cool effect with their pale grey-green leaves and white flowers; they are best in sun. Likewise for full sun and best treated as a herbaceous plant is the superlative new plant *Romneya* 'White Cloud'; the comparatively large glaucous leaves are fully complemented by the long succession of great white poppy-flowers. Among greyish climbers I know of nothing so satisfactory as *Hedera helix* 'Glacier', though it is really variegated.

Of grey-green, glaucous and silvery blue-green conifers there are many. As intimated in Group 6, they form a subject for special study; one has to get to know both the characters of the varieties and their uses in the garden.

PERENNIALS

Among the many herbaceous perennials the Seakale is outstanding (*Crambe maritima*); its great lobed convoluted leaves are what gladdens the eye, while the palate has the delectation of the young forced foliage, or, indeed, the young flower buds. Some buds should be left for their floral beauty and the charm of the glaucous seed-pods. This is a plant for full sun, in rough soil, whereas I need not caution you to give *Hosta sieboldiana* a cool spot in soil full of humus. Its great leaves, when it is well suited, are nearly a foot long and wide, whereas that other good, neglected, and seldom-recognized plant *Hosta fortunei hyacinthina* is better in flower though smaller in leaf. The leaves of glaucous hue have a tiny margin of a paler tint, as if a pale blue thread was close round them. The hybrids of *H. tardiflora*, known by the group name of *H. × tardiana*, are as yet very scarce but are likely to become favourites in smaller gardens; they include 'Halcyon', 'Buckshaw Blue', 'Hadspen Blue' and 'Harmony'. Other good glaucous leaves are *Kniphofia caulescens* (imperturbably hardy, unlike other large species and hybrids); *Iris pallida dalmatica* whose leaves remain in beauty until autumn; the unusual *Rudbeckia maxima*, a moisture lover; *Othonnopsis, Sedum, Sisyrinchium, Eryngium maritimum* and *Sanguisorba*.

Very woolly leaves are found in *Hieracium villosum* and *Salvia argentea* (beware slugs and wet in winter). The main mass of silvery silky or pubescent plants are found among the artemisias – and there are some really good plants of divergent beauty in this genus – achilleas, *Lychnis, Mertensia, Potentilla, Scabiosa, Veronica* and *Alyssum. Alyssum saxatile* makes such a display of yellow in spring that we are apt to forget its value as a grey plant. If its yellow is too bright for you I suggest trying the light lemon-yellow of 'Citrinum' ('Silver Queen') or the warm buttery tint of 'Dudley Neville'. The most prolific and invasive carpeter is *Cerastium tomentosum* or 'Snow in Summer'; for small areas in smaller gardens a more compact, even more silvery plant is *C. biebersteinii*. Apart from *Rudbeckia maxima*, mentioned above, another plant that flags in drought is *Anaphalis triplinervis*; it is useful to bear this in mind for moister parts of the garden where grey is needed but which might not suit other plants; plants of similar preferences are *Lysimachia ephemerum* and the *Pulmonaria*. Extra grey-leafed forms of *P. saccharata* (*P. picta*), sometimes labelled 'Margery Fish', are most useful for shady places; after their spring flowering they remain in good foliage until winter. Try the filigree of *Dicentra oregona* with them. For the very front of the border or bed is a whole range of hardy pinks, most with good glaucous foliage, particularly 'Bat's Double Red' and 'White Ladies'; these can grow alongside the almost prostrate *Artemisia stelleriana* and *Anthemis cupaniana*. All these, pinks included, need pulling apart and replanting from time to time.

I should have mentioned those splendid giants the species of *Cynara* before. They are magnificent in their deeply cut silvery foliage; the flowers are equally magnificent but the great height of the stems makes them rather unmanageable. They are best cut off unless intended for the cooking pot. Likewise I always remove promptly the spent flower stems of *Thalictrum speciosissimum* – which used to be known as *T. flavum glaucum* – leaving just the elegant grey leaves for the rest of the summer.

TREES	Country of origin	Height/ Width	Brief description
EUCALYPTUS			
coccifera	Tasmania	40 ft × 15 ft	Rounded; grey
gunnii	,,	100 ft × 40 ft	Rounded; grey-green
POPULUS			
alba White Poplar	Eurasia, N.Africa	60 ft × 40 ft	Lobed; grey-white beneath
PYRUS			
elaeagrifolia	S.E.Europe	20 ft × 10 ft	Narrow; grey-green
salicifolia	Caucasus		
— 'Pendula'		15 ft × 15 ft	Narrow; grey
SALIX			
alba White Willow	Europe etc		
— 'Sericea' ('Argentea')		50 ft × 15 ft	Silvery
exigua, see below			

SHRUBS

ARTEMISIA			
arborescens	S.Europe	3 ft × 3 ft	Laciniate; silvery
'Powis Castle'	Hybrid	3 ft × 5 ft	,,
tridentata	W.USA	3 ft × 3 ft	Small; grey
ATRIPLEX			
halimus Tree Purslane	S.Europe	6 ft × 4 ft	Small; silvery
BERBERIS			
dictyophylla	W.China	,,	Small; grey, also stems; autumn colour
temolaica	S.E.Tibet	10 ft × 10 ft	Blue-green
BUDDLEIA			
crispa	W.India	6 ft × 6 ft	Lobed, greyish
fallowiana	China	,,	Grey green, woolly
— 'Alba'		,,	,,

Deciduous or Evergreen	Colour of flower	Period of flower	Habit	Special conditions	Propagation
E	White; fruits glaucous	Summer	Erect, compact	W	S
E	White	Autumn	Erect, rounded	W	S
D	Green catkins	Spring	Graceful		C
D	White; fruits green	,,	,,		G
D	,,	,,	Weeping		G
D	Yellow catkins	,,	Erect, compact		C
E	Grey	Summer	Lax bush	W	C
E	,,	,,	,,	W	C
D	,,	,,	,,		C
D	Silvery grey	Inconspi- cuous	Erect	W	CS
D	Yellow; fruits red	Spring	Arching		C
D	,,	,,	Erect, arching		C
D	Lavender-blue	L.Summer	Open	W	C
D	,,	Summer/ Autumn	Compact	W	C
D	White	,,	,,	W	C

SHRUBS (cont.)	Country of origin	Height/ Width	Brief description
CALLUNA Ling, Heather			
vulgaris Heather, Ling	Europe, Asia Minor		
— 'Silver Queen'		18 ins × 2 ft	Minute silvery grey
— *tomentosa*		,,	Minute grey-green
CARYOPTERIS			
× *clandonensis*	Hybrid	2–3 ft × 2 ft	Lobed, grey-green
'Arthur Simmonds' is the form first named; 'Ferndown' and 'Heavenly Blue' are of subsequent naming			
incana (C. mastacanthus, C. tangutica)	Far East	4 ft × 3 ft	Lobed, grey-green
CISTUS			
albidus	S.W.Europe, N.Africa	5 ft × 4ft	Small, grey, woolly
CONVOLVULUS			
cneorum	S.E.Europe	18 ins × 18 ins	Small, silvery
CYTISUS			
battandieri	Morocco	15 ft × 12 ft	Three-lobed, silvery
ELAEAGNUS			
angustifolia Oleaster	Temperate Asia	18 ft × 18 ft	Narrow, grey-white, woolly white stems
commutata	N.America	5 ft × 3 ft	Narrow, silvery
macrophylla	Far East	8 ft × 10 ft	Broad, silvery above when young, silvery beneath
ERICA			
tetralix Cross Leafed Heath	Europe		
— 'Alba Mollis'		10 ins × 1 ft	Minute, grey-green
HALIMIUM			
atriplicifolium	Spain	6 ft × 4 ft	Small, scaly grey

Deciduous or Evergreen	Colour of flower	Period of flower	Habit	Special conditions	Propagation
E	Lilac-pink	L.Summer	Dense carpeter		CL
E	,,	,,	,,		CL
D	Lavender-blue; fruits glaucous	,,	Dense	W	C
D	Lavender-blue	,,	,,	W	C
E	Light mauve	Summer	,,	W	C
E	White; pinkish in bud	,,	,,	W	C
E	Yellow, fragrant	E.Summer	,,		CS
D	Minute, yellow, fragrant; fruits tiny yellowish	,,	,,		S
D	Silvery yellow, fragrant; fruits silvery	,,	Suckering, open		DS
E	Cream, fragrant	Autumn	Lax	W	CL
E	White	Summer	Dense		CL
E	Yellow	E.Summer	Open	W	CS

SHRUBS (cont.)	Country of origin	Height/ Width	Brief description
HALIMIUM (cont.)			
halimifolium	Mediterranean Region	4 ft × 4 ft	Narrow, grey green, woolly
lasianthum (*H. formosum*)	Spain, Portugal	3 ft × 4 ft	,,
ocymoides (*Helianthemum algarvense*)	,,	2 ft × 3 ft	Small, grey-green, woolly
HALIMODENDRON			
halodendron (*H. argenteum*)	Europe Asia	6 ft × 4 ft	Small, scaly grey
HEBE			
albicans	New Zealand	18 ins × 2 ft	Small, glaucous
carnosula	,,	18 ins × 3 ft	,,
colensoi 'Glauca'	,,	2 ft × 2 ft	,,
glaucophylla (*H. darwiniana*)	,,	3 ft × 3 ft	,,
pinguifolia 'Pagei'	,,	1 ft × 2 ft	Small, pale, glaucous
HELIANTHEMUM Sun Rose	Hybrids	1 ft × 2–3 ft	Small, grey green woolly

'The Bride' white, 'Rhodanthe Carneum' light pink, 'Mrs Croft' pink, 'Wisley Primrose' ('Praecox') yellow, are some of the best cultivars with greyish foliage

HELICHRYSUM			
splendidum (*H. triliniatum, H. alveolatum*)	S.Africa	3 ft × 3 ft	White, woolly
HIPPOPHAË Sea Buckthorn			
rhamnoides	Europe, Asia	10 ft × 8 ft	Narrow, scaly grey-green
LAVANDULA Lavender			
angustifolia — 'Hidcote'	Mediterranean Region	18 ins × 18 ins	Small, grey, woolly
Dutch (*L. vera* of gardens)	Hybrid	2 ft × 4 ft	,,
lanata (some forms are hardy)	Spain	3 ft × 3 ft	Narrow, white-woolly

The foliage of all lavenders is of greyish green; the above three are the most grey

Deciduous or Evergreen	Colour of flower	Period of flower	Habit	Special conditions	Propagation
E	Yellow	E.Summer	Dense	W	CS
E	,,	,,	,,	W	CS
E	,,	,,	,,	W	CS
D	Tiny, purplish pink	Summer	Open	W	CS
E	White, buds pinkish	,,	Dense		CL
E	White	,,	Prostrate		CL
E	,,	,,	Dense		CL
E	,,	,,	,,		CL
E	,,	,,	Carpeter		CL
E		E.Summer	,,		CL
E	Yellow	Summer/ Autumn	Dense	W	C
D	Inconspicuous; fruits orange on female plants		Open, suckering		S
E	Purple	Summer	Dense		CS
E	Light lavender	Summer/ Autumn	,,		C
E	Dark purple, small	Summer	,,	W	CS

SHRUBS (cont.)	Country of origin	Height/ Width	Brief description
LEPTOSPERMUM			
lanigerum	Australia,	6 ft × 5 ft	Tiny, silvery
(*L. pubescens*)	Tasmania		
OLEARIA			
mollis (of gardens)	Hybrid	2 ft × 2 ft	Small, grey-woolly
moschata	New Zealand	4 ft × 3 ft	,,
PEROVSKIA			
atriplicifolia	Asia	,,	Grey-green, woolly small; Grey-white stems

—'Blue Spire' is a desirable form; 'Blue Haze' is rather less grey, with less incised leaves

POTENTILLA			
'Beesii' (*P. nana argentea*)	Hybrid	2 ft × 2 ft	Small, silvery hairy
'Manchu' (*P. mandschurica* of gardens)	,,	1 ft × 3 ft	Small, grey-woolly
'Vilmoriniana' (of gardens)	,,	4 ft × 2 ft	Small, silvery grey
RHODODENDRON			
campanulatum aeruginosum	Bhutan, Sikkim	5 ft × 5 ft	Rounded, verdigris-blue
concatenans	Tibet	5 ft × 5 ft	Rounded, glaucous
lepidostylum	Burmah	18 ins × 3 ft	Narrow, glaucous

ROMNEYA   Californian Poppy
coulteri and *R. trichocalyx*, and the garden hybrid between them, all have glaucous leaves and large white flowers; they usually die to ground level in winter. The most conspicuous hybrid with larger glaucous leaves is

'White Cloud'	Hybrid	5 ft × 5 ft	Lobed, glaucous
ROSA			
beggeriana	W.Asia, China	8 ft × 8 ft	Pinnate, glaucous
fedtschenkoana	Turkestan	,,	Pinnate, glaucous; pinkish young shoots
glauca (R. rubrifolia)	Europe	8 ft × 6 ft	Glaucous in shade
murieliae	W.Asia, China	8 ft × 8 ft	Pinnate, glaucous
RUTA			
graveolens Rue	S.E.Europe		
— 'Jackman's Blue'		2 ft × 2 ft	Tiny, glaucous blue-green

Deciduous or Evergreen	Colour of flower	Period of flower	Habit	Special conditions	Propagation
E	White	Summer	Open	W	CS
E	,,	,,	Dense	W	CS
E	,,	,,	,,	W	CS
D	Lavender-blue	L.Summer	Erect		CD
D	Bright yellow	E.Summer/ Autumn	Dense		CL
D	White	,,	Prostrate		CL
D	Pale sulphur	Summer/ Autumn	Dense		C
E	Lilac	E.Summer	,,		CL
E	Orange	,,	,,		CL
E	Yellow	Summer	,,		CL
D	White	Summer/ Autumn	Erect		DR
D	,,	,,	Open		CG
D	,,	,,	,,		CDG Suckers
D	Pink; fruits red	E.Summer	,,		S
D	White	Summer/ Autumn	,,		CDG
E	Yellowish	Summer	Dense		CDL

SHRUBS (cont.)	Country of origin	Height/ Width	Brief description
SALIX Willow			
exigua Coyote Willow	Western N.America	9 ft × 5 ft	Narrow, silvery, hairy
lanata Woolly Willow	N.Europe, N.Asia	3 ft × 3 ft	Small, grey, woolly
— 'Stuartii'		2 ft × 3 ft	Broad, grey, woolly
lapponum	Europe, Siberia	3 ft × 4 ft	Small, grey, woolly
repens argentea	Europe, N.Asia	2 ft × 6 ft	Small, silvery, woolly
SALVIA Sage			
lavandulifolia	Spain	2 ft × 3 ft	Small, grey, woolly
officinalis	S.Europe		
— 'English Broad Leaf'		2 ft × 4 ft	Medium, grey, woolly
SANTOLINA Cotton Lavender, Lavender Cotton			
chamaecyparissus (*S. incana*)	Mediterranean Region	18 ins × 2 ft	Pinnate, tiny; white-woolly
'Nana', a useful dwarf variety, 1 ft × 1 ft			
pinnata	S.Italy		
— *neopolitana*		2 ft × 2 ft	Pinnate, tiny; very white-woolly
— 'Edward Bowles'		2 ft × 2 ft	Pinnate, tiny; grey-green
— 'Sulphurea'		2 ft × 2 ft	,,
SENECIO			
'Sunshine' (*S. greyi*, *S. laxifolius* of gardens)	Hybrid	4 ft × 6 ft	Broad, grey-green; stems white-woolly
leucostachys	Patagonia	2 ft × 3 ft	Divided; silvery white-woolly
SIBIRAEA (Spiraea)			
laevigata	S.Europe, Russia	4 ft × 5 ft	Medium, glaucous
TEUCRIUM			
fruticans Shrubby Germander	S.Europe, N.Africa	5 ft × 5 ft	Small grey-green; stems white

Deciduous or Evergreen	Colour of flower	Period of flower	Habit	Special conditions	Propagation
D	Catkins	Spring	Open, suckers		CD
D	,,	,,	Dense		CS
D	,,	,,	,,		CL
D	,,	,,	,,		CL
D	,,	,,	Prostrate		CL
E	Lavender-blue	Summer	Spreading		CL
E	,,	,,	,,		CL
E	Yellow buttons	,,	Dense		CD
E	Sulphur yellow	,,	,,		CD
E	Creamy-white	,,	,,		CD
E	Primrose yellow	,,	,,		CD
E	Bright yellow	E.Summer	,,		C
E	Pale yellow	Summer	Lax	W	C
D	White, small	E.Summer	,,		CL
D	Lavender-blue	Summer/ Autumn	Bushy	W	C

CLIMBER	Country of origin	Height/ Width	Brief description
LONICERA	Honeysuckle, climber for warm walls		
splendida		12 ft × 10 ft	Glaucous

CONIFERS

There are many conifers with grey or bluish colouring. Some of the most noteworthy and obtainable are the following, starting with the largest:

Abies concolor is always a grey tone but special forms have been named for their vivid tints.

Abies procera 'Glauca'. Achieves great height.

Cedrus atlantica 'Glauca'. A free-growing tree, faster but of shorter life than the Lebanon Cedar.

Chamaecyparis lawsoniana. The most voluminous and luxuriant is 'Triomf van Boskoop'; 'Pembury Blue' is a remarkable light grey-blue shade; 'Columnaris' is a good grey blue, narrow while young.

Chamaecyparis pisifera 'Squarrosa' is the most feathery of all conifers and displays a good contrast in its rich brown stems.

C.p. 'Boulevard' is a remarkable bluish colouring, and at present we cannot tell to what height it will grow. Deteriorates with age.

Cupressus glabra 'Pyramidalis' (*C. arizonica* 'Conica' of gardens) is a bright colour, with feathery narrow growth and quick growing.

C. lusitanica is mentioned in Group 12.

The junipers are many, from the slim outline of *Juniperus virginiana* 'Skyrocket' (see Group 13) to completely prostrate forms of *J. horizontalis*.

J. horizontalis excels in completely prostrate forms which, in full exposure, develop their brightest glaucous tints, such as 'Bar harbor'and 'Wilton'; 'Douglasii' turns to violet blue in winter; 'Hughes' is a brilliant steel-grey, almost silver white. They all make admirable ground-cover.

J. × media 'Pfitzeriana Glauca' adds a pleasant change to the over-planted 'Pfitzeriana'.

J. squamata 'Meyeri', though often sold as a dwarf, will achieve 10 feet or more or be bulky as well.

Juniperus virginiana 'Glauca' is narrowly erect while 'Grey Owl' is plumose and semi-prostrate or at least low growing; it is probably a hybrid. 'Blue Cloud' is equally glaucous and of flatter growth.

Picea pungens varies from dull grey green to a remarkable glaucous blue tint. Many forms have been named, such as 'Kosteri', 'Moerheimii', 'Endtz', 'Spekii', 'Erich Frahm', 'Thomsen'.

Pinus parviflora in its most glaucous forms is remarkable for its "Japanesque" habit, and for the freedom with which it bears lasting cones at an early age. It is perhaps the best pine for small gardens in its usual bushy type; some forms are more upright.

Pinus wallichiana. An informal tree with long drooping needles and cones.

Deciduous or Evergreen	Colour of flower	Period of flower	Habit	Special conditions	Propagation
D	Pinky-cream	Summer		W	C

PERENNIALS	Country of origin	Height/ Width	Brief description
ACHILLEA			
clypeolata of gardens	Hybrid	18 ins × 1 ft	Pinnate, feathery, white-woolly
'Moonshine'	,,	2 ft × 18 ins	Pinnate, feathery, grey-green
× *taygetea* of gardens	,,	,,	,,
grandifolia	S.E.Europe, Asia Minor	3 ft × 2 ft	Pinnatisect, silvery woolly
ALYSSUM			
saxatile	Europe	10 ins × 18 ins	Small, narrow, grey
ANAPHALIS			
triplinervis	Himalaya	15 ins × 2 ft	Broad, grey-green
ANTHEMIS			
cupaniana	Italy	1 ft × 3 ft	Deeply cut, silvery grey
ARTEMISIA			
absinthium	Europe		
— 'Lambrook Silver'		3 ft × 2 ft	Much divided, silvery grey
canescens (of gardens)		18 ins × 1 ft	Lacy, silvery grey
ludoviciana	N.America	4 ft × 2 ft	Silvery grey-white
— *latiloba*		2 ft × 2 ft	Silvery broad
— 'Silver Queen'		,,	Silvery grey-white, jagged
stelleriana	N.E.Asia, Eastern N.America	1 ft × 3 ft	Divided, silvery grey-white
— 'Mori's Form'		9 ins × 2 ft	Extra grey-white
valesiaca	S.Europe	18 ins × 18 ins	Lacy, silvery grey
BALLOTA			
pseudodictamnus	Crete etc	1 ft × 2 ft	Grey, woolly, small
CERASTIUM Snow in Summer			
biebersteinii	Crimea	6 ins × 1 ft	Silvery white
tomentosum	S. & E.Europe	9 ins × 2 ft	Silvery grey, small

Deciduous or Evergreen	Colour of flower	Period of flower	Habit	Special conditions	Propagation
D	Yellow	Summer	Clump		D
D	Sulphur-yellow	,,	,,		D
D	Sulphur-primrose	,,	,,		D
D	White	,,	,,		CDS
E	Yellow; primrose in "Citrinum" (Silver Queen)	Spring	Spreader		CS
D	White	L.Summer	Clump		D
	,,	E.Summer some later	Lax, spreader		DL
E	Grey	Summer	Bushy		CD
D	,,	,,	Dense		CD
D	,,	,,	Runner		D
D	,,	,,	,,		D
D	,,	,,	,,		D
D	,,	,,	Prostrate		CDL
D	,,	,,	,,		CDL
D	,,	,,	Dense		CD
D	Pale mauve, inconspicuous	,,	Bushy		CS
E	White	,,	Spreading		CD
E	,,	E.Summer	Carpeter, invasive		D

PERENNIALS (cont.)	Country of origin	Height/ Width	Brief description
CRAMBE Seakale			
maritima	Europe	2 ft × 3 ft	Large, curved and lobed; glaucous grey-white
CYNARA			
cardunculus	,,	6 ft × 4 ft	Deeply cut, silvery
Cardoon			white-woolly
scolymus Globe	,,	,,	Deeply cut, grey
Artichoke			woolly
DIANTHUS Pink, Carnation. Almost all kinds have good glaucous foliage			
DICENTRA			
oregona	Oregon	1 ft × 18 ins	Dainty filigree
ECHINOPS			
tournefortii	E.Mediter- ranean Region	5 ft × 2 ft	Prickly, white and grey-green
ERYNGIUM			
maritimum Sea	Europe	1 ft × 1 ft	Prickly, glaucous
Holly			grey
HIERACIUM			
lanatum	,,	2 ft × 1 ft	Broad, white-woolly
villosum	,,	1 ft × 1 ft	Broad, grey-woolly
HOSTA			
fortunei	Japan		
— *hyacinthina*		2½ ft × 2 ft	Broad, grey-green
sieboldiana	Japan	2½ ft × 2 ft	Broad, blue grey
— *elegans*		2½ ft × 2 ft	Broad, rounded blue-grey
tokudama	,,	18 ins × 18 ins	Broad, cupped, blue-grey
× *tardiana*	Hybrids	1 ft × 1 ft	

— 'Buckshaw Blue', 'Hadspen Blue', 'Harmony', 'Halcyon' are comparatively new, very glaucous blue named forms of this hybrid

IRIS			
pallida dalmatica	Europe	4 ft × 18 ins	Narrow, glaucous
KNIPHOFIA			
caulescens	S.Africa	4 ft × 2 ft	,,

Deciduous or Evergreen	Colour of flower	Period of flower	Habit	Special conditions	Propagation
D	White	E.Summer	Spreader		DR
D	Lavender-blue	Summer	Clump		D
D	,,	,,	,,		D
D	Pink	Spring/ Summer	Spreader	S	D
D	White	Summer	Clump		SR
D	Blue	,,	,,		SR
D	Yellow	,,	,,		S
D	,,	,,	,,		S
D	Lilac	L.Summer	,,	S	D
D	Lilac–white	Summer	Clump	S	DS
D	,,	,,	,,	S	DS
D	,,	,,	,,	S	DS
E	Lavender-blue	E.Summer	,,		D
D	Red to creamy	Autumn	,,		D

PERENNIALS (cont.)	Country of origin	Height/ Width	Brief description
LAMIUM			
maculatum	Europe		
— 'White Nancy'		6 ins × 18 ins	Silvery
LYCHNIS			
coronaria	S.Europe		
— 'Abbotswood Rose'	Hybrid	2½ ft × 2 ft	Grey-woolly
flos-jovis	Europe	18 ins × 18 ins	,,
LYSIMACHIA			
ephemerum	S.W.Europe	3 ft × 1 ft	Glaucous green
MERTENSIA			
ciliata	Rocky Mountains	2 ft × 1 ft	Rounded, glaucous green
— 'Blue Drop' is a popular selection			
virginica Virginian Cowslip (for spring display only)	Virginia	18 ins × 1 ft	Rounded, glaucous
OTHONNOPSIS			
cheirifolia	N.Africa	8 ins × 1 ft	Glaucous
POTENTILLA			
argyrophylla	Kashmir, Nepal	18 ins × 2 ft	Three-lobed, silvery
atrosanguinea	Himalaya	,,	,,
PULMONARIA Lungwort			
saccharata (P. picta)	Europe	1 ft × 2 ft	Some extra grey forms
RUDBECKIA			
maxima	Texas	4 ft × 2 ft	Large, glaucous
SALVIA			
argentea	E.Mediterranean Region	3 ft × 2 ft	Large, very woolly, grey-white
SANGUISORBA			
obtusa	Japan	4 ft × 2 ft	Pinnate, grey-green
SCABIOSA			
graminifolia	S.Europe	18 ins × 18 ins	Very narrow, silvery grey

Deciduous or Evergreen	Colour of flower	Period of flower	Habit	Special conditions	Propagation
E	White	Summer	Carpeter		D
D	Strong magenta-crimson	E.Summer	Clump		D
D	Pink	,,	,,		DS
D	Grey-white	Summer	,,		DS
D	Light blue	E.Summer	,,		DRS
D	,,	Spring	,,		DRS
E	Yellow	Summer	Carpeter		D
D	,,	E.Summer	Clump		DS
D	Red	,,	,,		DS
E	Blue/pink	E.Spring	,,		D
D	Yellow, black centre	L.Summer	,,	M	DS
E	White	Summer	,,		S
D	Pink spikes	,,	,,		D
D	Lilac	All Summer	,,		CDS

PERENNIALS (cont.)	Country of origin	Height/ Width	Brief description
SEDUM			
'Autumn Joy'	Hybrid	2½ ft × 2½ ft	Broad, toothed, glaucous
spectabile	China	18 ins × 18 ins	Broad, pale, glaucous
SENECIO			
cineraria	S.Europe	2 ft × 2 ft	Silvery woolly filigree
(Cineraria maritima)			
SISYRINCHIUM			
striatum	Chile	2 ft × 9 ins	Sword-like, grey-green
STACHYS Lamb's Ears			
olympica (S. lanata,	Caucasus to	2 ft × 2 ft	Grey-white woolly
S. byzantina)	Persia		
— 'Cotton Boll'		2 ft × 2 ft	,,
— 'Silver Carpet'		6 ins × 2 ft	,,
THALICTRUM			
speciosissimum	Spain, N.W.Africa	6 ft × 2 ft	Much divided, glaucous grey
VERONICA			
incana	Russia	1 ft × 1 ft	Small, silvery grey
— 'Wendy' is a good flowering plant but less grey in leaf			
ZAUSCHNERIA			
cana	California	18 ins × 18 ins	Small, grey

Deciduous or Evergreen	Colour of flower	Period of flower	Habit	Special conditions	Propagation
D	Coppery pink/red	Autumn	Clump		CD
D	Pink	L.Summer	,,		CD
E	Grey	,,	,,	W	CDS
E	Straw yellow	Summer	,,		DS
E	Woolly grey spikes, small magenta flowers	,,	Spreader		D
E	Woolly grey spikes, no flowers	,,	,,		D
E	Seldom flowers	,,	,,		D
D	Pale yellow	E.Summer	Clump		DS
E	Blue spikes	Summer	Spreader		D
D	Scarlet	Autumn	Clump		C

Group 9

Leaves of purple, brown, pink, etc.

I find it very difficult to describe the dark tints in this group. Everybody knows what is meant by a Copper Beech, but except for its delicate tints in spring, its normal summer colour is not the least like copper. Its other name 'Rivers' Purple' is equally confusing; no foliage of any hardy plant can really be called purple, though we get this tint in *Setcreasia* under glass. Furthermore the true Copper Beech is strictly *Fagus sylvatica* 'Cuprea', a plant that is never seen nowadays. So please bear with me if I ring the changes on copper and purple, meaning the rich dark tone of purple plum, copper beech and claret wine. All these dark tones need full sunshine not only to develop their colour, but to give them vibrancy; on a dull day they are apt to look lifeless and heavy. I think they – and in fact all foliage other than green – must have the sophistication of the garden to bring forth their value; they appear to me to be foreign and undesirable away from dwellings.

There is no noticeable decrease in vigour of the plants under review owing to the lack of chlorophyll as is the case with yellow and variegated plants.

Everyone, as I said, knows what is meant by a Copper Beech, but it is not always realized that some are raised from seeds and may vary in tint. They are often sold for hedging, being cheaper than grafted plants. Some indeed lose their early summer colour and turn to a greenish brown later. A noted best type is 'Rivers' Purple', which is always a grafted tree and will reach a large size. It is the king of all this Group. Next I think we should place *Acer platanoides* 'Crimson King', though only its emerging young foliage, when seen against the light, remotely resembles crimson. It matures to the darkness of 'Rivers' Purple' beech. A step down in size and magnificence is the *Betula*. Here the leaves are very small and dark and it needs a light background to make it noticeable, though the white stem helps considerably. The most freely planted of all these coppery trees are the forms of the Cherry Plum, *Prunus cerasifera*. The original was 'Pissardii', which I think remains my favourite because of the cloud of blush-white March blossom; I am, at that early time of the year, scarcely ready for the full pink of 'Nigra', though its foliage is a richer colour. The two doubles 'Moseri' and 'Blireiana' follow the same colour sequence, but are less vigorous trees. There is much to be said for the coppery-leafed Sloe, *Prunus spinosa* 'Purpurea': in the Red Borders at Hidcote we find it just right as a complement and contrast to all the full colours, and it is not so large and coarse in growth as the forms of the Cherry Plum. The purple-leaf Peach, *Prunus persica* 'Foliis Rubis', is a wayward and rather unsatisfactory small tree though its fruits are worth having and often breed true to leaf colour. The leaves are rich and dark in colour, but somewhat glossy. There are many cultivars of *Malus* whose foliage is attractive in coppery purple in spring, but their beauty fades by the summer and I have therefore omitted them. The purplish-leafed variants of *Cordyline australis*, mentioned in Group 2, are by no means hardy.

All the Japanese Maples are great favourites; I often hesitate before naming my favourite, but usually decide on *Acer palmatum* 'Linearilobum Atropurpureum'; it is well worth the long name, with narrow-fingered, dark leaves. But all are beautiful, and best on lime-free retentive soil, well away from frost pockets. Equally gorgeous in summer are the special forms of *Cotinus*. These can either be left to grow quite large, or pruned annually to achieve large leaves with less height. *Prunus* 'Cistena' is not always a satisfactory plant when grafted; it is best raised from cuttings. Perhaps the darkest note is struck in full summer by the copper-leafed Filbert (*Corylus*); it can be overpowering amongst greenery but is magnificent when the bushes are thinned out so that the light can shine through the leaves. As yet little known, though an old plant, is *Rhododendron ponticum* 'Purpureum', a compact grower with the usual lilac flowers – which can be picked off if you do not like them! It is known for its foliage: bronze-green in summer, turning at the onset of winter to a dark tint like that of the best Copper Beech. It is a wonderful contrast to yellow and bluish conifers, and in fact an invaluable plant. Last and least of these full-coloured plants are the big *Berberis × ottawensis* 'Purpurea' and *B. thunbergii* 'Atropurpurea Nana', a close clump-forming little bush of some excellence. A new compact richly coppery-coloured form is 'Dart's Red Lady', though the colour is far from red. Another small shrub is *Rhododendron* 'Elizabeth Lockhart', a remarkable sport of the pink-flowered 'Hummingbird'; its bell-shaped flowers are inherited from *R. williamsianum*. The foliage is a rich wine-red when young, turning to dark mahogany, even in the partial shade which it enjoys. Something of the same colouring for part-shade is 'Moser's Maroon' but this is a big sprawling shrub.

Now we will look at some items of less marked colouring. I do not want to linger over the Sycamore (*Acer pseudoplatanus*) with reddish purple undersides to the leaves, nor *Acer platanoides* 'Schwedleri' and 'Reitenbachii', but in full summer we should spare a moment to appreciate the unusual combination of almost black young foliage of *Catalpa × erubescens* 'Purpurea' when the tree – so good at Cambridge University Botanic Garden – is lit all over by its chestnut-like spikes of white blossom picked out with purple and orange. There is too that extraordinary Elder (*Sambucus*) which has cropped up in the wild in this country two or three times and whose foliage is clouded with a purple tone where warmed by the sun – a delightful setting for the flowers which have the wit to be of a pink tone. Something of this same sun-washed tint is found in *Rosa glauca (Rosa rubrifolia)* which we looked at in Group 8. On sunny walls the Claret Vine *Vitis vinifera* 'Purpurea' is a great delight; the young foliage is of a dusky greyish tint, but gathers to itself as the summer advances a dark purplish tone, turning to red in autumn, when contrasted by the bunches of almost black grapes. Lastly a very subdued shrub, *Weigela florida* 'Foliis Purpureis'. The dusky grey-purplish leaves make a delightful background for the soft pink flowers in June.

As a complete contrast to all this duskiness we can now look at three small trees whose young foliage is of a remarkable un-leaf-like colour for the Northern Temperate Zone, whatever may happen elsewhere. Often in hedgerows where Sycamores have seeded themselves we may spot one whose spring foliage is bright reddish or orange tinted. It may be presumed that this is how *Acer pseudoplatanus* 'Brilliantissimum' occurred. It is very slow in growth, even old trees achieve little more than 25 feet. The foliage in spring is a brilliant shrimp-pink, gradually losing this and becoming light green. 'Prinz Handjery' is rather stronger growing with some purplish undertones. Yet another is *Aesculus neglecta* 'Erythroblastos', of the same colouring as the first Maple. I am never sure that I really approve of *Berberis thunbergii* 'Rose Glow', but its mixture of coppery purple and pink is certainly appealing in late summer. I am quite sure that I do not approve of *Spiraea japonica* 'Gold Flame' when its pink flowers clash horribly with the sallow orange-green of the foliage, however appealing this may be in the spring. One has to be equally careful about some of the newer forms of *Calluna vulgaris* whose foliage is of bright red, orange and yellow: when the purply-pink heather flowers come out we have to shut our eyes and wait till winter, when their foliage colour is the brightest thing in the garden (on lime-free soils). A welcome exception is 'Gold Haze' which has white flowers. Referring again to *Spiraea japonica* 'Gold Flame', something of the same tint, but more of a khaki-yellow, is found in the spring foliage of *Diervilla sessilifolia* whose subsequent flowers are light yellow.

As to the Phormiums, in warm gardens they provide a wide variety of foliage colour but few of them would be hardy in Surrey, judging by the performance of *Phormium tenax* and *P. cookianum (P. colensoi)*. There is no doubt that the latter species is more hardy than the former, and after a very severe winter the species usually sprout from ground level, but the leaves take three years or more to achieve their full vigour. The new hybrids listed, all from New Zealand, provide something unrivalled by other garden plants. Moreover, as intimated in Group 2, they provide a link between shrubs and herbaceous plants.

PERENNIALS

The most magnificent purplish foliage among herbaceous perennials comes from *Canna* 'Le Roi Humbert', but this is only hardy in the warmer south-west. A remarkable new strain of *Heuchera micrantha diversifolia*, named 'Palace Purple', has been raised at Kew from the wild and plants are already in the Red Borders at Hidcote (a kind gift); their leaves are of uniform coppery red, quite different from the older *H. americana* which are greenish with glistening purplish central tinting. The rodgersias are noble plants; both are good in their seasons for moist ground, which is also needed by the statuesque *Rheum*, and the two kinds (practically identical) of *Ligularia*; their rich colouring is admirable with their vivid flower-colour. Also for moisture are those kinds of *Astilbe* with red flowers, notably 'William Reeves' (apt to revert to less colourful 'Granat'), 'Fanal' and 'Red Sentinel'.

For sunny, but reasonably moist spots in sheltered gardens is *Crocosmia* × *crocosmiiflora* 'Solfatare'. Its warm maize yellow is a good contrast to the dusky foliage, while at the back of the border, supported by pea-sticks, the *Clematis* gives another good contrast for its white flowers by having dark foliage. It is important to get a really good dark form; some, raised from seeds, are greenish. For really hot sunny borders the *Sedum* cannot be beaten. And as a carpeter (but apt to become a nuisance from self-sowing) for autumn bulbs there is the little Labrador Violet; its dull blackish-purple leaves make a lovely anti-splash background for autumn flowering crocuses and colchicums – particularly the large white *Colchicum speciosum* 'Album'. Also for autumn are the white flowers of *Saxifraga fortunei*; 'Wada's Variety' has rich dark glistening foliage. This needs a cool, moist, shady position. Almost anywhere will suit *Euphorbia amygdaloides* 'Purpurea' which contrasts its yellowish flower heads with dark purplish young leaves through the season.

There are many forms of the native Bugle, *Ajuga reptans*, with colourful foliage. I give top rank to 'Burgundy Glow' and 'Atropurpurea'; these both appreciate full sun in a reasonably moist soil.

One of the most spectacular of foliage plants for late summer and early autumn is *Ricinus communis*, the plant whose seeds yield castor oil; the strain named 'Gibsonii' has magnificent purplish foliage, resembling that of *Fatsia japonica* in shape. It must be treated as a half-hardy annual and has to be raised from seeds under glass, and planted out for the summer, as for the big-leafed coppery hybrid cannas, such as *Canna* 'Le Roi Humbert'.

TREES	Country of origin	Height/ Width	Brief description
ACER			
platanoides Norwegian Maple	Europe		
— 'Crimson King'		60 ft × 30 ft	Broad, dark
pseudoplatanus Sycamore	Europe, W.Asia		
— 'Atropurpureum' ('Spaethii')		80 ft × 40 ft	Broad, dark beneath
— 'Brilliantissimum'		25 ft × 12 ft	Broad, shrimp pink when young
— 'Prinz Handjery'		30 ft × 12 ft	Broad, pink when young, purplish beneath
AESCULUS			
neglecta	S.E.USA		
— 'Erythroblastos'		18 ft × 10 ft	Fingered, shrimp pink in spring
BETULA			
pendula Silver Birch	Europe		
— 'Purpurea'		60 ft × 15 ft	Dark, dull
CATALPA			
× *erubescens*	Hybrid	50 ft × 60 ft	Large leaves, purplish while young
CORDYLINE			
australis	New Zealand		
— 'Atropurpurea'		6 ft × 10 ft	Purplish brown, there are narrow and broad-leafed forms
FAGUS			
sylvatica Common Beech			
— 'Riversii'		90 ft × 50 ft	The best dark beech
— 'Purpurea Tricolor' ('Roseomarginata')		60 ft × 35 ft	Dark leaves, more or less edged with pink
PRUNUS			
× *blirieana*	Hybrid	15 ft × 12 ft	Dark, small
— 'Moseri' is similar, with blush-white flowers			
cerasifera Myrobalan or Cherry Plum	S.E.Europe, W.Asia		
— 'Nigra'		25 ft × 15 ft	Very dark

Deciduous or Evergreen	Colour of flower	Period of flower	Habit	Special conditions	Propagation
D	Reddish; fruits reddish	Spring	Open		G
D	Yellowish; fruits reddish	,,	Dense		GS
D	,,	,,	Dense, very slow		G
D	,,	,,	Dense, slow		G
D	Pale yellow	E.Summer	Slender, open		G
D	Catkins	Spring	Open, graceful		G
D	White, spotted purple	L.Summer	Open		G
E	Creamy, fragrant	E.Summer	Gaunt	W	CR
D			Dense		G
D			,,		G
D	Double, pink	Spring	,,		G
D	Creamy white	E.Spring	,,		S
D	Pink	Spring	,,		CG

TREES (cont.)	Country of origin	Height/ Width	Brief description
PRUNUS cerasifera (cont.)			
— 'Pissardii'		25 ft × 15 ft	Dark
padus Bird Cherry	Europe		
—'Colorata'		30 ft ?	Dark while young
persica Peach			
Long cultivated			
— 'Foliis Rubis'		15 ft × 10 ft	Dark
spinosa Sloe	,,		
— 'Purpurea'		,,	Dark, soft

SHRUBS

ACER			
palmatum Japanese Maple	Far East		
— 'Atropurpureum'		12 ft × 12 ft	Fingered, bright
— 'Dissectum Atropurpureum'		8 ft × 8 ft	Very fingered, dark
— 'Heptalobum Elegans Purpureum'		12 ft × 12 ft	Fingered, dark
— 'Linearilobum Atropurpureum'		10 ft × 10 ft	Thin fingered, dark
Several darker forms have been named			
BERBERIS			
× *ottawensis*	Hybrid		
— 'Superba'		7 ft × 7 ft	Small, dark
thunbergii	Japan		
— 'Atropurpurea'		5 ft × 5 ft	,,
— 'Atropurpurea Nana'		2 ft × 2 ft	,,
— 'Dart's Red Lady'		3 ft × 3 ft	,,
— 'Rose Glow'		4 ft × 4 ft	Small, purple and pink mottled

CALLUNA   Heather, Ling

vulgaris has many varieties of startling winter colour, orange to red. Unfortunately their late summer flowers of lilac-pink assort ill with the leaf tint. Some good ones are 'Blazeaway', 'Orange Queen', 'Robert Chapman', 'Tricolorifolia', 'Sir John Charrington', 'Spitfire'; 'Serlei Aurea' and 'Gold Haze' tone up their yellow foliage with white flowers. 'Serlei Rubra' has rich purplish foliage. All grow to about 1 foot high and wide, and are at their most brilliant in winter

Deciduous or Evergreen	Colour of flower	Period of flower	Habit	Special conditions	Propagation
D	Blush white	E. spring	Dense		CG
D	Pink	E. Summer	Open		G
D	Pink; fruits reddish	Spring	,,		GS
D	Pink	,,	Dense		G

D	Reddish; fruits reddish	Spring	Open		GS
D	,,	,,	Open, slow		G
D	,,	,,	Open		G
D	,,	,,	Open, slow		G
D	Yellowish	,,	Dense		C
D	Yellowish; fruits red	,,	,,		CS
D	Yellowish	,,	Very dense		C
D	,,	,,	,,		C
D	,,	,,	Dense		C

SHRUBS (cont.)	Country of origin	Height/ Width	Brief description
CORYLUS Filbert			
maxima	Balkans		
— 'Purpurea'		9 ft × 9 ft	Broad, very dark
COTINUS Venetian Sumach or Smoke Tree			
coggygria	S.Europe		
— 'Foliis Purpureis'		8 ft × 8 ft	Dark
— 'Royal Purple' and 'Notcutt's Variety' are two good selected forms			
DIERVILLA			
sessilifolia	S.E.USA	4 ft × 4 ft	Yellowish khaki
PRUNUS			
'Cistena'	Hybrid	,,	Rich colour
RHODODENDRON			
'Elizabeth Lockhart'		3 ft × 3 ft?	Dark, purplish
ponticum var. 'Purpureum'		6 ft × 7 ft?	Dark, purplish in winter
ROSA			
glauca (*R. rubrifolia*)		8 ft × 6 ft	Purplish in sun
SALVIA Sage			
officinalis	S.Europe		
— 'Purpurascens'		1 ft × 2 ft	Broad, purplish
— 'Tricolor'		10 ins × 18 ins	Pink, white and grey with purplish tips
SAMBUCUS Common Elder			
nigra	Europe etc		
— 'Purpurea'		7 ft × 6 ft	Dark, in sun
WEIGELA			
florida	Far East		
— 'Foliis Purpureis'		5 ft × 5 ft	Soft grey purple

Deciduous or Evergreen	Colour of flower	Period of flower	Habit	Special conditions	Propagation
D	Catkins	Spring	Open		CL
D	Fluffy, purplish	Summer	,,		CL
D	Yellow	E.Summer	Bushy		C
D	White; fruits dark	Spring	Dense		C
E	Pink	,,	,,		CL
E	Mauve	E.Summer	,,		CL
D	Pink; fruits red	Summer	Open		S
E	Violet	,,	Dense, sprawling		CL
E	,,	,,	,,		CL
D	Pinkish white	,,	Open		C
D	Pink	,,	Dense		C

CLIMBER	Country of origin	Height/ Width	Brief description
VITIS Grape Vine			
vinifera	S.E.Europe,		
— 'Purpurea'	W.Asia	15 ft × 15 ft	Soft, dark

PERENNIALS

AJUGA			
reptans	Europe,		
— 'Atropurpurea'	Britain	5 ins × 18 ins	Beetroot purple
— 'Burgundy Glow'		,,	Purple, pink and grey
ASTILBE			

garden hybrids: most of the red-flowered cultivars have young foliage of dark colouring, such as 'Fanal', 'Red Sentinel'

CANNA			
'Le Roi Humbert'	Hybrid	5 ft × 3 ft	Large, broad, purplish
CLEMATIS			
recta	Europe		
— 'Foliis Purpureis'		5 ft × 3 ft	Bipinnate, dusky
CROCOSMIA			
× *crocosmiiflora*	Hybrid		
— 'Solfatare'		2 ft × 9 ins	Grassy, brownish
HEUCHERA			
americana	N.America	18 ins × 1 ft	Variable, dark
micrantha diversifolia		2 ft × 2 ft	Broad dark leaves
'Palace Purple'			
LIGULARIA			
dentata (*Senecio clivorum*)	China		
— 'Desdemona' and 'Othello'		4 ft × 2 ft	Large, dark beneath and dark stems

PHORMIUM
tenax   New Zealand Flax

Deciduous or Evergreen	Colour of flower	Period of flower	Habit	Special conditions	Propagation
D	Inconspicuous; fruits nearly black	Summer	Climber (tendrils)		CL
E	Blue	Spring	Carpeter		D
E	,,	,,	,,		D
D	Various	Summer	Clump	M	D
D	Orange-red	L.Summer	Clump	W	D
D	White; fruits fluffy	Summer	,,		CD
D	Soft yellow	L.Summer	,,	W	D
E	Green	E.Summer	,,		D
E	,,	Summer	,,		DS
D	Orange	,,	,,		DS

PERENNIALS (cont.)	Country of origin	Height/ Width	Brief description
PHORMIUM *tenax* (cont.)			
'Purpureum'		5 ft × 2 ft	Purplish sheen
'Bronze Baby'	Hybrid	2 ft × 1 ft	Dark
'Dazzler'	,,	3 ft × 2 ft	Brown, striped red
'Maori Chief'	,,	4 ft × 2 ft	Greenish purple, red edges
'Maori Maiden'	,,	2 ft × 1 ft	Pink and fawn
'Maori Sunrise'	,,	3 ft × 2 ft	Pink and bronze
'Sundowner'	,,	,,	Purplish and pink
'Thumbelina'	,,	1 ft × 1 ft	Dark
RHEUM			
palmatum	China		
— 'Atrosanguineum'		6 ft × 6 ft	Jagged leaves, dark beneath
RICINUS			
communis	Africa		
— 'Gibsonii'		5 ft × 3 ft	Large, rounded, jagged; purplish
RODGERSIA			
pinnata 'Superba'		4 ft × 3 ft	Leaves dark while young
podophylla	Japan	,,	Leaves dark while young and again in late summer
SAXIFRAGA			
fortunei	China,		
— 'Wada's Variety'	Japan	18 ins × 1 ft	Rounded, dark
SEDUM			
maximum	Europe		
— *atropurpureum*		2 ft × 2 ft	Dark, bloomy
VIOLA			
labradorica	N.America	5 ins × 1 ft	Greenish purple

Deciduous or Evergreen	Colour of flower	Period of flower	Habit	Special conditions	Propagation
E	Red-brown	L.Summer	Clump	W	D
E	Greenish	,,	,,	W	D
E	,,	,,	,,	W	D
E	,,	,,	,,	W	D
E	,,	,,	,,	W	D
E	,,	,,	,,	W	D
E	,,	,,	,,	W	D
E	,,	,,	,,	W	D
D	Crimson	E.Summer	,,		D
D	Purplish	L.Summer	Single stem	W (Annual)	S
D	Pink	Summer	,,		D
D	Cream	,,	,,		D
D	White	Autumn	,,		D
D	Reddish	L.Summer	Clump		CD
D	Violet	Spring	,,		S

Group 10

The heath effect in gardens on limy or acid soils

We all like to have as large a garden as possible so long as its maintenance does not test us too greatly. Heaths and heathers are some of the best of plants for covering the ground with a mantle of foliage and providing floral and leaf colour throughout the year. With them can be assorted many dwarf plants such as species of *Cytisus* and *Genista*, prostrate junipers, dwarf hebes, *Arctostaphylos*, *Bruckenthalia*, *Cyathodes*, *Gaultheria*, dwarf and prostrate rhododendrons and potentillas. Some gardeners who wish for a heather garden find they are on the wrong soil; few heathers will tolerate lime, and certainly this is true of the rhododendron. But if the effect desired is a close-knit, weed-proof, dwarf covering of the soil, to act as a foreground to garden trees and shrubs, despair need not be the outcome of contemplation. There are plenty of dwarf shrubs which will admirably provide the same desired quiet, low effect and which will tolerate lime. Here is a brief list: prostrate *Juniperus* and *Picea* and a few other flat growing conifers; dwarf *Berberis*, *Bergenia*, *Betula nana*, *Ceanothus* (prostrate), *Cotoneaster* (prostrate), *Dryas*, *Euonymus fortunei*, *Genista*, *Halimium*, *Helianthemum*, *Hebe*, *Hyssopus*, dwarf lavender, *Iberis*, *Mahonia* (dwarf), *Polygonum affine*, *Potentilla* (shrubby dwarfs), *Ribes alpinum* 'Aureum', prostrate roses, *Ruta*, prostrate *Salix*, *Salvia officinalis* forms, *Santolina*, *Satureia montana*, *Spiraea* (dwarfs), *Teucrium chamaedrys*, *Vinca minor*.

In *Plants for Ground-Cover* I dealt exhaustively with all these plants and only mention them here because, from time to time, I have detected a despairing note in intending planters' voices when coping with limy or neutral soils. There is no doubt that these carpeting shrubs, used in generous groups and drifts, dispel that spotty effect that can so easily accrue from our modern tendencies. These tendencies are fostered by our small gardens and the collecting instinct, rife in so many of us, which results in our purchasing one only of a kind in shrubs. The sward, if I may so call what is not grass, has a unifying result, a quietening of effect. This list links with Group 14.

Group 11

Autumn colour and winter bark

Although I like to have flowers in the garden throughout the year, there comes a time in November when they are very scarce, and then is the turn of trees and shrubs which excel in autumn colour. I willingly and gratefully take what comes, but should need a very large garden if I wished to plant those items whose main attraction is the autumn leaf colour. Though in many ways autumn is the beginning of the gardener's year, it has for me a sadness which is not assuaged by brilliant colour. I am never so glad as when all deciduous leaves have fallen and one has the long prospect of the dark evergreens contrasting with the trees' bare branches – showing catkins and other buds – gradually opening to glorious spring. As to berries, of which so many are red, a few yellow and fewer still of other colours, I again take what comes, gratefully, but artistry as far as colour goes in the berries and the colourful leaves is not difficult. Almost all their tints enhance one another and on a bright day can provide as much brilliance as a summer garden. Therefore I do not propose to do more than call attention to a few shrubs of unusual colouring in both groups.

To take the autumn leaf colour first, there is usually plenty of red and scarlet tone, and the essential is to include plenty of clear yellow; a few give a pinkish or crimson tint, notably *Euonymus alatus* and *E. verrucosus*, and *Cotoneaster horizontalis* 'Variegatus'. Among berries there are the usual red ones, some yellow and some white ones; also the violet ones of *Callicarpa* and the blue of *Symplocos* – much loved by birds – and certain black or blackish fruits on shrubs with brilliant leaf colour.

It is when the leaves have all fallen that the bark of certain trees and shrubs comes into its own. As mentioned earlier in this book it is essential to plant such items, and also berrying plants, so that the southern light falls on them, otherwise they will be mere silhouettes of darkness. This applies to all colours other than white; Birch stems show up even against the light. To plant a garden for all sorts of winter colour, from bark and berry, to foliage and flowers, requires a lot of thought and research. If an area can be set aside for such abiding joys, almost all in defiance of frost and cold, the satisfaction – and surprise to one's visitors – is great. Since I have devoted a whole book to it, *Colour in the Winter Garden*, I will leave you to explore its pages to save repeating my thoughts here.

It should be borne in mind that no "colour" in winter is of value unless augmented by a choice of evergreen shrubs, and, I would add, there are valuable evergreen herbaceous plants as well. Without evergreens no garden worthy of the name can be devised.

Group 12

Weeping trees and shrubs

The conifers are not specially noted for weeping cultivars, though many species have pendulous side shoots, notably the two tall species of *Picea* listed and the Lawson's Cypress. Perhaps the most striking of weeping conifers is the Cedar which if left to itself will make a sort of irregular tent of almost vertically hanging branches. But I think before we look further into the lists I had better explain about the production and training of weeping trees. Nurserymen have a habit of grafting them on stems of the parent species, in which case the tendency of all is to grow downwards. While the tree is still young it is vital – in order to avoid this unnatural effect – to train upwards on a cane a pliable young leader and to go on giving it this attention for as long as possible. Then the tree will appear as if it had been grafted at ground level, producing its own stem, which is always desirable, instead of looking like an umbrella. In old days the Weeping Ash was sometimes grafted on 20 feet stems. There is however something very appealing in a weeping tree on its own sinuous stem and with lofty leading shoot, as opposed to a "top grafted" tree, which, however much training is given to it and however many branches are cut off at the union, always proclaims its artificial growth. If it had not been for this nursery practice, resulting in the production of younger trees of greater height and so more profit, many weeping trees would grace our sloping banks with a crinoline of elegant, drooping, even creeping branches.

But to return, following the grey Weeping Cedar, there is the less drooping but plumose *Cupressus lusitanica* 'Glauca Pendula', wide spreading and graceful, for our warmer counties. Getting very large in time is the horizontally-growing Dovaston Yew and its yellowish counterpart, though both will also make leading shoots of semi-upright growth. The long trusses of branchlets hang down like the fur on an anteater's tail, and they make remarkable bulky specimens. The *Picea* and *Tsuga* are comparatively small, and being usually grown from cuttings provide a mantle of greenery over the ground. Old specimens of the Larch are picturesque curiosities and although a conifer it leads us on to the next series.

There is a considerable range of weepers among the deciduous species. There are far more Weeping Willows planted than any other weeping tree; people sometimes plant the Golden Weeping Willow on small front lawns, oblivious of the size it will achieve. It is a thing of great beauty throughout the year in its yellowish tint. It loses its pendulous beauty in time on windy sites, or when its topmost branches reach up into the buffeting air. Its place is in still conditions, preferably by water, but it would be a mistake to think that one cannot have a sheet of water, or a river, without a Weeping Willow or Gunneras! There are so many things to choose from. A less hackneyed Weeping Willow (there are many) than the Golden one, *Salix × chrysocoma*, is *S. × sepulchralis* 'Salamonii', being green twigged and with more erect main branches giving it more of the effect of a high fountain. Little used, but of great beauty – partly because it is usually produced from layers – is the Alder, forming a wide tent-like shape, and exquisite in early spring when hung with yellowish catkins.

Reaching a great height is the green Weeping Beech. Anyone who has seen the immense specimens at Florence Court in Northern Ireland, or the two big trees at the main entrance to Westonbirt Arboretum, Gloucestershire, will still be in for a shock when seeing for the first time the almost incredible size and spread of the specimen at Knap Hill Nursery, Surrey. It can however be enjoyed for many years as a slim youngster. I have omitted the Elms since practically all have been killed by the prevalent disease, but I hope in some distant decades *Ulmus glabra* 'Pendula' – the big, wide, arching tree – and the smaller umbrella-shaped 'Camperdownii' will be seen in our gardens again. We do have a considerable variety to choose from for our larger gardens; for instance there is the old popular Weeping Ash, a stiff, bulky, masculine line, and the Birches. The ordinary Silver Birch (*Betula pendula*) very often in maturity develops long weeping branchlets, but one cannot be certain of this; to make sure, one might select 'Dalicarlica', the cut-leaf Swedish Birch, which coupled with a vertical stem exhibits a narrow outline of long drooping twigs. The finest truly Weeping Birch, *B.p.* 'Tristis', is little known or appreciated but should be the choice when a tree of fair size is needed, compared with the much more common 'Youngii' of comparatively small, irregular umbrella shape. In fact these two echo in many particulars the characters of the two elms but with more delicacy of outline, twig and leaf. The Weeping Poplar listed is seldom seen, but delights in moist ground and is of great beauty, with rattling leaves and remarkable long, greyish, furry catkins in spring, looking like overgrown hairy caterpillars. A most popular tree today is the Weeping Silver Pear, *Prunus salicifolia* 'Pendula'; no tree repays so well a yearly thinning of under-branches and the fostering of a leader. *Salix caprea* has produced decided weeping forms, female ('Pendula') and 'Kilmarnock' male, which latter should be grown to the exclusion of the former since its yellow catkins are so conspicuous. The summer foliage of both is rather dull and coarse.

All trees flower, as we all know, but we can now turn to those which are forms of our garden trees noted for their blossom. The largest is the arching form of the St Lucie Cherry, *Prunus mahaleb* 'Pendula'; then there are the two forms of *Crataegus*, the *Laburnum* (there are others than the single one listed), two *Malus* – 'Elise Rathke' has a stiff character all of its own, grey twigs and large edible fruits – and the various *Prunus* varieties. If only the bullfinches would leave it alone the weeping *Prunus subhirtella* would bid fair to outshine all the others in brilliance and delicacy. Lastly, whilst as explained above, any of these can make mounds of growth, clothing the ground, especially when grafted at ground level, there is *Exochorda × macrantha* 'The Bride', which makes a delightful low growth, bespangled with white in spring. It is also admirable for training on a wall. It qualifies, as many others do in maturity, for ground-cover for which the *Picea* and *Tsuga* are useful also. For banks I like to use graceful arching shrubs such as the *Holodiscus* and *Stephanandra*.

There are three other smallish trees – or at least of slow growth – which make comparatively compact, dense umbrellas of foliage: the *Sophora*, *Morus* and the Weeping Copper Beech. The first two are particularly self-controlled, needing an occasional thinning of branches. Possibly there is more than one cultivar of the beech; some remain admirably controlled and dome-shaped, others persist in throwing up erect branches; constant removal spoils the shape of the tree, which is usually small compared with a normal tree.

To reveal their full beauty weeping trees should be uncluttered with shrubs, and are best on otherwise untenanted ground, the lawn for instance. Their drooping growths are accentuated when they make a dome of greenery on a mound; pared away perhaps on one side they make a suitably shady place for a seat.

I have not added widths to the heights of the items in this Group because so much depends on the way they are trained. As a general rule the width will equal the height, except for *Fagus sylvatica* 'Pendula Purpurea', *Laburnum*, *Morus*, *Pyrus*, *Salix caprea* and *Sophora*, which are usually less wide than high. The same applies to *Chamaecyparis* and *Picea breweriana*, while the Dovaston Yew is much wider than high.

TREES AND SHRUBS	Country of origin	Height/ Width	Brief description
ALNUS Alder			
incana			
— 'Pendula'		10–15 ft	Medium, greyish green
BETULA			
pandula Silver Birch			
— 'Tristis'		50–60 ft	Small
— 'Youngii'		10–15 ft	,,
CRATAEGUS Hawthorn			
monogyna			
— 'Pendula' Weeping Thorn		,,	,,
oxyacantha			
— 'Punicea' ('Single Scarlet')		,,	,,
EXOCHORDA			
× *macrantha*			
— 'The Bride' (shrub)		4–5 ft	Medium, green
FAGUS			
sylvatica Common Beech			
— 'Pendula' Weeping Beech		40–80 ft	Medium
— 'Pendula Purpurea' Weeping Purple Beech		10–15 ft usually top-grafted	Medium, purplish
FRAXINUS Ash			
excelsior			
— 'Pendula' Weeping Ash		20–40 ft	Pinnate
GLEDITSIA			
triacanthos			
— 'Bujotii'		10–15 ft	Pinnate, small
HOLODISCUS (Spiraea)			
discolor Shrub		6–7 ft	Small, toothed
ILEX			
aquifolium 'Argenteomarginata Pendula'		10–20 ft	White edged
— 'Pendula'		10–12 ft	Dark green

Deciduous or Evergreen	Colour of flower	Period of flower	Habit	Special conditions	Propagation
D	Catkins	Spring	Arching		L
D	Yellow catkins	,,	Tall, arching		G
D	,,	,,	Umbrella-like		G
D	White; fruits red	,,	Umbrella-like		G
D	Crimson	,,	Semi-weeping		G
D	White	,,	Semi-prostrate arching		CL
D	Inconspicuous, yellowish	,,	Tall, arching		GL
D	,,	,,	Umbrella-like		G
D	Inconspicuous, purplish	,,	Tall, arching		G
D	Inconspicuous; long brown pods	Summer	Umbrella-like		G
D	Creamy, in feathery sprays	,,	Arching		CL
E	Inconspicuous; fruits red	,,	,,		C
E	,,	,,	,,		C

TREES AND SHRUBS (cont.)	Country of origin	Height/ Width	Brief description
LABURNUM			
alpinum Scotch Laburnum			
— 'Pendulum'		10–12 ft	Trilobed
MALUS			
prunifolia 'Pendula'		8–10 ft	Small
'Elise Rathke'		,,	Medium, greyish
'Red Jade'		,,	Small, toothed
MORUS			
alba White Mulberry			
— 'Pendula'		,,	Large, fresh green
POPULUS			
tremula 'Pendula'		10–15 ft	Small
PRUNUS			
'Kiku Shidare Sakura'		8–10 ft	Medium
mahaleb 'Pendula'		15–20 ft	Small
subhirtella 'Pendula'		10–15 ft	,,
× *yedoensis* 'Shidare Yoshino'		,,	,,
PYRUS			
salicifolia 'Pendula'		15 ft	Narrow, grey
SALIX			
caprea 'Kilmarnock'		8 ft	Dark green
× *chrysocoma (S. babylonica ramulis aureis)*		20–40 ft	Light green, narrow, yellow twigs
× *sepulchralis* 'Salamonii'		40–60 ft	Narrow, dark green
SOPHORA			
japonica 'Pendula'		8–15 ft	Pinnate, small, dark green
STEPHANANDRA			
tanakae (Shrub)		5–6 ft	Small, toothed

Deciduous or Evergreen	Colour of flower	Period of flower	Habit	Special conditions	Propagation
D	Yellow racemes	E.Summer	Umbrella-like		G
D	White; fruits red	Spring	,,		G
D	Pinky white apple blossom; fruits, greenish, large	,,	Rather horizontal and stiff		G
D	White; small red fruits	,,	Umbrella-like		G
D	Inconspicuous		,,		G
D	Large male catkins	,,	,,		G
D	Double, pink	,,	,,		G
D	Small, white	,,	Open		G
D	Small, pink	,,	Umbrella-like		G
D	Small, blush white	,,	,,		G
D	Small, white	,,	,,		G
D	Large yellow catkins in the female tree	,,	,,		CG
D	Yellow catkins	,,	Open		C
D	Catkins green	,,	Tall, arching		C
D	White, no flowers	L.Summer	Umbrella-like		G
D	Creamy, small	E.Summer	Arching bright brown stems		CL

CONIFERS	Country of origin	Height/ Width	Brief description
CEDRUS			
atlantica 'Glauca Pendula'		8–20 ft	Blue-grey
CHAMAECYPARIS			
lawsoniana 'Filiformis'		40–80 ft	Dark green, long hanging shoots
CUPRESSUS			
lusitanica 'Glauca Pendula'		20–40 ft	Blue-green plumose
LARIX			
decidua 'Pendula'		20–30 ft	Green needles
PICEA			
breweriana		30–50 ft	,,
smithiana		40–60 ft	Grey-green needles
TAXUS			
baccata 'Dovastoniana'		8–15 ft	Dark green, tiny
TSUGA			
canadensis 'Pendula'		6–15 ft	Dark green needles

Deciduous or Evergreen	Colour of flower	Period of flower	Habit	Special conditions	Propagation
E			Tall, arching		G
E			Columnar		CG
E			Wide, open	W	CG
D			Wide, open, arching		CG
E			Weeping branchlets		S
E			,,		S
E	Fruits red		Horizontal branches, weeping branchlets		CG
E			Umbrella-like		CG

Group 13

Fastigiate trees and shrubs

This term immediately brings to mind the most common of all fastigiate trees, the Lombardy Poplar, *Populus nigra* 'Italica'; there are good and bad forms as outlined in my *Trees in the Landscape*. In spite of its great size it is usually the first tree to which people turn in creating a screen – with regrets later when it becomes too tall and large and bare at the base, but slowly *P. simonii* 'Fastigiata' is becoming recognized as a desirable alternative for the more restricted areas. This has a unique vertical growth, like smoke from a bonfire on a still day. The two cultivars of *Acer*, the *Robinia* and *Liriodendron*, are all slender and beautiful, the last rather slow. The *Betula*, *Quercus* and *Carpinus* are considerably wider in maturity; the more slender of the two (or more) forms of the *Quercus* should be chosen, while the *Carpinus* is slow and dense. The besom-like *Crataegus* is almost a joke if one is thinking of the original beauty of trees, so unlike the parent it is, but its narrow, dense shape has its uses. The little *Berberis* also has a form with purplish leaves, *B. thunbergii* 'Red Pillar'.

Turning now to the evergreens, most conifers qualify for inclusion, but to mention all would make the list too long. I therefore propose only to call attention to a few which have vertical branches, or otherwise merit the term columnar. The ultimate in size is of course the very splendid rich green *Calocedrus (Libocedrus) decurrens*. My next in decreasing size would be *Chamaecyparis lawsoniana* 'Kilmacurragh'. These two have outward growing branches but retain a strictly columnar shape and should be carefully restricted to a single leader. Not so that most slender Lawson's Cypress, 'Witzeliana' (not to be confused with 'Wisselii'), which always makes many upright feathery growths. While this remains in fusiform shape, 'Ellwoodii' manages to provide a column in spite of side stems. The yellowish forms of the last are not decisive in their tint.

Thuja occidentalis has provided three good columnar forms, which turn to a khaki tint in winter. The Irish Yew and its yellow form are, like the Lombardy Poplar, a popular choice, but get very wide in time though preserving a vertical growth. Trees of some 40 feet in height may be 15 feet or more in width in congenial climates and soils. But for many years they preserve a slim outline and are frequently clipped. A tall and slender light grey-green feathery column is *Juniperus virginiana* 'Skyrocket'.

Coming down to much smaller plants we have the slow growing *Chamaecyparis thyroides* 'Andeleyensis' whose winter tint and small cones add to its attraction, while faster in growth (fusiform) there is the Irish Juniper, prickly-leafed, and needing some thinning and restriction with age; it is also, like the next, apt to suffer from red spider in dry positions in poor soil and both grow so densely that they become congested with dead leaves. If something really small is required *Juniperus communis* 'Compressa' should be the choice. I have left till last a bright yellow, slow growing feathery tapering column, *J. chinensis* 'Aurea'. It is a dominant plant wherever it is used.

I have omitted ultimate widths from the following table because I think that the descriptive terms in the penultimate column are sufficiently indicative of the habits.

TREES AND SHRUBS	Country of origin	Height/ Width	Brief description
ACER Maple			
× *lobelii*		40–60 ft	Large, palmate, green
platanoides 'Columnare'		30–50 ft	,,
rubrum 'Scanlon'		20–40 ft	Medium, lobed, green
BERBERIS			
thunbergii 'Erecta' (shrub)		2–4 ft	Small, bright green
BETULA Birch			
pendula 'Fastigiata'		40–50 ft	Small, bark white
CARPINUS Hornbeam			
betulus 'Columnaris'		10–20 ft	Medium
CRATAEGUS Hawthorn			
monogyna 'Stricta'		,,	Small
FAGUS Beech			
sylvatica 'Dawyck'		40–60 ft	Medium
LIRIODENDRON Tulip Tree			
tulipifera 'Fastigiata'		30–50 ft	Large, lobed
POPULUS Poplar			
nigra 'Italica'		60–80 ft	Medium
'Lombardy Poplar'			
simonii 'Fastigiata'		40–60 ft	,,
PRUNUS			
'Amanogawa'		10–30 ft	,,
× *schmidtii*		20–30 ft	,,
QUERCUS			
petraea 'Columnaris'		30–60 ft	,,
ROBINIA			
pseudacacia 'Pyramidalis'		40–60 ft	Pinnate

Deciduous or Evergreen	Colour of flower	Period of flower	Habit	Special conditions	Propagation
D	Yellowish	Spring	Divergent		G
D	Yellow		Columnar		G
D	Reddish	,,	,,		G
D	Yellow; fruits red	,,	Erect, but opening with age		C
D	Catkins	,,	Divergent		G
D	,,	,,	Narrow, but widening slowly		G
D	White; fruits red	,,	Dense, columnar		G
D	Inconspicuous	,,	Divergent		G
D	Greenish	Summer	Columnar		G
D	Greenish catkins	Spring	Divergent		C
D	,,	,,	Columnar, yet graceful		C
D	Pale pink, double	,,	Very divergent when old		G
D	Blush white	,,	Divergent		G
D	Yellowish	,,	Narrow pyramid		G
D	White	Summer	Columnar		G

CONIFERS	Country of origin	Height/ Width	Brief description
CHAMAECYPARIS			
thyoides 'Andeleyensis'		4–8 ft	Tiny, purplish in winter
JUNIPERUS			
chinensis 'Aurea'		8–15 ft	Tiny, bright yellow, feathery
— 'Columnaris Glauca'		4–10 ft	Tiny, blue grey
communis 'Hibernica'		6–9 ft	Tiny, blue green
— 'Compressa'		1–4 ft	,,
virginiana 'Skyrocket'		10–15 ft?	Grey-green

Deciduous or Evergreen	Colour of flower	Period of flower	Habit	Special conditions	Propagation
E			Very narrow cone, slow		C
E			Columnar, slow		C
E			Very narrow cone		C
E			Columnar		C
E			Columnar, slow		C
E			Columnar		C

Group 14
The horizontal line

Fastigiate plants reveal their potential in the garden landscape while quite young; weeping trees take rather longer. Plants of horizontal growth demand many years before their line assumes any importance. Take for instance that most superb of trees with horizontal branches, the Lebanon Cedar; seventy-five or more years must pass before the plant becomes characterful. The Blue Atlas Mountains Cedar, though quicker in growth, never develops this remarkable shape. There are many great houses and gardens through the country which depend much on a Lebanon Cedar or two for their timeless serenity. Introduced to this country towards the end of the seventeenth century, it is doubtful if many trees are still alive from this date, but there are many about of 200 or more years of age. It is so accepted in the English landscape that we should go on planting it whenever possible; it thrives best in the southern half of this country.

One of the most magnificent evergreen shrubs of large size for our list is the West Felton or Dovaston Yew, *Taxus baccata* 'Dovastoniana'. If after many years it achieves 15 ft in height it is likely to be 50 ft across, the pendulous branchlets hanging from the thrusting horizontal branches. Having started with the conifers I will continue with them, though the remainder are but small fry by comparison. There are many Junipers that qualify, the largest being also the most common, the feathery semi-horizontal *Juniperus* × *media* 'Pfitzeriana'. It is frequently used unsuitably in restricted spaces and is speedily ruined by pruning. By the time it is 5 ft high it is likely to be 15 ft across. As with many such characterful shrubs which are spoiled by pruning, it is best to plant closely with a view to quick achievement of effect, followed by subsequent thinning. It has a yellowish variant; so far no blue-grey form of like growth has appeared. The next most common is a compact, comparatively slow plant, *Juniperus sabina tamariscifolia*. Every overlapping shoot has a horizontal line. *J. chinensis* 'Parsonsii' and *J. virginiana* 'Chamberlaynei' are two remarkable plants of stiff horizontal habit, while the remainder, giving though they do a low, carpeting effect, achieve this by interlacing and overlapping twigs, such as *J. communis* forms, *J. horizontalis* (remarkable for its violet-blue winter colour in some forms), *J. procumbens* and, rather taller, the grass-green *J. conferta*. *Picea abies* 'Reflexa' is also rich green and specially bright in its young early summer growth; it is a completely prostrate Spruce Fir.

Apart from *Phellodendron* and *Cornus* I cannot call to mind any deciduous trees of striking horizontal growth. Phellodendrons are not often seen, but the profuse flowering and autumn fruiting and colouring of the several *Cornus* species is well known.

Best appreciated of all horizontal-growing shrubs is undoubtedly *Viburnum plicatum tomentosum*; the branches appear to be covered with white tablecloths at flowering time and with red shawls in autumn. Other shrubs of fair size for our list are the popular *Cotoneaster horizontalis* and *Ceanothus thyrsiflorus repens*, an evergreen which has proved remarkably hardy in the warmer counties. Several rhododendrons perhaps just qualify for inclusion; they grow somewhat in tiers if not horizontally, from the tall *R. calophytum* and *R. fortunei* for sheltered woodlands to the nearly evergreen Japanese Azalea *R. obtusum* whose crimson purple flowers are tiny but make a virulent mass of colour.

For shade or sun the Cherry Laurel variant *Prunus laurocerasus* 'Zabeliana' has much to commend it, but in old age it can be as high as it is broad; much smaller, *Lonicera pileata* is a useful dwarf shrub, again for sun or shade, while the broad, deeply ribbed leaves of *Viburnum davidii* have long since passed into the planter's repertoire; to achieve the bright blue berries one male is required to a half-dozen females, or thereabouts.

The kinds of *Salix* listed are not distinguished shrubs but add to the list and there is no doubt that, also deciduous, *Symphoricarpos* × *chenaultii* 'Hancock' will become a general favourite. It develops its small pink fruits sparsely.

We have whittled down the list until we have come to carpeting shrubs, such as kinds of *Rosa*, *Euonymus*, *Sarothamnus* (*Cytisus*), *Jasminum nudiflorum*, which in their carpeting create a quiet flat line without being horizontal in their twigs. These and many others are listed in my *Plants for Ground-Cover*, which gives many details of their habits and requirements, and I will refer you to its pages for the further use of such plants, since "carpeting" is not really what this Group is about.

TREES AND SHRUBS	Country of origin	Height/ Width	Brief description
CEANOTHUS *thyrsiflorus*			
— *repens*		3 ft × 8 ft	Dark green, small, glossy
CORNUS *controversa*		20 ft × 30 ft	Mid green
— 'Variegata'		15 ft × 10 ft	Beautiful white variegation, slow
kousa		10 ft × 12 ft	Mid green, autumn colour
— *chinensis*		20 ft × 15 ft	,,
macrophylla		30 ft × 20 ft	Mid green
COTONEASTER *horizontalis*		2 ft × 6 ft	Tiny, dark green, autumn colour
LONICERA *pileata*		2 ft × 3 ft	Small, dark green
PHELLODENDRON several species		30 ft × 30 ft	Green, pinnate
PRUNUS *laurocerasus* 'Zabeliana' (Cherry Laurel)		7 ft × 10 ft	Narrow, shining dark green
SALIX *arbuscula* (*S. formosa* in part)		1 ft × 3 ft	The more prostrate forms make carpets of rich green
× *gillotii*		1 ft × 5 ft	Shining green, small
SYMPHORICARPOS × *chenaultii* 'Hancock'		3 ft × 8 ft	Small, light green
VIBURNUM *davidii*		2 ft × 3ft	Broad, dark, veined

Deciduous or Evergreen	Colour of flower	Period of flower	Habit	Special conditions	Propagation
E	Blue, small, in fluffy heads	Spring	Low hummock		C
D	Small, white; fruit blue-black	,,	Tabular formation		S
D	Small, white	,,	,,		G
D	Large white bracts, red fruit, autumn colour	,,	Somewhat tabular		CL
D	,,	,,	,,		CL
D	Small, white; bluish fruits	,,	,,		S
D	Tiny; red fruits	,,	Wide fanlike growth		CS
E	Tiny; purplish berries	,,	Somewhat tabular		CLS
D	Small, yellowish-green	E.Summer	,,		S
E	Spikes of small white flowers	Spring	Arching		C
D	Yellow catkins	,,	Carpet, rooting		CL
D	,,	,,	Vigorous carpeter		CL
D	Tiny; pink fruits	,,	Horizontal		CL
E	Tiny pinky-white; blue berries on females	Summer	Hummock		C

TREES AND SHRUBS (cont.)	Country of origin	Height/ Width	Brief description
VIBURNUM (cont.)			
plicatum tomentosum			
— 'Lanarth' and 'Mariesii'		6 ft × 15 ft	Broad, autumn colour
— 'Pink Beauty'		6 ft × 4 ft	,,
— 'Rowallane'		6 ft × 6 ft	,,

CONIFERS

CEDRUS			
libani Lebanon Cedar		80 × 80 ft	Dark green
JUNIPERUS chinensis			
— 'Parsonsii'		6 ins × 2 ft	Clear green, tiny
communis (Common Juniper)			
— 'Hornibrookii'		9 ins × 4 ft	Needle-like grey-green
conferta (*J. litoralis*)		1 ft × 5 ft	Bright green needles
horizontalis		6 ins × 3 ft	Tiny leaves, appressed
— 'Glauca', 'Bar Harbor' and 'Douglasii' are desirable forms whose leaves turn to brilliant violet-blue in winter			
× *media*			
— 'Pfitzeriana'		3 ft × 8 ft	Tiny, greyish-green
— 'Pfitzeriana Aurea'		3 ft × 8 ft	Tiny, yellowish-green
procumbens		5 ins × 2 ft	Tiny, grey-green
sabina (Savin)			
— *tamariscifolia*		10 ins × 2 ft	Grey-green
virginiana 'Chamberlaynii'		1 ft × 3 ft	Pale green, tiny
PICEA abies (Spruce Fir)			
— 'Reflexa'		1 ft × 3 ft	Bright green

Deciduous or Evergreen	Colour of flower	Period of flower	Habit	Special conditions	Propagation
D	Conspicuous, white	E.Summer	Tabular		CL
D	Conspicuous, pale pink	,,	,,		CL
D	Conspicuous, white	,,	,,		CL
E	Cones		Tabular		S
E			Flat		C
E			Carpeter		CL
E			Flat carpet		CL
E			,,		CL
E			Plumose, arching		C
E			,,		C
E			Flat		C
E			,,		C
E			,,		C
E	Cones, perhaps		Hummock or carpet		C

CONIFERS (cont.)	Country of origin	Height/ Width	Brief description
TAXUS baccata (English Yew) 'Dovastoniana' and 'D. Aurea'		9 ft × 15 ft	Dark green or yellowish-green

Deciduous or Evergreen	Colour of flower	Period of flower	Habit	Special conditions	Propagation
E	Red berries if female		Tabular		C

Part V

Chronological flowering lists of a working gardener, from early spring to late autumn

15

Chronological lists of a working gardener

Long work it were,
Here to account the endless progeny
Of all the weeds, that bud and blossom there;
But so much as doth need, must needs be counted here.

EDMUND SPENSER, 1552–1599
from *The Garden of Adonis*

Quite early in my long term of work in helping to look after the gardens of the National Trust I found I needed an *aide-mémoire* for planting. Seldom a visit was made without the necessity of some new planting, occasioned perhaps by losses, or the need for obscuring unsightly things, or just generally enriching the gardens. I started making notes of principal trees, shrubs and plants which were in flower at the time of visits to gardens throughout the growing year. This eventually became a loose-leaf book with the flowering periods divided roughly into two lists every month; there was little point in adding the actual date because the seasons vary so much in the early half of the year, and because what might be in flower one week in the south-west might not open for a fortnight in the colder north. The last thing I wanted to do was to plant the same things in every garden to brighten them in any particular week of the year, but, horticulture being the involved subject that it is, and many of our gardens being widely separated, a little repetition would not matter. There was another danger that my favourites might appear too often; but I learnt long ago that there is little point in adhering to my personal favourites in gardens except my own for the simple reason that my choice might not please other people. Suitability, not personal preference, is the key, as stated in Chapter 2.

Each visit to a garden would reveal a weak point in a special position, which, with the addition perhaps of a shrub or plant – or the exchange of one for another – would help to make nearly the whole of every garden floriferous throughout the visiting season. Our National Trust gardens have to be on parade, so to speak, from April to October, and apart from gardens where a vast number of plants is grown this is no easy task. As I have been at

284

pains to suggest elsewhere in this book, colour from flowers is not essential everywhere; green is equally important but even in wholly green vistas a little variation of leaf shape and colour is an advantage.

And so, to help my sometimes fuddled brain, I devised the idea that lists of plants which flower or give other colour during each fortnight of the year would be a help in thinking of a suitable plant – or plants – for a given spot. This list has indeed proved invaluable to me. Nobody can guarantee when a plant will flower; its season is governed by the weather, the state of the soil, and its aspect, but generally I found that when A is at its best in any one district, so should I find B and C also in flower.

Dates, as I said, would have been of little use, but by dividing the lists into fortnights, roughly – or into an early and late section for each month – I have found my *aide-mémoire* of great help. Even so there had to be much give and take; flowers do not necessarily fit conveniently into a given fortnight, but in some seasons may be at their best at the junction of two months, or in the middle of one.

With all their imperfections, therefore, I offer my lists as a possible help to intending planters. The plants listed are those which I admire. Who knows but that at some future date one of you will edit and augment the lists to everyone's benefit! I submit the lists in all diffidence as something to build upon through the years. So far as I know this is the first effort that has been made in any detail to help intending planters.

The lists include the bulk of trees, shrubs, climbers and perennial plants which I should expect to thrive in Surrey. Reference to my *Perennial Garden Plants* and *Colour in the Winter Garden*, together with Hillier's *Manual of Trees and Shrubs* or Bean's *Trees and Shrubs*, will provide notes about their individual requirements.

CULTURAL NOTE

* = requires lime-free soil.

w = is not hardy in Surrey without the protection of a warm wall. This also applies to most evergreen ceanothuses; with regard to fuchsias I only grow those which are considered hardy. Early flowering rhododendrons mostly need woodland or sheltered conditions.

The early year: January–February

TREES AND SHRUBS

Acer opalus
Chimonanthus praecox
Clematis cirrhosa
Corylus avellana
— maxima
Erica herbacea
— × darleyensis
Garrya elliptica
* Hamamelis
Jasminum nudiflorum
Lonicera × purpusii
Mahonia japonica
Parrotia
Prunus mume
— subhirtella 'Autumnalis'
* Rhododendron dauricum
* — mucronulatum
* — Nobleanum
Sarcococca
* Sycopsis sinensis
Viburnum farreri
— × bodnantense
— foetidum
— grandiflorum
— tinus

PERENNIALS

Bergenia × schmidtii 'Ernst
    Schmidt'
Crocus chrysanthus
— imperati
— sieberi
— tomasinianus
Eranthis
Galanthus
Helleborus atrorubens
— niger
— orientalis kochii
Iris danfordiae
— histrioides
— 'Katharine Hodgkin'
— unguicularis
Narcissus asturiensis
— bulbocodium 'Romieuxii'
— 'Cedric Morris'
— 'Jana'
— 'Rijnvelt's Early Sensation'
Pulmonaria rubra

(For a fuller list, see my Colour in
the Winter Garden)

Earliest spring: late February/end March

TREES AND SHRUBS

Acer opalus
— platanoides
— rubrum
Alnus incana 'Aurea'
w Azara microphylla
* Camellia japonica 'Nobilissima'
w* — reticulata
* — 'Cornish Snow'
* — × williamsii
Cornus mas

Corylopsis glabrescens
* — pauciflora
Daphne mezereum
w — odora
Erica × darleyensis
— herbacea
w — mediterranea
Forsythia
Mahonia japonica
* Pieris floribunda
* — japonica

* *Pieris taiwanensis*
  Prunus cerasifera
  — *conradinae*
  — *dulcis*
  — *incisa* 'Praecox'
  — *mume*
  — *subhirtella* 'Autumnalis'
* *Rhododendron* 'Bo Peep'
  — *calophytum*
  — 'Christmas Cheer'
  — *ciliatum*
  — Cilpinense
  — *eclecteum*
  — *fargesii*
  — *leucaspis*
  — *lutescens*
  — *moupinense*
  — Praecox
  — *stewartianum*
  — *sutchuenense*
  — 'Tessa'
  Ribes laurifolium
  Salix caprea
  — *medemii*
  Stachyurus

PERENNIALS
Bergenia × *schmidtii* 'Ernst
      Schmidt'
Cardamine asarifolia
— *trifolia*
Chionodoxa
Chionoscilla
Crocus, Dutch hybrids
— 'Vanguard'
— *vernus*

Cyclamen orbiculatum
— *vernum*
Erythronium dens-canis
Helleborus corsicus
— *foetidus*
— *guttatus*
— *lividus*
— *orientalis* hybrids
— *purpurascens*
Iberis sempervirens
Iris reticulata
Lysichitum
Narcissus 'Beryl'
— *bulbocodium hiemalis*
— 'Dove Wings'
— 'February Gold'
— 'Forerunner'
— 'Jana'
— 'March Sunshine'
— *obvallaris*
— 'Piper's Barn'
— *pseudonarcissus*
— *pumilis*
Primula acaulis
— *denticulata*
— × *julianae*
— *rosea*
Pulmonaria
Scilla bifolia
— *sibirica*
Symphytum grandiflorum
Tulipa greigii and hybrids
— *kauffmanniana* and hybrids
— *praestans*
Viola alba
— *odorata*

Daffodil period: late March and April
(The 'Blackthorn Winter' occurs in early April;
tender flowers like rhododendrons are at risk)

TREES AND SHRUBS

Acer negundo
Alnus incana 'Aurea'
Amelanchier
* Andromeda polifolia
Berberis darwinii, hybrids and
    relatives
* Camellias
Ceanothus impressus
Chaenomeles
Clematis alpina
— armandii
— macropetala
Cytisus × beanii
— ratisbonensis
Daphne blagayana
— × burkwoodii
— retusa
* Erica arborea alpina
* — australis
— × darleyensis
w* — lusitanica
 w — erigena (E. mediterranea)
* Fothergilla
Kerria japonica
Malus × purpurea
Magnolia campbellii, and hybrids
— — mollicomata, and hybrids
— dawsoniana
— heptapeta (M. conspicua)
— kobus and hybrids
— sargentii
— × soulangiana
— sprengeri
— stellata
Mahonia aquifolium
— 'Undulata'
Osmanthus × burkwoodii
— delavayi

Paulownia
Paeonia delavayi
— lutea
* Pieris 'Forest Flame'
* — formosanum
Prunus 'Accolade'
— 'Amanogawa'
— incisa
— 'Kiku-shidare Sakura'
— persica
— sargentii
— 'Shirotae'
— subhirtella 'Pink Shell'
— tenella
— × yedoensis
w* Rhododendron augustinii
— 'Blue Diamond'
— 'Blue Tit'
w — 'Boddaertianum'
— 'Carex'
— 'Carita'
— cinnabarinum
— concatenans
— concinnum
— 'Damaris Logan'
— 'Elizabeth'
w — fargesii
— fulvum
— hippophaeoides
— 'Jacksonii'
— 'Little Ben'
— pemakoense
— 'Pink Drift'
— racemosum
— repens
— russatum
Ribes
Rosmarinus
Salix hastata 'Wehrhahnii'

Salix lanata 'Stuartii'
Skimmia
w Sorbus megalocarpa
Spiraea × arguta
— × vanhouttei
Ulex europaeus 'Flore Pleno'
Viburnum alnifolium
— × burkwoodii
— carlesii
— 'Fulbrook'
— furcatum
— × juddii

USEFUL EARLY FOLIAGE
Crataegus (Quickthorn)
Ligustrum ovalifolium 'Aureum'
* Nothofagus obliqua
Osmanthus armatus (purplish)
Philadelphus coronarius 'Aureus'
Photinia × fraseri 'Robusta' and
        other cultivars
Physocarpus opulifolius 'Luteus'
Populus × canadensis 'Robusta'
— maximowiczii
— trichocarpa
Prunus cerasifera
Salix, many
* Tetracentron sinense
Viburnum farreri

PERENNIALS
Adonis vernalis
Alyssum saxatile
Anemone apennina
— blanda
— coronaria
— nemorosa
Aubrieta
Bergenia
Caltha
Cheiranthus (Wallflowers)
Chionodoxa
* Chionoscilla
w Cyclamen libanoticum

Dentaria
Doronicum 'Miss Mason'
Epimedium
Erythronium, American species
Euphorbia polychroma
Fritillaria imperialis
— meleagris
— pallidiflora
Iberis sempervirens
Lysichitum
Muscari
Narcissus
Ornithogalum nutans
Oxalis acetosella
— oregona
Podophyllum
Primula auricula
— denticulata
— 'Garryarde'
— rosea
— vulgaris and Polyanthus
— 'Wanda'
— Polyanthus
Pulmonaria saccharata
Pulsatilla vulgaris
Ranunculus 'Speciosus Plenus'
Saxifraga, Mossy
Scilla lilio-hyacinthina
— messeniaca
— sibirica 'Spring Beauty'
Symphytum grandiflorum
* Trillium
Tulipa praestans
Tulips, early species and hybrids
Viola 'Huntercombe Purple'
— septentrionalis
Waldsteinia ternata

USEFUL EARLY FOLIAGE
Colchicum
Hemerocallis fulva etc.
Iris, Bearded
— pallida dalmatica
Valeriana phu 'Aurea'

Pheasant eye and bluebell period: May

TREES AND SHRUBS

Aesculus carnea
— hippocastanum
* Azalea kaempferi × malvatica
— Japanese
Berberis calliantha
— × stenophylla
— — 'Corallina' etc.
— — 'Irwinii'
— thunbergii
Ceanothus, evergreen
Chaenomeles 'Phylis Moore'
Choisya ternata
Clematis montana
Crataegus, most
Cytisus 'Golden Showers'
— × kewensis
— × praecox
— purgans
Daphne × burkwoodii
— cneorum
— collina neapolitana
— retusa
— tangutica
w Drimys winteri
* Erica arborea alpina
w* — australis
Exochorda
* Fothergilla
* Halesia
Japanese Azaleas, early kinds
Kerria japonica
* Leucothoë fontanesiana
Magnolia liliiflora
— × soulangiana etc.
— × veitchii
Malus, many, and apples and
        crabs
Osmanthus decorus
Prunus avium
— Japanese Cherries
— laurocerasus

* Rhododendron ambiguum
— amoenum
w — augustinii
— 'Blue Diamond'
— bureavii
— 'Butterfly'
— 'Carita'
— 'Cowslip'
— 'Damaris Logan'
— 'David'
— 'Daydream'
— 'Earl of Athlone'
— 'Electra'
— 'Fred Rose'
— 'Hummingbird'
— 'Loder's White'
w — Loderi
— luteum (Azalea pontica)
— 'Matador'
— 'May Day'
— mollis (Azaleas)
— 'Naomi'
— orbiculare
w — 'Penjerrick'
— 'Pink Pearl' etc., starting
w — 'Raoul Millais'
— reticulatum
— 'Sapphire'
— schlippenbachii
— scintillans
— 'Susan'
— 'Unique'
— vaseyi
— wardii
— xanthocodon
— 'Yellow Hammer'
— yunnanense
Rosa banksiae
— 'Cantabrigiensis'
— 'Frühlings' varieties
— hugonis
— spinosissima

Salix triandra
Spiraea × arguta
— nipponica
— prunifolia
Syringa 'Buffon'
— × chinensis
— 'Glory of Horstenstein'
— 'Lamartine'
— meyeri 'Palibin'
— microphylla
— vulgaris

USEFUL EARLY FOLIAGE
Acer, Japanese
— pseudoplatanus
        'Brilliantissimum'
— — 'Prinz Handjery'
Aesculus neglecta 'Erythroblastos'
Berberis thunbergii 'Atropurpurea'
        etc.
Philadelphus coronarius 'Aureus'
* Pieris 'Forest Flame'
Photinia × fraseri cultivars
Pyrus salicifolia 'Pendula'
Sorbus aria 'Lutescens'

PERENNIALS
Alyssum saxatile
Anemone pavonina
Aquilegia alpina hybrids
— vulgaris
Aubrieta
Brunnera macrophylla
Camassia
Cardamine latifolia
Cheiranthus (wallflowers etc.)
Convallaria majalis
Cytisus ardoinii
Dicentra
Dodecatheon
Doronicum plantagineum
Endymion hispanicus
Epimedium

Euphorbia epithymoides
— griffithii
— palustris
— robbiae
— wulfenii and relatives
Fritillaria meleagris
Gentiana acaulis
Geranium malviflorum
— phaeum
— punctatum
— sylvaticum
Geum rivale
Hylomecon japonicum
Iberis sempervirens
Iris, Intermediates
— pumila etc.
Lathyrus aureus
Leucojum aestivum
Libertia
* Lithospermum (Lithodora) diffusum
— purpureo-caeruleum
Lunaria annua
— rediviva
Narcissus gracilis
— 'Hawera'
— poeticus recurvus
— 'Silver Chimes'
Omphalodes cappadocica
Paeonia 'Early Bird'
— mlokosewitschii
— tenuifolia
Phlox douglasii
— subulata
Primula auricula
— Polyanthus
Ranunculus aconitifolius
Saxifraga, Mossy
* Smilacina racemosa
Symphytum
* Trillium
Trollius
Tulips, Darwins, etc.
Violas

USEFUL EARLY FOLIAGE
Eryngium alpinum

Hemerocallis
Milium effusum 'Aureum'

Lilac period (Chelsea Show): late May/early June

TREES AND SHRUBS
Aesculus carnea
Caragana arborescens
Ceanothus, many evergreens
Cercis siliquastrum
Colutea arborescens
* *Cornus florida*
— *kousa*
* — *nuttallii*
Crataegus crus-galli
— × *lavallei*
— *monogyna*
— *oxyacantha*
Cytisus albus
— hybrids
Davidia
Decumaria
Deutzia × *elegantissima*
— *gracilis*
— × *kalmiiflora*
Dipelta
w* *Embothrium*
* *Enkianthus*
w *Fabiana*
w *Fremontodendron*
Genista lydia
* *Laburnocytisus adamii*
Laburnum anagyroides
* *Ledum*
* *Leiophyllum buxifolium*
* *Leucothoë davisiae*
Lonicera syringantha
Malus coronaria 'Charlottae'
— *ioensis* 'Plena'
Magnolia liliiflora
Paeonia lutea ludlowii
— *suffruticosa*
Philadelphus coronarius

— *magdalenae*
Prunus serrulata 'Albo Plena'
— — 'Fugenzo'
* *Rhododendron* Ghent hybrids
(Azaleas)
— Hardy Hybrids
— 'David'
— *keleticum*
— 'J. G. Millais'
— Knap Hill hybrids
— 'Leo'
— 'Mayday'
— 'Naomi'
— *occidentalis* hybrids
— 'Siren'
— *wardii*, late forms
— 'Winsome'
Rosa 'Canary Bird'
— 'Fruhling's' varieties
— 'Headleyensis'
— 'Helen Knight'
— *moyesii*
— *rugosa*
— *sericea*
Rubus deliciosus
— Tridel
Staphylea
Syringa microphylla
— *vulgaris*
Tamarix tetrandra
Viburnum plicatum
Weigela 'Abel Carrière', 'Le Printemps'
w — *middendorfiana*
Xanthoceras sorbifolium

PERENNIALS
Achillea, alpine

Aethionema
Ajuga
Allium bulgaricum
Anthemis cupaniana
Aquilegias
Camassia leichtlinii
Centaurea dealbata
— hypoleuca
— montana
Cheiranthus allionii
Convallaria majalis 'Fortin's
    Giant'
Euphorbia griffithii
— palustris
Geranium himalayense
— 'Johnson's Blue'
— macrorrhizum
— pratense
— renardii
Geum 'Borisii'
— 'Lady Stratheden'
— 'Mrs Bradshaw'
— rivale
Hemerocallis dumortieri
— flava
— 'Gold Dust'
— middendorfianum
Iberis sempervirens
Iris Bearded, starting
— douglasii
* — innominata

— missouriensis
— setosa
— Lathyrus aureus
Lupinus arboreus
— polyphyllus, starting
Lychnis flos-jovis
* Meconopsis grandis
* — × sheldonii
* — villosa
Nepeta × faassenii
— gigantea
Ornithogalum nutans
Paeonia emodi
— officinalis
— veitchii
Polygonatum
Primula, Candelabra section
Pyrethrum coccineum
Ranunculus acris 'Flore Pleno'
— amplexicaule
— repens 'Flore Pleno'
Rheum palmatum
Saxifraga caespitosa
— Encrusted section
— geum
— × urbium
Stylophorum diphyllum
Symphytum × uplandicum
Tulipa sprengeri
Veronica gentianoides

Iris and lupin period: June

TREES AND SHRUBS
Aesculus flava
— indica
— × mutabilis 'Induta'
— octandra
* Azaleodendron Fragrans
Buddleia alternifolia
w Cistus

Cotoneaster multiflorus
— salicifolius
w Dendromecon
Deutzia
Diervilla
Fraxinus mariesii
— ornus
w Fremontodendron

Genista cinerea
Hebe macrantha
Kolkwitzia
Laburnum × watereri
Lonicera periclymenum 'Belgica'
— × tellmannianum
w — tragophylla
Magnolia 'Charles Coates'
— liliiflora
— sieboldii
— × thompsoniana
— × watsonii
— wilsonii and relatives
Philadelphus 'Belle Étoile'
— 'Conquête'
— coronarius
— delavayi
— 'Enchantress'
— magdalenae
Phlomix fruticosa
Potentilla fruticosa and relatives
Ptelea trifoliata
Pyracantha rogersiana
* Rhododendron arborescens
— 'Earl of Donoughmore'
— Fabia
— 'Fairy Light'
— 'Gomer Waterer'
— Hardy Hybrids early in
     month
— 'Lady Clementine Mitford'
— 'Mayday'
— 'Moser's Moon'
— 'Naomi'
— 'The Warrior'
— 'Vanessa'
— viscosum
— wardii L. & S.
Robinia, starting
Rosa 'Gloire de Dijon'
— 'Lawrence Johnston'
— macrophylla
— 'Madame Grégoire Staechelin'

— most species
— moyesii and relatives
— 'Nevada'
— Old French, end of month
— rugosa
— spinosissima
Schizandra
Senecio 'Sunshine'
w Solanum crispum
Spartium
* Styrax
Viburnum opulus
— sargentii 'Orondaga'
Weigela
Wisteria

BRILLIANT FOLIAGE
Fraxinus excelsior 'Jaspidea'
Quercus rubra

PERENNIALS
Alchemilla
Allium rosenbachianum
— stipitatum
Anchusa
Anthericum
Aquilegia
Armeria
Aruncus
Baptisia australis
Bergenia 'Morgenrote' (second
     flowering)
Camassia leichtlinii 'Plena'
Centranthus
Codonopsis clematidea
Crambe cordifolia
— maritima
Cynoglossum nervosum
Dactylorrhiza (Orchis)
Dianthus
Dictamnus
Digitalis
Eremurus

Erigeron, starting
Geranium × magnificum
— psilostemon
— sanguineum
Geum
Gladiolus byzantinus
Helianthemum
Hemerocallis dumortieri
— flava
— middendorfiana
— minor
— thunbergii
Heuchera
Incarvillea
Iris aurea
— Bearded, tall
— kerneriana
— orientalis
— pallida dalmatica
— sibirica
— spuria
Lathyrus grandiflorus
— rotundifolius
— undulatus
Lilium hansonii
— 'Marhan'
— martagon
— monadelphum
— szovitzianum
Lindelofia longifolia
Linum

Lupinus arboreus
— polyphyllus
Lychnis 'Abbotswood Rose'
— chalcedonica
— viscaria
* Meconopsis betonicifolia
Mertensia virginica
Nepeta
Paeonia
Papaver orientale
— pilosum
Polemonium
Polygonum sphaerostachyum
Potentilla
Ranunculus acris 'Flore Pleno'
Rhazia orientalis
Salvia haematodes
— interrupta
— 'Mainacht'
Saxifraga cotyledon
— longifolia
Scabiosa caucasica
Scilla peruviana
Stipa gigantea
Thalictrum aquilegifolium
Thymus nitidus
Valeriana
Verbascum Cotswold varieties
— 'Gainsborough'
— 'Pink Domino'
Veronica 'True Blue'

Midsummer rose period: late June/early July

TREES AND SHRUBS
w Abelia floribunda
w Abutilon × suntense
w — vitifolium
  Aesculus indica
  Carpenteria californica
  Chionanthus
  Clematis patens and florida hybrids

Deutzia discolor
— monbeigii
Fraxinus spaethiana
w Fremontodendron
  Genista tinctoria
— virgata
  Hebe macrantha
— many hybrids

w *Hebe* × *speciosa*, starting
   Lavandula 'Munstead'
   Lonicera × *americana*
   — *periclymenum* 'Serotina'
* *Magnolia globosa*
   — *liliiflora*
   — *obovata*
* — *sieboldii*
   — × *thompsoniana*
   — × *watsonii*
   Neillia longiracemosa
   Ononis fruticosa
   Philadelphus
   Potentilla fruticosa and relatives
* *Rhododendron* 'Albatross'
   — 'Angelo'
   — *arborescens*
   — 'Arthur Osborn'
   — 'Azor'
   — 'Beau Brummel'
   — 'Bonito'
   — Fabia
   — 'Fairy Light'
   — 'Firebird'
   — 'Fusilier'
   — 'Grenadier'
   — 'Grosclaude'
   — 'Impi'
   — 'Inamorata'
   — 'Iviza'
   — 'Kilimanjaro'
   — 'Lava Flow'
   — 'Mrs John Kelk'
   — 'Romany Chai'
   — 'Romany Chal'
   — 'The Warrior'
   — 'Vesuvius'
   Late-flowering Azalea species
   Rosa 'Albéric Barbier' and
      relatives
   — 'Bobbie James'
   — 'Fritz Nobis'
   — 'Gloire de Dijon'

   — 'Gold Bush'
   — 'Golden Wings'
   — Old French
   — 'Paul's Himalayan Rambler'
   — 'Paul's Lemon Pillar'
   — *rubus*
   — *rugosa*
   — 'Souvenir de Claudius
      Denoyel'
w — Tea Noisettes
w *Solanum crispum*
   Spartium
* *Stuartia*
* *Styrax*

PERENNIALS
Alchemilla
Allium cernuum
   — *christophii*
   — *schubertii*
Alstroemeria aurantiaca
   — *haemantha*
   — *ligtu*
Arisaema candidissima
Aruncus
Astrantia major
Calamintha grandiflora
Campanula alliariifolia
   — *carpatica*
   — *glomerata*
   — *latifolia*
   — *latiloba*
   — *sarmatica*
   — 'Van Houttei'
Cardiocrinum
Centaurea macrocephala
   — *montana*
   — 'Pulchra Major'
   — *rhaponticum*
   — *ruthenica*
Centranthus
Cephalaria gigantea
Clematis × *durandii*

Clematis × *eriostemon*
Coreopsis verticillata
Delphinium belladonna
Dianthus
Dictamnus
Erigeron
Eryngium dichotomum
— *giganteum*
Festuca glauca
Filipendula hexapetala
Geranium endressii
— *pratense*
Gillenia trifoliata
Hemerocallis hybrids, starting
Hosta crispula
— *sieboldiana*
Iris aurea
* — *laevigata*
— *orientalis*
— *spuria*
Kniphofia 'Atlanta'
Lathyrus grandiflorus
— *undulatus*

Lavandula 'Munstead'
Lilium, early hybrids
— × *hollandicum*
— *martagon*
Morina
Paeonia, late hybrids
Penstemon ovatus
— *pubescens*
Phlomis russeliana
Rhazia
Scabiosa caucasica
— *graminifolia*
Selinum tenuifolium
Stachys macrantha
Stipa gigantea
Thalictrum speciosissimum
Tropaeolum polyphyllum
Verbascum vernale
Veronica incana
— *longifolia*
Viola cornuta
Zantedeschia aethiopica

Linden period: early to mid July

TREES AND SHRUBS
Buddleia davidii (if unpruned)
Catalpa fargesii
— *speciosa*, starting
Clematis 'Étoile Rose'
— *patens* and *florida* hybrids
— *viticella* varieties
Cytisus battandieri
Deutzia monbeigii
Escallonia
w *Fremontodendron*
Fuchsia
Genista aetnensis
— *tinctoria*
Hebe
Hedysarum multijugum
Hoheria glabrata

Hydrangea arborescens
— *cinerea*
* — *paniculata* 'Praecox'
Hypericum calycinum
— *patulum* relatives
Indigofera
Jasminum humile
* *Kalmia latifolia*
Lavandula 'Hidcote'
— *spica*
Ligustrum sinense
Lonicera × *americana*
— *etrusca*
— *japonica*
— *periclymenum* 'Serotina'
— *sempervirens*
w — *tragophylla*

Magnolia × thompsoniana
— virginiana
Meliosma cuneifolia
Ononis fruticosa
Philadelphus
— incanus, starting
Potentilla fruticosa and relatives
* Rhododendron 'Aladdin'
— 'Bustard'
w — elliottii
w — eriogynum
— 'Josephine'
— 'Polar Bear'
Late-flowering Azalea species
Rosa centifolia
— 'Cerise Bouquet'
— filipes
— Floribunda varieties
— Hybrid Tea varieties
— mulliganii
— multibracteata
— Ramblers
Sambucus canadensis
Santolina
w Solanum crispum
Spartium junceum
Spiraea
* Stuartia
Tilia, most species

PERENNIALS
Acanthus, starting
Achillea clypeolata and hybrids
— filipendula
Alchemilla mollis
Anthemis santi-johannis
— tinctoria
Astilbes, early varieties
Astrantia
Campanula lactiflora
— persicifolia
Catananche
Chrysanthemum maximum

— parthenium
Clematis × durandii
— × eriostemon
— integrifolia
Coreopsis verticillata
Delphinium
Deschampsia caespitosa
w Eccremocarpus scaber
Erodium manescavii
Filipendula palmata
— purpurea
Fuchsia
Galega orientalis
Geranium endressii
— nodosum
— 'Russell Prichard'
— sanguineum
— wallichianum
Gypsophila
Helictotrichon sempervirens
Hemerocallis hybrids
Hosta decorata
— elata
— 'Thomas Hogg'
— undulata erromena
Iris × fulvala
* — kaempferi
Kniphofia 'Enchantress'
—'Maid of Orleans'
— 'Royal Standard'
— 'Sunningdale'
Lathyrus grandiflorus
— latifolius
— rotundifolius
Ligularia palmatiloba
— przewalskii
Lilium candidum
— croceum
— martagon dalmaticum
— testaceum
Linum
Lychnis chalcedonica
Lysimachia ephemerum

Lysimachia punctata
Lythrum
Malva moschata
Nepeta × faassenii
— sibirica
Oenothera biennis
— tetragona
w Osteospermum
w Penstemon
Phlox maculata
Primula florindae
Rodgersia
Romneya, starting

Salvia nemorosa
Sanguisorba obtusa
Scabiosa caucasica
— graminifolia
Stachys olympica
Tradescantia
Trollius stenopetalus
* Tropaeolum speciosum
Verbascum vernale
Verbena bonariensis
Viola cornuta
Zantedeschia aethiopica

Clematis viticella period: late July

TREES AND SHRUBS
Abelia × grandiflora
Aesculus californica
— parviflora
Buddleia davidii
w — fallowiana
Catalpa bignonioides
Ceanothus 'Autumnal Blue'
w — × burkwoodii
— × delilianus
Clematis fargesii soulei
— × jackmanii
— viticella
Cotinus coggygria
Cytisus nigricans
Deutzia chunii
— pulchra
— setchuenensis
* Erica ciliaris
* — cinerea
* — tetralix
w* Eucryphia, starting
Fuchsia
Hebe × speciosa
Hedysarum multijugum
Holodiscus discolor

Hydrangea arborescens
— cinerea
* — × hortensis 'Générale
           Vicomtesse de Vibraye'
* — paniculata
— petiolaris
* — 'Preziosa'
— sargentiana
Indigofera
Jasminum humile
— officinale
Lavandula, Dutch
— 'Hidcote Giant'
— spica 'Alba'
— 'Twickel Purple'
Ligustrum confusum
w Magnolia delavayi
— virginiana
Meliosma cuneifolia
Microglossa albescens
Ononis fruticosa
Philadelphus incanus
Phygelius
Pileostegia
Potentilla fruticosa and relatives
* Rhododendron auriculatum

w *Rhododendron crassum*
— *discolor* and *decorum*, late
    cultivars
— 'Polar Bear'
Rosa 'Crimson Shower'
— Floribunda
— Hybrid Tea
— 'Laughter'
— 'Rose d'Amour'
— 'Sander's White'
— *virginiana*
— *wichuraiana* (species)
Santolina
w *Solanum crispum*
Sorbaria
Spartium
Spiraea japonica
* *Stuartia*
Tamarix pentandra
Tilia euchlora
— *oliveri*
Yucca filamentosa
— *flaccida*
— 'Ivory'
— 'Vittorio Emmanuele'

PERENNIALS
Acanthus
Achillea ptarmica
Aconitum × *bicolor* 'Spark's
    Variety'
— *napellus*
— × *vulparia*
Agapanthus campanulatus
Allium montanum
Anaphalis
Anemone tomentosa
Astilbe 'King Albert'
— 'Lili Goos'
— 'Salland'
— *taquetii*
Catananche
Chrysanthemum maximum

Cimicifuga racemosa
Clematis × *durandii*
— × *eriostemon*
— *recta*
Curtonus
w *Cynara*
w *Dierama*
Echinops ritro and relatives
Erodium manescavii
Eryngium
— *planum*
— *tripartitum*
— × *zabelii*
Fuchsia
Gaillardia
Galega officinalis
Galtonia
Gazania (bedding)
Gentiana septemfida
Geranium 'Mavis Simpson'
Helenium pumilum
Helianthus
Heliopsis
Hemerocallis
Hosta ventricosa
Houttuynia cordata
Inula
Knautia macedonica
Lavatera cachemiriana
— *olbia*
Liatris
Lilium 'Destiny'
— 'Enchantment'
— 'Maxwill'
— 'Viking'
Lysimachia ephemerum
Lythrum
Macleaya
Malva moschata
Monarda
Penstemon
Phlox paniculata
Platycodon

Polygonum amplexicaule
— *campanulatum*
Primula florindae
Sanguisorba obtusa
Scabiosa caucasica
Solidago 'Goldenmosa'
* *Solidaster*
Thalictrum delavayanum

Tradescantia
Tritonia rosea
Verbena bonariensis
Veronica longifolia
— *spicata*
— *virginica*
Yucca
Zantedeschia aethiopica

Clematis × jackmanii period: early August

TREES AND SHRUBS

w *Abelia × grandiflora*
w — *schumannii*
Aesculus parviflora
w* *Berberidopsis*
Buddleia davidii
w — *fallowiana*
Calycanthus
Catalpa × erubescens
— *ovata*
Ceanothus × delilianus
Clematis fargesii soulei
— *flammula*
— *× jackmanii*
— *× jouiniana*
— *orientalis*
— *tangutica*
* *Clethra alnifolia*
* — *barbinervis*
Deutzia setchuenensis
w *Dorycnium hirsutum*
Erica terminalis
* — *vagans*
w *Escallonia* 'Iveyi'
* *Eucryphia glutinosa*
w* — *× intermedia*
w — *× nymansensis*
Euonymus sachalinensis (fruits)
w *Eupatorium ligustrinum*
Fuchsia
w *Hoheria sexstylosa*

Hydrangea aspera
w* — Hortensia
w* — *macrophylla*
— *paniculata*
w* — *serrata*
w *Hypericum chinense*
— *kouytchense*
— *patulum* relatives
Indigofera
Jasminum officinale
Koelreuteria
Lavandula 'Dutch'
— 'Hidcote Giant'
Leycesteria
Ligustrum japonicum
Phygelius
Pileostegia
Potentilla fruticosa and relatives
Rosa 'Crimson Shower'
— *foliolosa*
— *moschata*
— *moyesii* etc. (fruits)
— *wichuraiana*
Schizophragma
Tamarix pentandra
Tilia petiolaris
— *tomentosa*
w *Trachelospermum asiaticum*

PERENNIALS

Aconitum vulparia

Agapanthus
Althaea rosea
Anaphalis
Anemone × hybrida, starting
— tomentosa
Aster × frikartii
— thomsonii 'Nanus'
Buphthalmum
w Canna iridiflora
Cautleya 'Robusta'
Cimicifuga cordifolia
w Commelina caelestis
Crinum, starting
Crocosmia
Curtonus
Dianthus, Clove Carnations
Echinops niveus
— 'Taplow Blue'
Epilobium rosmarinifolium
Fuchsia
Geranium 'Mavis Simpson'
— 'Russell Prichard'
— wallichianum
Helianthus
Heliopsis
Hemerocallis, hybrids
Hosta lancifolia
— ventricosa
Inula

Kniphofia 'Wrexham Buttercup'
Lavatera cachemiriana
— olbia
Ligularia 'Gregynog Gold'
— veitchiana
Lilium × aurelianense
— henryi
Lilium tigrinum 'Splendens'
— wardii
Limonium latifolium
Macleaya
Monarda
Nepeta govaniana
Oenothera missouriensis
w Penstemon
Phlox maculata
— paniculata
Polygonum affine
— amplexicaule
— campanulatum
Sidalcea
Thalictrum delavayanum
Tradescantia
Tritonia rosea
Urospermum dalechampii
Veratrum
Verbena bonariensis
Veronica virginica (Veronicastrum)

Hydrangea villosa period: late August

TREES AND SHRUBS
w Abelia × grandiflora
w — schumannii
Aralia elata
w* Berberidopsis
w Buddleia fallowiana
 * Calluna, starting
Calycanthus
w Campsis
w Caryopteris × clandonensis

Ceratostigma willmottiana
Clematis campanulata
— flammula
— × jouiniana
— 'Lady Betty Balfour'
— rehderiana
— veitchiana
 * Daboecia
w Dorycnium hirsutum
w Ehretia thyrsiflora

Erica terminalis
* — tetralix
* — vagans
w Eupatorium ligustrinum
Fuchsia
Hebe × speciosa
w Hoheria sexstylosa
Hydrangea bretschneideri
w* — Hortensia
w* — macrophylla
* — paniculata
— quercifolia
w* — serrata
— villosa
Hypericum kouytchense
Indigofera
w Itea ilicifolia
Leycesteria
Malus, early fruiting
Olearia, several
Pileostegia
Potentilla fruticosa and relatives
Rosa moyesii etc. (fruits)
Schizophragma
w Solanum crispum
w — jasminoides
Sophora japonica
Spartium junceum
Syringa microphylla
Tamarix pentandra
Yucca gloriosa

PERENNIALS
Acanthus
Achillea millefolium
Actaea alba
— rubra
Allium glaucum
— tuberosum
Anemone × hybrida
Artemisia lactiflora
— ludoviciana
Aster × frikartii

— macrophyllus
— thomsonii 'Nana'
Astilbe 'Dunkellachs'
Buphthalmum salicifolium
Cautleya 'Robusta'
w Cestrum parqui
Cimicifuga dahurica
Clematis heracleifolia
— recta
Colchicum autumnale
— byzantinum
— 'Princess Astrid'
Crinum
Crocosmia
Curtonus
Cyclamen neapolitanum
Deinanthe caeruleum
Echinacea purpurea
Fuchsia
Gentiana asclepiadea
— makinoi
Geranium 'Mavis Simpson'
— 'Russell Prichard'
— wallichianum
Helenium 'Mahogany'
— tall hybrids
Helianthus
Heliopsis
Hosta 'Honeybells'
— lancifolia
— 'Royal Standard'
Hyssopus aristatus
Knautia macedonica
Kniphofia, some tender
Ligularia dentata
* Lilium auratum
* — speciosum
Limonium latifolium
w Lobelia cardinalis
w — fulgens
w — tupa
— × vedrariensis
Oenothera missouriensis

Pennisetum orientale
— villosum
w Penstemon
Perovskia
Phlox paniculata
Polygonum affine
— amplexicaule
Rudbeckia fulgida
— maxima
— nitida

Scutellaria canescens
Sedum maximum
— populifolium
Senecio tanguticus
Solidago 'Golden Gates'
Strobilanthes atropurpureus
Tradescantia
Tricyrtis, starting
Veronica exaltata
Zauschneria

Japanese anemone period: early September

TREES AND SHRUBS
w Abelia chinensis
w — × grandiflora
w — schumannii
w Buddleia crispa
 * Calluna
w Campsis
w Caryopteris × clandonensis
w — incana
Ceratostigma willmottiana
Clematis fargesii soulei
— 'Huldine'
— 'Lady Betty Balfour'
— orientalis
— rehderiana
— tangutica
— veitchiana
Clerodendron trichotomum
— — fargesii
 * Clethra tomentosa
Elsholtzia stauntonii
w* Eucryphia × intermedia
w — × nymansensis
Euonymus sachalinensis (fruits)
w Eupatorium ligustrina
Fuchsia
w Hibiscus sinosyriacus

— syriacus
w* Hydrangea Hortensia
w* — macrophylla
Leycesteria
Ligustrum lucidum
— quihoui
Polygonum baldschuanicum
Rosa moyesii etc. (fruits)
Schizophragma
Viburnum opulus (fruits)

PERENNIALS
Agapanthus inapertus
w Amaryllis belladonna
Anaphalis
Anemone × hybrida
Aster acris
— amellus
— divaricatus
— × frikartii
— macrophyllus
— thomsonii 'Nanus'
Astilbe 'Sprite'
Calamintha nepetoides
Chelone obliqua
Clematis heracleifolia
— 'Robert Brydon'

Colchicum
Crocus kotschyanus
— speciosus
Eupatorium ageratoides
— purpureum
Fuchsia
Gentiana asclepiadea
Helenium autumnale
* Kirengeshoma
Kniphofia caulescens
— triangularis, starting
* Lilium speciosum
Liriope
w Lobelia cardinalis
w — fulgens
— syphilitica
— × vedrariensis
Mertensia ciliata
Miscanthus sinensis 'Silver Fern'
Pennisetum alopecurioides
w Penstemon

Physostegia virginiana
Polygonum affine
— amplexicaule
— campanulatum
— paniculatum
Poterium canadense
Rudbeckia fulgida
— laciniata
— nitida
— subtomentosa
Salvia involucrata
Schizostylis
Sedum 'Ruby Glow'
— spectabile
— telephium
— 'Vera Jameson'
Senecio tanguticus
Stipa arundinacea
— pennata
Tritonia rosea
Zauschneria

Arbutus unedo period: late September/early October

TREES AND SHRUBS
w Abelia chinensis
w — × grandiflora
w — schumannii
w Arbutus unedo
w Buddleia auriculata
w — fallowiana
— × pikei
Caryopteris incana
Ceanothus 'Autumnal Blue'
Clematis orientalis

— rehderiana
— tangutica
— veitchiana
Fuchsia
w* Hydrangea macrophylla
w Hypericum 'Rowallane'
Lespedeza
Ligustrum lucidum
Polygonum baldschuanicum
* Rhododendron 'Yellow Hammer'
Vitex

Colchicum period: late September/early October

PERENNIALS
Aconitum carmichaelii
Anemone × hybrida
Aster cordifolius

— ericoides
— × frikartii
— lateriflorus
— novae-angliae

Aster novi-belgii
— thomsonii 'Nanus'
— turbinellus
w Boenninghausenia
Boltonia
Campanula 'Burghaltii' (second
    crop)
Chrysanthemum Korean
— nipponicum
— rubellum
— uliginosum
Cimicifuga simplex
Colchicum speciosum
Crocus kotschyanus
— speciosus
Cyclamen hederifolium
Fuchsia
Galanthus octobrensis
Geranium 'Mavis Simpson'
— 'Russell Prichard'
— wallichianum
Hemerocallis middendorfiana
    (second crop)

— multiflora
Kniphofia caulescens
w — snowdenii
— triangularis
— 'Underway'
— uvaria
— — 'Grandiflora'
* Lilium speciosum
Liriope muscari
Polygonum affine
— amplexicaule
— campanulatum
— paniculatum
Poterium canadense
Salvia involucrata
w — guaranitica
w — uliginosa
Schizostylis
Tricyrtis
Vernonia

Mahonia period: late October/November

TREES AND SHRUBS
Alnus nitida
w* Camellia sasanqua
Choisya ternata
Elaeagnus × ebbingii
— macrophyllus
Euonymus kiautchovicus
Fatsia japonica
Jasminum nudiflorum
Mahonia japonica
w — lomariifolia
— × media
Osmanthus heterophyllus
Prunus subhirtella 'Autumnalis'

Viburnum × bodnantense
— farreri
— grandiflorum
— tinus

PERENNIALS
Aster tradescantii of gardens
Chrysanthemum
Cimicifuga simplex ramosa
Crocus banaticus
— laevigatus fontenayi
Iris unguicularis
Liriope
Saxifraga fortunei

Bibliography

BIBLIOGRAPHY

Abercrombie, John. *Everyman his own garden.* 1816. London.

Bacon, Sir Francis. *Essay: On gardens* ⎫
   Essay: Of Masques and Triumphs ⎬ 1561–1626

Blomfield, R., and Thomas, F.I. *The formal garden in England.* 1901. Macmillan & Co. Ltd, London.

Bloom, Adrian. *Guide to garden plants*, Book 2, Conifers. Jarrold Colour Publications, Norwich.

Burbidge, F.W. *The book of the scented garden.* 1905. John Lane, London.

Chambers, Sir William. *A dissertation on oriental gardening.* 1773. W. Griffen, London.

Colour Chart, The. The Royal Horticultural Society. 1940. London.

Farrer, Reginald. *The English rock garden.* 1919. T.C. & E.C. Jack, London.

Freeman-Mitford, A.B. *The bamboo garden.* 1896. Macmillan & Co. Ltd, London.

Hampton, F.A. *Flower scent.* 1925. Dulau, London.

Jekyll, Gertrude. *Colour schemes for the flower garden.* 1910. Country Life, London.

   Wood and garden. 1899. Longman & Co., London.

   Flower decoration in the house. 1907. Country Life, London.

Jekyll, Gertrude, and Mawley, Edward. *Roses for English gardens.* 1902. Country Life, London.

Kornerup, P., and Wanscher, J.H. *Handbook of colour.* 3rd edition, 1978. Eyre, Methuen, London.

Lawson, William. *A new orchard and garden.* 1631. John Harrison, London.

Loudon, J.C. *An encyclopaedia of gardening.* 1827. Longman, Rees, London.

Newman, L.H., and Savonius, M. *Create a butterfly garden.* 1967. John Baker, London.

Nicol, Walter. *The gardener's kalendar.* 1812. Archibald Constable, Edinburgh.

Repton, H. *The art of landscape gardening.* Ed. by J. Nolen. 1907. Archibald Constable & Co. Ltd., London.

Robinson, William. *The English flower garden.* 1889. John Murray, London.

Robinson, William. *The wild garden.* 1870. John Murray, London.

Temple, Sir William. *Miscellanea.* 1690.

    Sir William Temple upon the gardens of Epicurus . . . Ed. by A.F. Sieveking. 1908. Chatto and Windus, London.

Thomas, G.S. *Gardens of the National Trust.* 1979. Weidenfeld & Nicolson, London.

    The old shrub roses. 1957 et seq. J.M. Dent & Sons Ltd, London.

    Shrub roses of today. 1962 et seq. J.M. Dent & Sons Ltd, London.

    Climbing roses, old and new. 1965 et seq. J.M. Dent & Sons Ltd, London.

    Perennial garden plants. 1976, 1982. J.M. Dent & Sons Ltd, London.

    Plants for ground-cover. 1970 et seq. J.M. Dent & Sons Ltd, London.

    Trees in the landscape. 1983. Jonathan Cape Ltd, London.

    Three gardens. 1983. Collingridge Books, London.

    Colour in the winter garden. 1957 et seq. J.M. Dent & Sons Ltd, London.

Tipping, H. Avray. *English gardens.* 1925. Country Life, London.

Verity, Enid. *Colour.* 1967. Leslie Frewin, London.

Waterfield, Margaret H. *Corners of grey old gardens.* 1914. T.N. Foulis, London.

Waterfield, Margaret H. *Flower grouping in English, Scotch and Irish gardens.* 1907.

Whateley, Thomas. *Observations on modern gardening.* 1770. John Exshaw, Dublin.

Index

Index

INDEX OF PLANTS

The plants included in this index are those which are in the Descriptive Tables (Groups 1–14). Some occur in more groups than one. Page references are not given for the plants mentioned in the Introduction to each Group; it is presumed that corroborative details will be looked for in these Introductions.

Plants mentioned earlier in the book, and in Chapter 14: Fragrance, and also in the Chronological Lists are not indexed. It is presumed that the chapter on Fragrance and the Chronological Lists will be used only when searching for seasonal plants.

DATE DUE

JUL 1 7 1991